CHILD ABUSE

INDICATORS, PSYCHOLOGICAL IMPACT AND PREVENTION

CHILDREN'S ISSUES, LAWS AND PROGRAMS

Additional books in this series can be found on Nova's website
under the Series tab.

Additional e-books in this series can be found on Nova's website
under the e-book tab.

PSYCHOLOGY OF EMOTIONS, MOTIVATIONS AND ACTIONS

Additional books in this series can be found on Nova's website
under the Series tab.

Additional e-books in this series can be found on Nova's website
under the e-book tab.

CHILDREN'S ISSUES, LAWS AND PROGRAMS

CHILD ABUSE

INDICATORS, PSYCHOLOGICAL IMPACT AND PREVENTION

RAYMOND A. TURNER
AND
HENRY O. ROGERS
EDITORS

Nova Science Publishers, Inc.
New York

NOTICE TO THE READER

The Publisher has taken reasonable care in the preparation of this book, but makes no expressed or implied warranty of any kind and assumes no responsibility for any errors or omissions. No liability is assumed for incidental or consequential damages in connection with or arising out of information contained in this book. The Publisher shall not be liable for any special, consequential, or exemplary damages resulting, in whole or in part, from the readers' use of, or reliance upon, this material. Any parts of this book based on government reports are so indicated and copyright is claimed for those parts to the extent applicable to compilations of such works.

Independent verification should be sought for any data, advice or recommendations contained in this book. In addition, no responsibility is assumed by the publisher for any injury and/or damage to persons or property arising from any methods, products, instructions, ideas or otherwise contained in this publication.

This publication is designed to provide accurate and authoritative information with regard to the subject matter covered herein. It is sold with the clear understanding that the Publisher is not engaged in rendering legal or any other professional services. If legal or any other expert assistance is required, the services of a competent person should be sought. FROM A DECLARATION OF PARTICIPANTS JOINTLY ADOPTED BY A COMMITTEE OF THE AMERICAN BAR ASSOCIATION AND A COMMITTEE OF PUBLISHERS.

Additional color graphics may be available in the e-book version of this book.

Library of Congress Cataloging-in-Publication Data

Child abuse : indicators, psychological impact and prevention / editors, Raymond A. Turner and Henry O. Rogers.
       p. cm.
   Includes index.
   ISBN 978-1-62257-113-0 (hbk.)
   1.Child abuse. 2. Abused children. I. Turner, Raymond A. II. Rogers, Henry O.
   HV6626.5.C4953 2011
   362.76--dc23
                                                                                    2012020011

Published by Nova Science Publishers, Inc. ✝ New York

CONTENTS

Preface		**vii**
Chapter 1	Child Maltreatment: Incidence, Consequences and Mediating Factors *Maureen C. Kenny, Lindsay Fernandez, and Roberto Abreu*	**1**
Chapter 2	Bonc Disease and Fractures in Early Childhood *Colin R. Paterson*	**27**
Chapter 3	Child Sexual Abuse Prevention Programs for Parents: Beyond Protective Behaviours *Georgia Babatsikos*	**53**
Chapter 4	Link Between Mistreatment and Obesity during the Childhood *J. Foucart*	**71**
Chapter 5	A Conspiracy of Silence? Addressing Childhood Trauma in Malta: An Empirical Review *Michael Galea*	**85**
Chapter 6	The Role of Child Sexual Abuse in the Development of Psychopathology *Roberto Maniglio*	**99**
Chapter 7	Childhood Sexual Abuse and Borderline Personality Disorder *Randy A. Sansone and Lori A. Sansone*	**133**
Index		**147**

PREFACE

In this book, the authors present current research in the study of child abuse indicators, psychological impact and prevention. Topics discussed in this compilation include the link between mistreatment and obesity in childhood; child maltreatment prevalence and consequences of victimization; bone disease and fractures in early childhood and their relation to child abuse; managing the risk of child sexual abuse including prevention and intervention strategies; addressing childhood trauma in Malta; the role of child sexual abuse in the development of psychopathology and borderline personality disorder.

Chapter 1 - Child maltreatment poses a significant threat to the children and youth in the United States (U.S.). All 50 states and the District of Columbia have mandatory child abuse and neglect reporting laws that require certain professionals (generally those who have regular contact with children) to report suspected maltreatment to a child protective services (CPS) agency (United States Department of Health and Human Services, (U.S. DHHS, 2011)). Although each state defines child abuse and neglect individually, the laws are based on standards established by the federal law, *Child Abuse Prevention and Treatment Act* (CAPTA, 2010) (42 U.S.C.A. §5106g). These provide a minimum definition of child abuse and neglect: "at a minimum, any recent act or failure to act on the part of a parent or caretaker which results in death, serious physical or emotional harm, sexual abuse or exploitation; or an act or failure to act which presents an imminent risk of serious harm."

There are four major types of child maltreatment that are identified and reportable in most states: neglect, physical abuse, sexual abuse and psychological (or emotional) abuse. Some states are beginning to require reports of other forms of abuse such as substance-exposed newborns, lack of supervision and abandonment. Victims may suffer from one form of abuse/neglect or may be victims of multiple abuse, often referred to as polyvictimization.

Chapter 2 - It was, at one time, assumed that, when a child was found to have fractures that the parents could not explain, the cause was inevitably a non-accidental injury. In recent years however it has become increasingly clear that a wide variety of bone disorders may present with unexplained fractures in young children. These include osteogenesis imperfecta, vitamin D deficiency rickets, scurvy, copper deficiency, Menkes' syndrome, bone disease of prematurity and, more controversially, temporary brittle bone disease. The review outlines the various disorders that need to be considered in such cases. It also outlines the factors that have in the past played a part in contributing to the misdiagnosis of abuse and the avoidable damage to otherwise normal families.

Chapter 3 - While there are some child sexual abuse prevention programs for parents, these tend to focus solely on protective behaviours and urging parents to report abuse to authorities. The current focus of the majority of prevention programs on teaching children protective behaviours has been criticised for placing the burden of responsibility for prevention on children while overlooking the critical population of parents. Parents are responsible for the protection and care of children and are in a powerful position to make a difference in terms of prevention and early detection. There is a need for parents to take more responsibility for prevention given the extent of known sexual abuse of children, particularly by persons known to families, and there is a need for more prevention programs targeting parents due to the scarcity of such programs. This research was undertaken to better understand the knowledge, attitudes and behaviours of parents around child sexual abuse prevention and to inform the development of effective prevention programs for parents.

This study explored how parents manage the risk of child sexual abuse, including prevention as well as intervention strategies when sexual boundaries had been crossed with their children. Using a social constructivist philosophy and grounded theory methods, qualitative in-depth interviews were conducted with 28 parents (16 mothers and 12 fathers) from two cities in Australia, Cairns and Melbourne, between 2006 and 2008.

The findings from this primary research provide a range of prevention strategies that parents used to reduce the risk of sexual abuse to their children, including not only protective behaviours but also an array of important early intervention strategies. These include general communication skills with children to begin conversations on a range of challenging topics, including but not limited to child sexual abuse prevention, as well as specific communication strategies with children about child sexual abuse, including initiating conversations with children about sexual abuse. Other strategies included investigating social situations for safety, engaging with an extended support network to protect children and monitoring and respecting children's comfort levels with other persons within their social networks.

Early intervention strategies reported by parents once they believed sexual boundaries had been crossed included: making the person who had crossed the boundary aware, through verbal and non-verbal communication, that the parent was cognisant of what they were doing; limiting contact with that person; confidentially warning others in their social networks of potential boundary-crossing risks from that person and reporting boundary-crossing incidents to authorities. Each of these prevention and early intervention strategies are discussed in detail in this chapter.

Recommendations from this research include the need for further research to understand parental knowledge attitudes and behaviours relevant to child sexual abuse prevention, research to understand models of prevention from different countries on so as to expand and improve prevention education for parents and the development of appropriate and accessible prevention programs for parents.

Chapter 4 - These past ten years, numerous studies have established a link between mistreatement (physical, sexual, or of type deficiency) in childhood and obesity. The risk of becoming obese would be multiplied by 9 in children living in situations of abuse or neglect. In order to verify and clarify the relationship which may exist between a failed family environment and obesity, study was conducted in three parts.

1 part: study of the demographic profile, medical, family, psychological and psycho-pathological perspective of a population of adolescents suffering from severe obesity. Those informations have been collected with the help of questionnaires and by observation of 164

adolescents satisfying the criteria of severe obesity. A pedo-psychiatric diagnosis according to the CFTMEA's R 2000 has been asked for each subject and included a study of the factors of ill-treatment. Results of this first part stressed the multiple causes of the obesity of the subjects but especially have confirmed the importance of the factors of unfavourable family environment (deficiencies, neglect, maltreatment) such as described in the literature.

2 part: a factor analysis on data in order to clarify the links between the data collected. Highlighting a correlational relationship between the presence of non favorable environmental factors (mental disorders in the family, deficiencies, child abuse), the severity of the obesity and the development of a psycho-pathological perspective profile in the child.

3 part: identify the linkages between these different elements through a more thorough analysis of the psychological profile of the subjects. This is done by means of case analysis and with the aid of a Rorschach, the questionnaire of the image of the body of Bruschon-Schweitzer, and from a drawing by itself, evaluated the presence of disorder of the body-image among 10 subjects and their evolution during the care taking in link with the loss of weight. Our results have highlighted the presence of disorder of the body-image with an image of itself uncertain, undifferentiated, the limits disseminated very specific to subjects suffering from obesity in comparison with a population with average weight.

The authors concluded that the severe obesity develops more particularly in the context of a cloudy psycho-pathological perspective including a disorder of the image of the body induced by the presence of environmental factors faulty for the child. Obesity installs itself in bodies with poor care, which can barely be changed imposing the necessary construction of barriers (obesity) between the "inside weakened" and the outside perceived as dangerous.

Chapter 5 - Childhood maltreatment is a heterogeneous domain, full of complexities. It occurs in all socioeconomic, religious and ethnic groups. Child abuse carries one universal denominator: abuse of power. Childhood maltreatment consists of sexual, emotional, and physical abuse, and neglect.

The purpose of this review was to underline the potential effects of childhood maltreatment on the holistic development and well-being of victims. More specifically, these studies looked at key psycho-social variables which directly and indirectly affect victims of childhood maltreatment among a relatively new culture: Malta. Results suggested that this phenomenon is well present in Malta, which is uniform to related studies done elsewhere. A total of 11% in these studies qualified as 'severely' abused and neglected.

Maltreatment may have a sequential effect on individuals' lives, impacting directly their personality and cognitive evaluation of life, which in turn influences other variables, such as the participants' emotional sense of well-being.

This review intends first to foster greater social awareness of maltreatment in Malta in the hope it may spur more research. Such research should contribute to serious discussions around how best to develop public policies and laws to protect children. Furthermore, these studies suggest that the healing process has to be holistic in scope to be true to its name, including other variables in the equation that could have been sidelined for various reasons in the past.

Chapter 6 - Child sexual abuse is a primary focus of research investigating the development of psychopathology. Indeed, a growing number of studies and literature reviews investigating the potential link between child sexual abuse and a large variety of psychological problems have been published over the past twenty years. The largest number of these studies and literature reviews have suggested that child sexual abuse is related to a variety of mental disorders. However, there are fundamental questions regarding the nature of the relationship between early sexual abuse and subsequent psychological problems that remain unanswered. To prevent interpretative difficulties, mistaken beliefs, or confusion among all professionals who turn to this literature for guidance, this chapter aims to clarify the nature of the associations between child sexual abuse and the most commonly reported forms of psychological problems by estimating the significance and strength of such associations as well as the potential effects of third variables, such as moderators, mediators, or confounders. In addition, this chapters addresses the results of a number of reviews that have investigated the etiology and risk factors of those psychiatric disorders that are most commonly reported as potential outcomes in survivors of child sexual abuse. Evidence to date suggests that child sexual abuse is a significant risk factor for a variety of psychiatric disorders, but not the only important one. There is emerging evidence that child sexual abuse might promote other biological or psychological conditions, such as alterations in brain structure or function, information processing biases, and painful internal states, which, in turn, might predispose to the onset of psychopathology. Further evidence suggests that in some cases, certain biological and psychosocial factors, especially genes and the adverse environmental factors that might accompany child sexual abuse, such as other forms of child maltreatment and dysfunctional family relationships and climate, may contribute to the onset of psychopathology in people with a history of child sexual abuse.

Chapter 7 - This chapter discusses the relationship between childhood sexual abuse and borderline personality disorder (BPD), beginning by presenting an overview of BPD, including the epidemiology, working definition of the disorder, diagnostic approaches, treatment strategies, and outcome. Next, discuss the difficulties in assessing trauma in clinical populations, regardless of the individual's Axis II diagnosis. The literature regarding the role of sexual abuse in BPD is then discussed, which is generally conceptualized as one of several contributory variables to the development of the disorder. Chapter 7 is concluded by integrating childhood sexual abuse into the other known causal factors for BPD.

In: Child Abuse
Editors: Raymond A. Turner and Henry O. Rogers

ISBN: 978-1-62257-113-0
© 2012 Nova Science Publishers, Inc.

Chapter 1

CHILD MALTREATMENT: INCIDENCE, CONSEQUENCES AND MEDIATING FACTORS

Maureen C. Kenny, Lindsay Fernandez, and Roberto Abreu

Florida International University, Miami, Florida, US

OVERVIEW OF CHILD MALTREATMENT

Child maltreatment poses a significant threat to the children and youth in the United States (U.S.). All 50 states and the District of Columbia have mandatory child abuse and neglect reporting laws that require certain professionals (generally those who have regular contact with children) to report suspected maltreatment to a child protective services (CPS) agency (United States Department of Health and Human Services, (U.S. DHHS, 2011)). Although each state defines child abuse and neglect individually, the laws are based on standards established by the federal law, *Child Abuse Prevention and Treatment Act* (CAPTA, 2010) (42 U.S.C.A. §5106g). These provide a minimum definition of child abuse and neglect:

> "at a minimum, any recent act or failure to act on the part of a parent or caretaker which results in death, serious physical or emotional harm, sexual abuse or exploitation; or an act or failure to act which presents an imminent risk of serious harm."

There are four major types of child maltreatment that are identified and reportable in most states: neglect, physical abuse, sexual abuse and psychological (or emotional) abuse. Some states are beginning to require reports of other forms of abuse such as substance-exposed newborns (see Matthews and Kenny, 2008, for a review), lack of supervision and abandonment. Victims may suffer from one form of abuse/neglect or may be victims of multiple abuse, often referred to as polyvictimization (Brady and Caraway, 2002; Briere and Elliott, 2003; Finkelhor, Ormrod and Turner, 2007, 2009; Finkelhor, Ormrod, Turner, and Hamby, 2005).

The extent of the problem of child maltreatment is alarming. According to the U.S. DHHS, Administration for Children and Families, Administration on Children, Youth and Families, Children's Bureau (U.S. DHHS, 2011) during the federal fiscal year 2010, an estimated 3.3 million referrals, involving the alleged maltreatment of approximately 5.9 million children, were received by CPS agencies in the U.S. Based on the *Child Maltreatment* report for 2010 (U.S. DHHS, 2011), 60.7 percent of reports of maltreatment were screened in, with a range of 25.2 to 98.7 percent among the states and 39.3 percent were screened out, with a range of 1.3 to 74.8 percent among the states. Of the almost 2 million reports that were screened in and received a CPS response, 90.3 percent received an investigation response and from these, 436,321 were substantiated. It is important to note that these investigations resulted in more than 3.6 million duplicate children who were the subjects of at least one report and received one or more dispositions. In the *Child Maltreatment* report, duplicate is the term used to refer to the counting of a child victim each time he or she was found to be a victim.

In addition to the human toll of child maltreatment, the associated costs are staggering. The total lifetime estimated financial costs associated with just one year of confirmed cases of child maltreatment (neglect, physical abuse, sexual abuse and psychological abuse) are approximately $124 billion (Fang, Brown, Florence, and Mercy, 2012). When child abuse turns fatal, the estimated average lifetime cost per death of a child is about $1.3 million, which is largely an estimate of the money the child would have earned over a lifetime if alive. The estimated average lifetime cost per victim of nonfatal child maltreatment is $210,012, which includes childhood health care costs, adult medical costs, lost productivity, child welfare costs, criminal justice costs and special education costs. The costs associated with every victim of child maltreatment who lives is comparable to other costly health conditions such as stroke, which has a lifetime cost per person estimated at $159,846 or type 2 diabetes, which is estimated between $181,000 and $253,000 (Fang, et al., 2012). These figures are a conservative estimate since not all children who are abused are identified and receive treatment and only those costs related to victims are included (e.g. offender related costs are excluded).

The goal of this chapter is to provide an overview of the four major forms of child maltreatment by first defining what constitutes each form of abuse, examining incidence (number of new cases or occurrences of an event within a time frame), prevalence (the overall number of cases within a specific time frame), short and long term consequences of victimization (behavioral and emotional), and to explore risk and mediating factors. It is our hope that with a greater understanding of the problem of child abuse, we may all work creatively and innovatively toward prevention.

CHILD NEGLECT

Definition

Child neglect, which is the most prevalent form of maltreatment, is defined as "the failure by the caregiver to provide needed, age-appropriate care although financially able to do so or offered financial or other means to do so," (U.S. DHHS, 2011, p. 130) and is characterized by an ongoing damaged and inadequate parent-child relationship (Scannapieco, 2008). It occurs in many different ways, and experts have suggested implementing subcategories that more specifically describe the child's experience, including physical, psychological, and environmental neglect (Dubowitz, Pitts, and Black, 2004) as well as emotional, cognitive, and supervisory neglect (Kaufman Kantor et al., 2004).

According to the U.S. DHHS (2011), medical neglect occurs when a child's parent or caregiver fails to provide sufficient health care for the child despite the presence of financial means to do so. Many states categorize medical neglect under general neglect, while other states like California and Louisiana have laws that differentiate between the two categories.

Defining child neglect can be challenging due to complications with respect to context (McSherry, 2007), as well as threshold for what constitutes neglect (Mennen, Kim, Sang, and Trickett, 2010). Mennen et al. (2010) assert that guidelines for what qualifies as neglect need to be more specific in order to understand its consequences, because very different situations can be considered neglect. Other experts suggest differentiating between supervisory neglect and care neglect (Knutson, DeGarmo, and Reid, 2004; Knutson, DeGarmo, Koeppl, and Reid, 2005). Care neglect includes lack of attention to a child's hygiene, dangerous living conditions, and insufficient medical care, while supervisory neglect consists of lack of attention to a child's activities and requests, and a child's involvement in risky behaviors which are the result of lack of supervision.

Incidence and Prevalence

Child neglect is the most commonly reported form of abuse to CPS, with more than 78% of child victims of maltreatment suffering from it (U.S. DHHS, 2011).

About 10% of all victims of maltreatment experienced "other" types of maltreatment such as "abandonment," and "threats of harm to the child," both of which fall under the definition of neglect in many states. Understanding prevalence in other terms, approximately 7 out of every 1,000 children in the U.S. experience neglect (DePanfilis, 2006). More than one-third (32.6%) of child fatalities are attributed exclusively to neglect and approximately 68% of child fatalities are due to either neglect alone or neglect in conjunction with another form of maltreatment (U.S. DHHS, 2011).

Consequences

Children who are victims of neglect demonstrate a variety of emotional, cognitive, and physical impairments. Neglected children show diminished academic achievement, significantly lower IQ, weak language, visual-spatial, and memory skills, and poor attention span (De Bellis, Hooper, Spratt, and Woolley, 2009). Victims as young as three years of age show signs of depression and withdrawal (Dubowitz, Papas, Black, and Starr, 2002). Compared to victims of child physical abuse, victims of neglect demonstrate more severe problems with cognition and socialization, as well as a tendency toward internalizing behaviors rather than externalizing behaviors (Hildyard and Wolfe, 2002).

Implications for Adolescence

Victims of neglect also exhibit a higher predisposition toward violent behavior, drug and alcohol use and criminal offenses, and other risky behaviors during adolescence (Brook, Balka, Rosen, Brook, and Adams, 2005; Chenn, Propp, deLara, and Corvo, 2011; Hofstra, Van der Ende, and Verhulst, 2000; Moran, Vuchinich, and Hall, 2004). The severity of parental rejection predicts the extent to which adolescents with histories of neglect engage in the use of illicit drugs (Pires and Jenkins, 2007). Though research investigating negative health outcomes in neglected children is limited (Hussey, Chang, and Kotch, 2006), evidence suggests that the developmental consequences of neglect may be a contributing factor in adolescents' self care.

Neglect also appears to have devastating effects on children and youths' physical health. A study by Knutson, Taber, Murray, Valles, and Koeppl (2010) showed that 15% of neglected children were overweight and 16.3 percent were obese. Care neglect significantly predicted child body mass index (BMI) for younger children, while supervisory neglect predicted BMI for older children. These findings replicate those by other studies that show an increased risk of obesity in both childhood and young adulthood for victims of neglect (Whitaker, Phillips, Orzol and Burdette, 2007).

Long Term Consequences

Adults who are neglected as children show a wide range of long-term consequences resulting from their traumatic histories. Dubowitz (2007) reports that childhood neglect leads to different consequences than other forms of maltreatment that are no less severe, and there is a need for more research that investigates the effects of neglect alone, rather than in combination with other forms of maltreatment such as child physical abuse or child sexual abuse. According to Briere (1996), neglect can lead to several issues with attachment in adulthood, as well as problems related to symptoms of posttraumatic stress, maladaptive coping skills, and negative cognitive patterns. Young, Lennie, and Minnis (2011) report that children's perceptions that parents are emotionally inattentive are linked to future psychiatric illness and that such children should be seriously considered for being at risk for future psychopathology. Child neglect has also been shown to predict a higher likelihood of risky sexual behavior in adulthood (Wilson and Widom, 2011), as well as higher instances of unemployment, poverty, and low income (Zielinski, 2009). Dube et al. (2003) report that the severity of child abuse or neglect predicts the likelihood of victims' use and abuse of illicit drugs during adulthood. Repetti, Taylor, and Seeman (2002) suggest that the nature of being raised in a neglectful environment leads to deficits in victims' emotional control and expression, social competence, and physiological regulation, all of which lead to risky behaviors and poor decision-making in adult life.

Risk Factors

Studies suggest that there are several predictors of child neglect, many of which involve stressors for parents and caregivers. Stith et al. (2009) identify five risk factors for neglect, including poor parent–child relationship, parent perceiving the child as a problem, high stress level in the parent, parent anger or hyper-reactivity, and low parent self-esteem. Vorrasi, de

Lara, and Bradshaw (2005) suggest that parents with mental health issues have a tendency toward hostile, impulsive, inconsistent, and socially inappropriate behavior, all of which stifle their ability to provide sufficient care for their children and consequently impede normal child development. Parents' perceptions of poor neighborhood conditions can also lead to hostile parenting due to stress and depression (Gutman, McLoyd, and Tokoyawa, 2008; Kohen, Leventhal, Dahinten, and McIntosh, 2005). Similar studies suggest that parents' stress level and lack of personal control are associated with risk of neglect (Haskett, Ahern, Ward, and Allaire, 2006; Rodriguez and Richardson, 2007). Slack et al. (2011) report similar findings, indicating that there is a higher risk of neglect in families of caregivers with higher depression scores and more health problems.

Families with economic stressors also appear to be at increased risk for neglect. Factors such as having received recent financial assistance from family members, use of food donations, inability to see a doctor, recent change of residence, having utilities shut off, and eating smaller meals all predict the likelihood of future CPS reports for neglect-related issues. Stith et al. (2009) stress the importance of studying neglect as a sole factor, due to findings that neglect is related to distinctive factors such as parent unemployment and family size, while child physical abuse is related to factors involving parent self-esteem and stress. Slack et al. (2011) lend support to this notion, asserting that enough attention has not yet been given to studying risk factors and protective factors associated with child neglect, especially with respect to young children and infants, who are more at risk of severe neglect (U.S. DHHS, 2011). Specifically, it appears that young age is a risk factor for neglect as approximately 48% of child maltreatment fatalities in 2010 were infants (U.S. DHHS, 2011).

Mediating Factors

Some victims of neglect do not exhibit the same adverse consequences demonstrated by many victims due to the presence of protective factors such as adaptive coping mechanisms or supportive environments. According to Cicchetti and Rogosch (2009), "the pathways to either psychopathology or resilience are influenced in part by a complex matrix of the individual's level of biological and psychological organization, experience, social context, timing of adverse events and experiences, and developmental history" (p.49). Perhaps due to the complexity of measuring this construct, as well as the common co-occurrence of neglect with other forms of maltreatment, research is limited with respect to protective factors of neglect alone.

Studies suggest that maltreated children who demonstrate resilience show higher levels of academic engagement, more developed social skills, average or above average intellectual ability, and secure relationships with their caregivers. Children who demonstrate higher self-esteem and an internal locus of control for positive events also show more adaptive functioning despite early trauma (Cicchetti and Valentino, 2006).

Cicchetti and Rogosch (2009) report that additional predictors of resiliency in maltreated children include ego resiliency and ego overcontrol, perhaps because ego overcontrol involves a controlled and rational way of relating to others, which can be protective in detrimental living conditions. Results also suggest that maltreated children with higher levels of self-esteem, self-reliance, emotion regulation, and adaptable personalities demonstrate higher levels of resilience due to their ability to adjust their emotional expression when necessary.

While personal characteristics such as self-esteem and ego control are important factors in resilience, the environment in which child victims are raised also plays an important role with respect to buffering neglects' negative consequences. Yonas et al. (2010) reported that 12 year-old victims of earlier neglect from neighborhoods with higher levels of collective efficacy (neighborhood collective trust; tendency for individuals to maintain social control and neighborhood cohesiveness) showed lower externalizing scores, suggesting that neighborhood-level factors can serve a protective function for victims of neglect.

CHILD PHYSICAL ABUSE

Definition

Child physical abuse (CPA) is defined as a "type of maltreatment that refers to physical acts that caused or could have caused physical injury to a child" (U.S. DHHS, 2011, p. 131). Paavilainen and Tarkka (2003) provide common examples of CPA such as hitting, kicking, burning, shaking by the hair, strangling, and in extreme cases, homicide. Resulting physical injuries can include pain, bruises, burns, soreness, and permanent or temporary damage to the child's physical functions, such as head injuries, fractures, or internal injuries. May-Chahal and Cawson (2005) categorize three different kinds of CPA based on level of endangerment, including serious/continuous physical abuse, intermediate/intermittent physical abuse, and cause for concern. Serious/continuous physical abuse includes violence by parents or caregivers that either resulted in injuries or continued regularly over time, usually causing marks or pain lasting more than one day. Intermediate/intermittent physical abuse describes parent or caretaker violence that occurred irregularly and caused no serious injury, and/or regular use of other physical treatments (such as spanking or pushing) over time that led to physical injury. Cause for concern includes situations in which physical injury or potential for harm was not urgently serious but demonstrated problems in the child's quality of care that could have become harmful or caused ongoing suffering, such as parents who use corporal punishment too severely but do not pose a serious imminent threat to the child.

Incidence and Prevalence

According to *Child Maltreatment 2010*, 17.6% of all reported cases of maltreatment consisted of victims who were physically abused, comprising the second largest category of child maltreatment (U.S. DHHS, 2011). In another large sample of 3,780 cases of substantiated maltreatment, CPA was reported in 18% of cases, some of which (4%) were severe enough to require medical attention (Trocmé, MacMillan, Fallon, and De Marco, 2003). Fortunately, severe CPA that resulted in broken bones and head trauma occurred in less than 1% of the reported substantiated cases (Trocmé et al., 2003).

In a non-clinical sample of 2,869 children, 25% report suffering from CPA at least once in their life (May-Chahal and Cawson, 2005). When examining these children for the type of

CPA categorized by May-Chahal and Cawson (2005) (serious/continuous physical abuse, intermediate/intermittent physical abuse, and cause for concern), results show that 7% of reported CPA was considered to be serious (6% boys and 8% girls). Comparatively, 14% of CPA reports were categorized as intermediate (15% boys, 12% girls), while an additional 3% of reports fell under the category of cause for concern (May-Chahal and Cawson, 2005). Similarly, Hussey et al. (2006) found that physical assault by a parental figure, such as being slapped, hit, or kicked accounted for 28.4% of participants in their study, which would appear consistent with the category of intermediate abuse.

Consequences

While there is an extensive amount of research studying the long-term consequences of other kinds of abuse, such as child sexual abuse, studies investigating the long-term effects of CPA are more uncommon (Fergusson, Boden, and Horwood, 2008). The research that is available demonstrates that CPA has been linked to aggressive behavior, emotional and behavioral problems, and educational difficulties in children (Finkelhor, 2008). It has also been found to be related to several physical, cognitive, emotional, and behavioral problems that often continue into victims' adult lives and impact future relationships, including those with their children. Victims can experience neurological problems and physical injuries such as pain, disability or, in extreme cases, death (Finkelhor, 2008).

With regard to short term consequences, CPA can result in different forms of physical injury, especially when abuse occurs in a child's first three years (Vinchon, Defoort-Dhellemmes, Desurmont, and Dhellemmes, 2005). Two-thirds of infant subdural hemorrhages are a result of physical abuse (Vinchon et al., 2005) and 10 percent of pediatric burn and reconstructive surgery cases are related to child maltreatment (Chester, Jose, Aldlyami, King, and Moiemen, 2006). Children's neurological functioning can also become impaired, commonly as a result of vigorous headshaking (Christian and Block, 2009). Victims of CPA also demonstrate several manifestations of emotional distress. Children often learn to imitate abusers' violent behavioral patterns, as fear, anger, and distrust are instilled in them (Paavilainen and Tarkka, 2003). Physically abused children also demonstrate increased withdrawal, apathy, low self-esteem, conduct disorder, and aggressiveness (Miller-Perrin and Perrin, 2007). Furthermore, adolescents with histories of physical abuse demonstrate higher levels of diminished health, violent behavior, problems with weight, as well as both regular use and abuse of substances such as cigarettes, marijuana, illicit inhalants, and alcohol (Hussey et al., 2006).

While victims of CPA often experience immediate consequences as a result of their abusive experiences, several exhibit even more serious consequences later in life (Springer, Sheridan, Kuo, and Carne, 2007). Permanent physical injury, including scarring or neurological damage, is a common consequence of CPA (Paavilainen and Tarkka, 2003). Adult victims of CPA also show higher instances of cognitive impairment, including brain damage, intellectual deficits, learning disabilities, language and comprehension issues, and diminished academic ability (Kolko, 2002). Physical abuse predicts higher instances of depression, anxiety, and drug and alcohol use in adulthood (Schneider, Baumrind, and Kimerling, 2007; Springer, e al., 2007; Thompson, Arias, Basile, and Desai, 2002; Walsh, Jamieson, Macmillan, and Boyle, 2007).

A longitudinal population-based study of 2,800 middle-aged men and women by Springer et al. (2007) showed that CPA victims reported more diagnoses of physical illness and more symptoms of poor health than 90% of the sample while controlling for several confounding factors, including other types of abuse such as child sexual abuse. Having a history of physical abuse also predicts various long-term trauma symptoms including anxious arousal, depression, anger and irritability, intrusive experiences, defensive avoidance, dissociation, sexual concerns, dysfunctional sexual behavior, impaired self-reference, and tension reduction behavior (Briere and Elliot, 2003). Another severe consequence of CPA is increased risk for suicidal behavior (Pompili et al., 2009), as a history of physical victimization has been associated with suicide attempts in both large community samples (Afifi et al., 2008; Dube et al., 2001) and in mentally ill adult populations (Ystgaard, Hestetun, Loeb, and Mehlum, 2004).

Risk Factors

Research shows a variety of different risk factors that affect physically abused children, including psychological factors, marital status and the father-mother relationship, paternal education, children with chronic conditions, and the child's age (Lee, Guterman, and Lee, 2008; Svensson, Bornehag, and Janson, 2011; U.S. DHHS, 2011; Vitale, Squires, Zuckerbraun, and Berger, 2010).

With regard to psychological factors, there is a direct relationship among the level of parental involvement and the presence and frequency of CPA (Lee et al., 2008). Research shows that higher levels of paternal involvement result in lower incidences of CPA, such as spanking (Lee et al., 2008). Parental involvement refers to the support provided by a father and mother that directly affects the well being of a child either positively or negatively. Maternal support was associated with a lower incidence of spanking by the father (Lee et al., 2008). The majority of CPA is perpetrated by parents (49% mothers, 40% fathers), and is less commonly perpetrated by non-parental figures, such as brothers (10%), sisters (3%), and peers and other young individuals (14%) (May-Chahal and Cawson, 2005).

Marital status and father-mother relationship also play an important role in the presence or absence of CPA. Although varying among different ethnic backgrounds, cohabitating relationships versus married relationships show different levels and frequency of CPA (Lee et al., 2008). Regardless of economic and psychosocial factors, married mothers are at higher risk of engaging in maternal CPA than non-married mothers. Moreover, married African American fathers in cohabitating relationships engage less in CPA, including spanking, in comparison to married African American fathers who are not cohabitating (Lee et al., 2008). It is important to note that fathers, regardless of their ethnic background, who spend more time involved in their child activities engage in CPA less (Lee et al., 2008). There also appears to be cultural differences with regard to child rearing practices. For example, Hispanic parents are more likely to see spanking as a normal behavior rather than as CPA (Lee et al., 2008).

Research suggests that parent educational level may play an important role in the presence of CPA. A study conducted by Lee et al. (2008) demonstrated that, from a sample of 1,257 participants, parents without high school diplomas showed lower levels of CPA (26% for mothers and 26% for fathers) than parents with some college education (45% for mothers and 47% for fathers). However, Haskett, Allaire, Kreig, and Hart (2008), reported that 16.3% of parents (N=153) with less than a high school diploma engaged in CPA, 30.1% with a high school diploma engaged in CPA, 28.8% with some college education engaged in CPA, and 29.2% with a college degree engaged in CPA. Thus, it is evident that further research is needed to form solid conclusions about the relationship between CPA and parent educational level.

There may also be certain personal and familial characteristics that put children at risk for CPA. According to Svensson, Bornehag, and Janson (2011), chronically ill children are more vulnerable to CPA. In addition, when parental income was compared to chronic conditions (a disease or disorder resulting in long-term disability), research shows that children from parents of lower income were more vulnerable to CPA than children from families with higher incomes (Svensson et al., 2011). The age of the child appears to play a role in the risk for CPA as well. As reported by the U.S. DHHS (2011), older children are at a lower risk of physical abuse than younger children, and children 4 years old or younger make up more than 75% of fatalities resulting from physical abuse (U.S. DHHS, 2011). Infants in larger families also appear to be more at risk for CPA, as Vitale, et al. (2010) reported that infants with siblings are more prone to being physically abused than infants who are only children.

Research suggests that a history of physical abuse is a risk factor for perpetrating CPA. Kim (2009) reported that from a national sample of 2,977 participants, 1,367 (45%) were victims of some type of abuse as a child (including neglect, sexual abuse, and physical abuse). Approximately, 17% of participants who reported prior abuse, experienced physical abuse exclusively, and 16% reported physically abusing their own children. Therefore, as described by Narang and Contreras (2005), physical abuse frequently becomes a cycle in which victims later become abusive to their own children.

Mediating Factors

Though CPA clearly has devastating short-term and long-term effects on its victims, several factors can lessen some of the damage it causes. Some adult victims of CPA may be able to withstand its negative effects and "maintain relatively stable, healthy levels of psychological and physical functioning" (Bonanno, 2004, p. 20). Reinert and Edwards (2009) suggest that the strength of mother-daughter attachments can buffer some of the negative emotional effects experienced by female victims of physical abuse, and a study by Teague, Mazerolle, Legosz, and Sanderson (2008) demonstrated lower instances of adult criminal offenses in CPA victims who experienced higher levels of maternal support. Kim and Cicchetti (2010) suggest that abused children with more developed emotion regulation skills fair better socially, which contributes to lower levels of future psychopathology. The mediating effects of social support were replicated in another study in which victims with higher instances of peer acceptance and friendships demonstrated lower instances of behavior problems (Criss, Pettit, Bates, Dodge, and Lapp, 2002). The presence of self-control in physical abuse victims can also be a mediator, possibly because it contributes to higher levels of emotional support (Pitzer and Fingerman, 2010). It is also helpful for victims to remain positive about their future, as abuse victims who show dispositional optimism demonstrate lower levels of distress (Brodhagen and Wise, 2008).

CHILD SEXUAL ABUSE

Definition

All states in the U.S. have laws against the sexual abuse of children (Mustaine, 2011). However, definitions vary from state to state, with each state labeling and prohibiting certain actions and imposing criminal statutes accordingly. However, for research and reporting purposes, there are some commonly agreed upon elements that constitute child sexual abuse. Typically, childhood sexual abuse (CSA) is a "type of maltreatment that refers to the involvement of the child in sexual activity to provide sexual gratification or financial benefit to the perpetrator, including contacts for sexual purposes, molestation, statutory rape, prostitution, pornography, exposure, incest, or other sexually exploitative activities" (U.S.DHHS, 2011, p. 133).

CSA involves a range of sexual victimization experiences that carry varying levels of risk for different mental health problems (Saunders, 2012). Saunders (2012) provides a good understanding of just how complex sexual abuse is:

> "Today, child sexual abuse…may indicate a wide range of sexual victimization experiences encountered by children and adolescents, such as being the subject of pornographic pictures distributed on the Internet, sexual assault by a peer or dating partner, children being made to observe adults engaging in sexual activity or watch pornography, drug- or alcohol-facilitated rape, exploitation through prostitution, or a long list of other sexually related victimization experiences" (p. 173).

Goodyear-Brown, Fath, and Myers (2012) expand the definition of CSA by stating that "any behavior involving a child that results in the premature activation of that child's sexual development qualifies as abuse" (p. 3). These broad definitions include sexual contact that may or may not involve force, regardless of the age of the participants, and all sexual contact between an adult and a child, with the understanding that children are not able to consent to sexual activity.

Although the age of consent varies by state, the age of 18 is used in most states (Goodyear-Brown, et al., 2012). Whether perpetrated by adults or teenagers, sexual abuse involves the exploitation of children's naïveté, trust, and obedience. Exploitation implies an inequality of power between abusers and children who inherently lack the emotional, maturational, and cognitive capacity to understand or to consent to such acts.

CSA can include physical contact between a perpetrator and victim. Examples of this include sexual touching, oral, anal, or genital penetration. In some cases, the child victim may be forced to touch the adult or conversely, the adult may fondle or touch the child. There are also "sexual interactions" where there is no physical contact. These include exposure (exhibitionism), voyeurism, or photographing a child for pornographic purposes. Exposing a child to pornographic or sexually explicit material is another non-contact form of abuse. Sexual abuse can also be perpetrated by someone in the child's family (intra-familial; mother, father, brother, uncle) or someone outside of the child's family (extrafamilial; babysitters, family friends). Incest is typically used to refer to cases of intrafamilial sexual abuse.

Incidence and Prevalence

Since many cases of CSA are not reported immediately, gaining an accurate understanding of incidence is difficult. Although incidence and prevalence estimates vary depending on the participant sample and definition of sexual abuse used, it is clear that CSA is a serious and pervasive public health problem (Hammond, 2003; Satcher, 2001). In the U.S., reports of suspected child maltreatment included in the National Child Abuse and Neglect Data System revealed that there were an estimated 63,527 confirmed cases of CSA reported to CPS in 2010 (U.S. DHHS, 2011). This figure likely underestimates the true incidence, given that these numbers reflect cases that were reported and substantiated and only cases where the perpetrators were parents or caregivers. Additionally, it is estimated that less than 10% of child sexual abuse is reported to authorities (Lyon and Ahern, 2011). Compared to physical abuse and neglect, fewer CSA cases are reported, and most CSA is *not* perpetrated by parents or caregivers (e.g., Bolen (2001) estimates that 70% of all CSA is extrafamilial).

Prevalence studies suggest a much larger scope of CSA. Prevalence studies determine the scope of the CSA problem by asking adults if they had experienced sexual abuse as children. According to a recent meta-analysis of CSA prevalence studies conducted in 65 countries, 20% of women and 8% of men report suffering some form of sexual abuse before the age of 18; U.S. rates were 25% of women and 8% of men (Pereda, Guilera, Forns, and Gomez-Benito, 2009). Although CSA remains a serious and pervasive social problem, affecting thousands of American children, and no doubt millions worldwide, each year, recent data has shown a decline in reported victims. Compared to 149,800 cases in 1992, in 2010 an estimated 63,527 children were victims of sexual abuse (U.S. DHHS, 2010, 2011), indicating a 57% decline, which coincides with a more general decline in crime rates in U.S.

Consequences

Sexual victimization can result in a broad range of negative short- and long-term outcomes. The consequences of sexual victimization vary for victims based on frequency, relationship to perpetrator, duration, and use of force (Kendall-Tackett, Williams, and Finkelhor, 1993), but CSA almost always results in emotional and behavioral difficulties for the child. Research has documented the link between CSA and deleterious outcomes in a wide range of domains, including psychological, interpersonal, and physical health during childhood and into adulthood (e.g., Berliner, 2011; Kilpatrick et al., 2003; Noll, Trickett, and Putnam, 2003; Paolucci, Genuis, and Violato, 2001; Roberts, O'Connor, Dunn, Golding, and The ALSPAC Study Team, 2004; Tyler, 2002). These consequences can include emotional disorders (e.g., depression, anxiety), cognitive disturbances (e.g., poor concentration, dissociation), academic problems, physical problems (e.g., sexually transmitted diseases, teenage pregnancy), post-traumatic stress disorder (Berliner, 2011), acting-out behaviors (e.g., prostitution, running away from home), and interpersonal difficulties (Berliner and Elliott, 2002; Kilpatrick et al., 2003; Maniglio, 2009; Noll, et al., 2003; Paolucci, et al., 2001; Roberts et al., 2004; Tyler, 2002).

Although a victim's response to the abuse varies, numerous studies have documented long-term negative effects of CSA (Beitchman, et al., 1992). Evidence is growing that CSA increases one's risk for experiencing sexual dysfunctions, substance addictions, suicidal behaviors, and revictimization in adulthood (Arata, 2000; Barnes, Noll, Putnam, and Trickett, 2009; Classen, Palesh, and Aggarwal, 2005; Dube et al., 2001; Fargo, 2009; Raghavan, Bogart, Elliott, Vestal, and Schuster, 2004). Kendall-Tackett et al. (1993) report that the effects of CSA tend to differ depending on the developmental level of the child. These authors note the difficulty in isolating the effects due solely to CSA and not other associated maltreatment or family environment factors.

Despite the constant struggle for many victims, it is important to note that a substantial minority (about 20–40%) of victims of CSA show no clinical symptoms (Bahali, Akçan, Tahiroglu, and Avci, 2010; Finkelhor and Berliner, 1995; Kendall-Tackett et al., 1993). As Saunders (2012) reports, a large portion of CSA victims will develop serious and long term mental health problems, however some will not. For reasons yet unknown, there are children who are resilient to the potentially severe impact of childhood victimization.

Along with robbing children of their innocence and causing psychological, physical, and behavioral difficulties, CSA also affects families, communities, and the entire nation. Although costs are difficult to estimate, the Minnesota Department of Health (2007) reported that the cost *per* sexual assault victimization of youth (aged 0-17) was $184,000 (which includes medical and mental health care, lost work, property damage, suffering and lost quality of life, criminal justice and several other costs). However, they note that these costs are only a fraction of what is spent since other costs, such as the heightened fear and mistrust in communities, are difficult to gauge. The authors further note that more money was spent on those accused of sexual assault than those who were victimized and recommend policies aimed at prevention.

Risk Factors

Although CSA can affect anyone, there are some identifiable risk factors. Black, Heyman, and Smith Slep (2001) report on the difficulty discerning between risk factors for intrafamilial versus extrafamilial CSA because most studies combine these types, although there appear to be different risk factors for each. Where possible, this chapter will delineate the differences. Obviously, children are not responsible for their sexual victimization, however, there are certain child characteristics that may put a child at risk. These characteristics may be helpful identifying those children who are in high risk categories and targeting them for prevention (Black, et al., 2001).

Among the demographic characteristics that put a child at risk for CSA, gender plays an important role. Simply, females are at a higher risk than males (Berliner, 2011; Gault-Sherman, Silver and Sigfusdottir, 2009). Age also seems important, as most studies have found that the majority of victims are teenagers (13-17 years) (Boney-McCoy and Finklehor, 1995; Finkelhor, Moore, Hamby, and Straus, 1997). Race and ethnicity do not appear to place a child at risk for CSA; however, research has shown that the resultant symptoms displayed by a victim may vary due to cultural factors (Mennen, 1995; Shaw, Lewis, Loeb, Rosado, and Rodriguez, 2011).

Certain family environment factors have been shown to be associated with CSA. A child living in a home in which there is substance abuse appears to be at a higher risk than a child from a home where there is no substance abuse. Interestingly, Fleming, Mullen and Bammer (1997) found that intrafamilial sexual abuse occurred more often when an alcoholic father was present and extrafamilial sexual abuse occurred more frequently when an alcoholic mother was present. Thus, having either parent suffering from an alcohol addiction seems to increase the possibility of CSA. In addition, Boney-McCoy and Finklehor (1995) found that children from dangerous communities were at an increased risk for CSA, compared to those from other communities. Two studies based on nationally representative samples, found that families with lower income, compared to other families, were at an increased risk for CSA (Finkelhor, et al., 1997; Sedlak, 1997). Finkelhor, et al. (1997) further found that parents with a history of CSA were at 10 times higher risk for having a sexually abused child than parents without a history of sexual victimization. Finally, the absence of a mother in the home or the presence of a stepfather has long been cited as a risk factor for CSA (Friedrich, 1990).

Mediating Factors

As previously stated, some children do not demonstrate the same level of symptomatology following victimization as others. In fact, a fair amount of victims show no symptoms. It is possible that a combination of familial support, a positive social support system and inherent resiliencies can serve as protective factors for children who have suffered CSA (Goodyear-Brown et al., 2012). Early identification and swift treatment aid in the recovery from CSA. Berliner (2011) lists three main groups of factors that contribute to risk of persistent harm from sexual abuse: (1) preabuse risk factors (e.g., prior trauma, family problems); (2) nature of the abuse (violence, injury, multiple episodes); and 3) response when a child discloses CSA (unsupportive response). In examining these factors more closely, it is already apparent how family problems (SES, substance abuse, parental victimization) can lead to an increased risk of victimization of the child. With regard to the second factor cited by Berliner (2011), the severity of abuse has been found to influence the impact of sexual abuse in the majority of studies (Kendall-Tacket et al., 1993), with victims who suffer more violent abuse, faring worse than those who do not. Finally, factor three has been examined in the literature. Maternal support following disclosure of abuse has been identified as a mediating factor in the child's adjustment to the abuse (Browne and Finkelhor, 1986; Everson, Hunter, Runyon, Edelsohn, and Coulter, 1989), with those children receiving the most support faring the best emotionally after the abuse.

CHILD PSYCHOLOGICAL ABUSE

Definition

Child psychological abuse is a commonly used term to describe a form of maltreatment that is psychological or mental in nature. Often referred to in the literature by other terms such as emotional abuse, mental abuse, psychological maltreatment or psychological battering, psychological abuse will be used here. Although definitions for child psychological abuse vary from one study to another, there are some key components that characterize this type of child maltreatment. Presently, a victim of psychological abuse is defined as a "child that has suffered or was at substantial risk of suffering from mental, emotional, or developmental problems caused by overtly hostile, punitive treatment, or habitual or extreme verbal abuse" (Trocmé, et al., 2011, p. 833). This broad definition includes threat of violence, verbal abuse, isolation, exploitation, and inadequate affection.

The definition of psychological abuse covers a wide range of activities. The threat of violence refers to repeated incidences of placing a child in an unbearable situation where the child feels frightened and bullied, such as threatening to use physical violence against a child (Trocmé, et al., 2011). Threats against the child's own wellbeing, as well as the wellbeing of those with whom the child has a close relationship, also fall under the category of psychological abuse. This may occur when a child is threatened with harm or the child's caregiver is threatened with harm in the presence of the child. Verbal abuse is a type of psychological abuse that places the child in a hostile environment through humiliating, inflicting marked distress, ridiculing, and extreme rejection of the child's actions (Moran, Bifulco, Ball, Jacobs, and Benaim, 2002). This includes using harsh verbal statements that may escalate to physical abuse (Slep, Heyman, and Snarr, 2011). While isolation refers mostly to locking children in a confined area, it also includes cutting off all social ties to children, making them believe they are alone in the world, and depriving children of basic needs (Moran, et al., 2002; Trocmé, et al., 2011). Child psychological abuse can also be observed through exploitative behaviors such as allowing or encouraging a child to engage in criminal and antisocial actions. Inadequate affection refers to the deliberate negation of affection by being detached, uninvolved in the child's daily routines, denial of love and affection, and lack of interaction when most needed by the child.

Psychological abuse can also be understood along a continuum of mild to severe. Mild cases of child psychological abuse include yelling, while placing a child in time-out is considered to be moderate child psychological abuse (Slep, et al., 2011; Wolfe and McIsaac, 2011). Severe psychological abuse refers to a parent threatening the child with serious physical harm (Loue, 2005).

Incidence and Prevalence

According to the U.S. DHHS (2011), of the 436,321 cases of substantiated child maltreatment in 2010, 8.1% were reports of psychological abuse. In contrast to other forms of child maltreatment, which remained static or declined, child psychological abuse increased by .5% from 2009 to 2010 (U.S. DHHS, 2011). A fairly common type of maltreatment, research suggests that approximately 19% of mothers and 23% of fathers engage in one or a combination of child psychological abuse behaviors defined above (Slep et al., 2011).

With regard to age at time the abuse began, Moran and colleagues (2002), found that 38% of victims were 5 years or below, 25% were between 6 and 10 years, and 25% were between 11 and 17 years (N=301). The frequency and severity of the abuse did not differ among the different age groups, with mild cases accounting for 55%, moderate cases accounting for 75%, and severe cases accounting for 64%. While both mothers and fathers perpetrate psychological abuse, research comparing psychological abuse from mothers and fathers individually shows that fathers engage in psychological abuse of children more often than mothers (Slep et al., 2011). It is important to mention that although psychological abuse is more often perpetrated by women than men, when comparing the severity of the abuse, mild, moderate, or severe, there was no difference between men and women (Moran et al., 2002).

Consequences

Although all types of child maltreatment lead to emotional consequences, there are some unique factors surrounding child psychological abuse that must be addressed (U.S. DHHS, 2011). Consequences for psychological abuse, both short-term and long-term, can be separated into two subcategories: resultant psychopathology of the child and the child's competence.

Child competence refers to childrens' emotional ability to successfully interact with their environment and adjust to different social circumstances. The consequences of psychological abuse may scar the individual through different developmental life stages, creating a pattern of aggression, substance abuse, criminal behavior, teen pregnancy, and abuse toward their future children (California Childcare Health Program (CCHP), 2010). To understand the effect of psychological abuse on children, a brief review of attachment theory is helpful. This theory holds that variations in the quality of infant-mother interaction lead to an internal working model (IWM) of self in relation to others that can be classified as belonging to one of three distinct attachment styles: secure, ambivalent, or avoidant (Ainsworth, Blehar, Waters, and Wall, 1978). Young children who have attachment figures who sensitively respond to their needs and feelings develop IWMs that foster views of others as dependable and trustworthy, while viewing themselves as loveable, competent, and attractive; hence, they are secure (Bretherton, 1992; Levy and Blatt, 1999). When analyzing the relationship between child psychological abuse and attachment theory, research shows that continuous persistent unavailability and hostility from a child's primary caregiver will lead to pathological consequences such as anxiety, depression, interpersonal violence in relationships, and potentially the development of personality disorders (Yates, 2009). The negative emotional view, low self-esteem, and anxiety symptoms that are sometimes present in victims of child psychological abuse may be fatal, leading to suicidal thoughts or even suicide (Kairys and Johnson, 2002). The effects of child psychological abuse also impact learning, leading to "low academic achievement, learning impairments, and impaired moral reasoning" (Kairys and Johnson, 2002, p. 2). Children who have suffered psychological abuse consistently show lower grades and test scores, as well as problematic school performance than children that have not been victims of maltreatment (U.S. DHHS, 2003). According to Yates (2009), psychological abuse also results in withdrawal from social interactions during middle childhood (ages 6 – 11), as the child feels inferior to peers. With regard to long term consequences, failure to thrive physically and having an unhealthy life style as an adult are other observable consequences of childhood psychological abuse (Kairys and Johnson, 2002).

Risk Factors

There are certain experiences to which children may be exposed that may put them at risk for psychological abuse. Risk factors that will be addressed in this section include social and environmental risk factors, caregiver risk factors, and paternal socio-demographic factors. Social and environmental risk factors include factors in the immediate environment of the child and family including socio economic status, housing struggles, and immigration conflicts (Glaser, 2011).

Direct caregiver risk factors include the caregiver's mental health, alcohol and drug abuse, domestic violence, and maternal depression. It is important to mention that these caregiver factors often do not take place on their own, but, rather a combination of such factors contribute to child psychological abuse. When analyzing paternal socio-demographic factors, research shows that the older the parental figure, the less likely the child is to experience psychological abuse (Lee, et al., 2008). Also, children that are raised in a single-parent household have a 74% higher risk of suffering from child psychological abuse than those raised in a two parent household (U.S. DHHS, 2006). Slep et al., (2011) confirm this with their finding that parents that are married engage in less child psychological abuse than unmarried parents, indicating a correlation between marital status and the frequency of such abuse by parental figures. Finally, it is important to mention that child psychological abuse is a cycle, where most abusive parents were abused themselves as a child and/or teenager (Glaser, 2011).

Mediating Factors

Not every child that experiences child psychological abuse shows the same level of adjustment. Research demonstrates an array of important mediating factors, or circumstances that may allow the child to live a healthier life while coping with the effects of the abuse. According to Iwaniec, Larkin, and Higgins (2006), "personal characteristics [of the child], such as optimism, high self-esteem, high intelligence, or a sense of hopefulness" (p. 7), are important mediating factors in recovery from psychological abuse. Also, being rescued from an abusive household and/or getting mental health treatment serves as an important mediating factor (Iwaniec, et al., 2006). Resilience is another important mediating factor that must be addressed. Child resilience refers to the ability of a child to thrive and mature under circumstances that would normally cause distress and impairment (U.S. DHHS, 2006). Research shows that resilience does not stem from a single factor but rather from various factors such as parenting skills, community involvement, and personal motivation to do better (U.S. DHHS, 2006).

Research shows that social support including the child's skills and interests, relationship with peers, siblings, and non-abusive adults, community resources, and parent-child secure attachment encompass a broad range of mediating factors (Iwaniec et al., 2006), which can moderate the mental consequences of child psychological abuse that occurs early in life (Hill, Kaplan, French, and Johnson, 2010).

The school environment provides the psychologically abused child with an opportunity to build social support (Iwaniec, et al., 2006). Skills and interests in certain academic areas and/or extracurricular activities can increase the child's self-esteem. Research shows that an academic environment provides an escape from the child's abusive environment and allows them to be independent and make their own decisions, enhancing their self-esteem (Iwaniec, et al., 2006). Being part of an organization and/or religious community and having supportive siblings, pets, and toys can shift the focus from the abuse and provide a sense of belonging (Iwaniec, et al., 2006). According to U.S. DHHS (2006), "parental religiosity has been linked to greater involvement, warmth and positivity in parent-child relationship" (p.33). Essentially, parents who are involved in their religious community may experience high levels of social support and likewise, their children may experience this social support, which may serve as a buffer from childhood psychological abuse. Community resources may provide a stable environment outside the home where the abuse takes place. In such community activities, child victims of psychological abuse find a safe haven and can engage in sports and interest clubs, which can contribute to their feeling appreciated and wanted (Iwaniec et al., 2006).

CONCLUSION

The incidence and prevalence of child abuse in the U.S. has reached epidemic proportions and affects millions of families each year. This chapter has provided an overview of the four main categories of child maltreatment: neglect, physical abuse, sexual abuse and psychological abuse. Although definitions of types of maltreatment vary, they can all be understood as harm to a child which results from acts of omission or commission. Given the continuum on which abusive acts may occur, it is important to examine all maltreatment both in terms of how it affects the child presently and may in the future. Most researchers would agree that there are several factors that need to be considered when evaluating the effects of abuse on the victim. These include the severity of the abuse, the chronicity, age of onset and the frequency with which the abuse has taken place. Although there is no identifiable "at risk" child, for each type of abuse, there exists both environmental and family factors that appear to contribute to the risk of abuse. Fortunately, just as there are factors that may increase the likelihood of abuse for a child, there are mediating factors, which help to mitigate the impact of the abuse. The outcome for most victims includes both short and long term consequences which can cause emotional, behavioral and psychological difficulties that extend well into adulthood. Providing children who have been victimized with treatment is critical to their recovery. Often intensive interventions aimed at the individual or the family can assist in recovery and hopefully thwart the cycle of abuse in subsequent generations.

REFERENCES

Afifi, T. O., Enns, M. W., Cox, B. J., Asmundson, G. J. G., Stein, M. B., and Sareen, J. (2008). Population attributable fractions of psychiatric disorders and suicidal ideation and attempts associated with adverse childhood experiences. *American Journal of Public Health, 98,* 946-952.

Ainsworth, M. S., Blehar, M. C., Waters, E., and Wall. (1978). Patterns of attachment: A psychological study of the Strange Situation. Hillsdale, NJ: Erlbaum.

Arata, C. M. (2000). From child victim to adult victim: A model for predicting sexual revictimization. *Child Maltreatment, 5,* 28-38.

Bahali, K., Akçan, R., Tahiroglu, A. Y., and Avci, A. A. (2010). Child sexual abuse: Seven years in practice. *Journal of Forensic Sciences, 55*(3), 633–636.

Barnes, J. E., Noll, J. G., Putnam, F. W., and Trickett, P. K. (2009). Sexual and physical revictimization among victims of severe childhood sexual abuse. *Child Abuse and Neglect, 33,* 412-420.

Beitchman, J. H., Zucker, K. J., Hood, J. E., daCosta, G. A., Akman, D., and Cassavia, E. (1992). A review of the long-term effects of child sexual abuse. *Child Abuse and Neglect, 16,* 101-118.

Berliner, L. (2011). Child sexual abuse: Definitions, prevalence, and consequences. In J. E. B. Myers (Ed.), The APSAC handbook on child maltreatment (3rd ed., pp. 215-232). Thousand Oaks, CA: Sage Publications.

Berliner, L., and Elliott, D. M. (2002). Sexual abuse of children. In J. E. B. Myers, L. Berliner, J. Briere, C. T. Hendrix, T. Reid, and C. Jenny (Eds.), The APSAC handbook on child maltreatment (2nd ed., pp. 55–78). Newbury Park, CA: Sage Publications.

Black, D., Heyman, R., and Smith Slep, A. (2001). Risk factors for child sexual abuse. *Aggression and Violent Behavior*, 6, 203-229.

Bolen, R. M. (2001). Child sexual abuse: Its scope and our failure. New York: Kluwer Academic/Plenum Publishers.

Bonanno, G. (2004). Loss, trauma, and human resilience. *American Psychologist, 59,* 20–28.

Boney-McCoy, S. and Finklehor, D. (1995). Prior victimization: A risk factor for child sexual and for PTSD-related symptomotology among sexually abused youth. *Child Abuse and Neglect, 19,* 1401-1421.

Brady, K. L., and Caraway, S. J. (2002). Home away from home: Factors associated with current functioning in children living in a residential treatment setting. *Child Abuse and Neglect, 26*(11), 1149-1163.

Bretherton, I. (1992). The origins of attachment theory: John Bowlby and Mary Ainsworth. *Developmental Psychology, 28,* 759-775.

Briere, J. (1996). A self-trauma model for treating adult survivors of severe child abuse. In J. Briere, L. Berliner, J. A. Bulkley, C. Jenny, and T. Reid (Eds.), *The APSAC handbook on child maltreatment,* (pp. 175–203). Thousand Oaks, CA: Sage.

Briere, J., and Elliott, D. M. (2003). Prevalence and psychological sequelae of self-reported childhood physical and sexual abuse in a general population sample of men and women. *Child Abuse and Neglect, 27*(10), 1205-1222.

Brodhagen, A. and Wise, D. (2008). Optimism as a mediator between the experience of child abuse, other traumatic events, and distress. *Journal of Family Violence, 23,* 403-411.

Brook, J. S., Balka, E. B., Rosen, Z., Brook, D. W., and Adams, R. (2005). Tobacco use in adolescence: Longitudinal links to later problem behavior among African American and Puerto Rican urban young adults. *Journal of Genetic Psychology, 166,* 133–151.

Browne, A., and Finkelhor, D. (1986). Impact of child sexual abuse: A review of the research. *Psychological Bulletin, 99*(1), 66-77.

California Childcare Health Program (CCHP). (2010). Child Care Health Connections: A Health and Safety Newsletter for California Child Care Professionals. San Francisco, CA: University of California, San Francisco (UCSF) School of Nursing (UCSF).

Chen, W., Propp, J., deLara, E., and Corvo, K. (2011). Child neglect and its association with subsequent juvenile drug and alcohol offense. *Child and Adolescent Social Work Journal, 28*(4), 273-290.

Chester, D. L., Jose, R. M., Aldlyami, E., King, H., and Moiemen, N. S. (2006). Non-accidental burns in children—are we neglecting neglect? *Burns, 32*, 222-228.

Child Abuse Prevention and Treatment Act (CAPTA), CAPTA Reauthorization Act of 2010, 42 U.S.C.A. §5106g (2010).

Christian, C. W. and Block, R. (2009). Abusive head trauma in infants and children. *Pediatrics, 123*(5), 1409-1411.

Cicchetti, D., and Rogosch, F. A. (2009). Adaptive coping under conditions of extreme stress: Multilevel influences on the determinants of resilience in maltreated children. In E. A. Skinner and M. J. Zimmer-Gembeck (Eds.), Coping and the development of regulation. New Directions for Child and Adolescent Development, 124, pp. 47–59. San Francisco: Jossey-Bass.

Cicchetti, D., and Valentino, K. (2006). An ecological transactional perspective on child maltreatment: Failure of the average expectable environment and its influence upon child development. In D. Cicchetti and D. J. Cohen (Eds.), *Developmental psychopathology* (2nd ed., Vol. 3, pp. 129–201). Hoboken, NJ: Wiley.

Classen, C.C., Palesh, O., and Aggarwal, R. (2005). Sexual revictimization: A review of the empirical literature. *Trauma, Violence and Abuse: A Review Journal, 6*(2), 103-129.

Criss, M. M., Pettit, G. S., Bates, J. E., Dodge, K. A. and Lapp, A. L. (2002). Family adversity, positive peer relationships, and children's externalizing behavior: a longitudinal perspective on risk and resilience. *Child Development, 73*(4), 1220-1237.

DeBellis, M. D., Hooper, S. R., Spratt, E. G. and Woolley, D. P. (2009). Neuropsychological findings in childhood neglect and their relationships to pediatric PTSD. *Journal of the International Neuropsychological Society, 15*, 868–878.

DePanfilis, D. (2006). Child neglect: A guide for prevention, assessment and intervention. Retrieved on January 17, 2012 from http://www.childwelfare.gov/pubs/usermanuals/neglect/chaptertwo.cfm.

Dube, S. R., Anda, R. F., Felitti, V. J., Chapman, D. P., Williamson, D. F., and Giles, W. H. (2001). Childhood abuse, household dysfunction, and the risk of attempted suicide throughout the life span: Findings from the Adverse Childhood Experiences Study. *Journal of the American Medical Association, 286*, 3089-3096.

Dube, S. R., Felitti, V. J., Dong, M., Chapman, D. P., Giles, W. H., and Anda, R. F. (2003). Childhood abuse, neglect, and household dysfunction and the risk of illicit drug use: The Adverse Childhood Experiences study. *Pediatrics, 111*(3), 564-572.

Dubowitz, H. (2007). Understanding and addressing the "neglect of neglect:" Digging into the molehill. *Child Abuse and Neglect, 31*(6), 603-606.

Dubowitz, H., Pitts, S. C., and Black, M. M. (2004). Measurement of three major subtypes of child neglect. *Child Maltreatment, 9*(4), 344-356.

Dubowitz, H., Papas, M. S., Black, M. M., and Starr, R.H. (2002). Child neglect: Outcomes in high-risk urban preschoolers. *Pediatrics, 109*(6), 1100-1107.

Everson, M. D., Hunter, W. M., Runyon, D. K., and Edelsohn, G. A. (1989). Maternal support following disclosure of incest. *American Journal of Orthopsychiatry, 59*(2), 197-207.

Fang, X., Brown, D., Florence, C., and Mercy, J. (2012). The economic burden of child maltreatment in the United States and implications for prevention. *Child Abuse and Neglect, 36*(2), 156-165.

Fargo, J. D. (2009). Pathways to adult sexual revictimization: Direct and indirect behavioral risk factors across the lifespan. *Journal of Interpersonal Violence, 24,* 1771-1791.

Fergusson, D.M., Boden, J.M., and Horwood, L.J. (2008). Exposure to childhood sexual and physical abuse and adjustment in early adulthood. *Child Abuse and Neglect, 32,* 607–619.

Finkelhor, D. (2008). Childhood victimization. Violence, crime and abuse in the lives of young people. Oxford: Oxford University Press.

Finkelhor, D., and Berliner, L. (1995). Research on the treatment of sexually abused children: A review and recommendations. *Journal of the American Academy of Child and Adolescent Psychiatry, 34*(11), 1408-1423.

Finkelhor, D., Ormrod, R. K., and Turner, H. A. (2007). Poly-victimization: A neglected component in child victimization. *Child Abuse and Neglect, 31*(1), 7-26.

Finkelhor, D., Ormrod, R. K., and Turner, H. A. (2009). Pathways to poly-victimization. *Child Maltreatment, 14*(4), 316-329.

Finkelhor, D. Moore, D., Hamby, S.L. and Straus, M.A. (1997). Sexually abused children in a national survey of parents: Methodological issues. *Child Abuse and Neglect, 21,* 1-9.

Finkelhor, D., Ormrod, R. K., Turner, H. A., and Hamby, S. L. (2005). Measuring poly-victimization using the Juvenile Victimization Questionnaire. *Child Abuse and Neglect, 29*(11), 1297-1312.

Fleming, J., Mullen, P., and Bammer, G. (1997). A study of potential risk factors for sexual abuse in childhood. *Child Abuse and Neglect 21*(1), 49-58.

Friedrich, W. (1990). Psychotherapy of sexually abused children and their families. New York: NY. Norton.

Gault-Sherman, M., Silver, E. and Sigfusdottir, I.D (2009). Gender and the associated impairments of childhood sexual abuse: A national study of Icelandic youth. *Social Sciences and Medicine, 69,* 1515-1522.

Glaser, D. (2011). How to deal with emotional abuse and neglect—Further development of a conceptual framework (FRAMEA). *Child Abuse and Neglect, 35,* 866-875.

Goodyear-Brown, P. , Fath, A., and Myers, L. (2012). Child sexual abuse: The scope of the problem. In Paris Goodyear-Brown (Ed.) *Handbook of Child Sexual Abuse: Identification, Assessment, and Treatment.* (pp. 3-28). Hoboken, NJ: Wiley Press.

Gutman, L. M., McLoyd, V. C., and Tokoyawa, T. (2008). Financial strain, neighborhood, stress, parenting behaviors, and adolescent adjustment in urban African American families. *Journal of Research on Adolescence, 154*(4), 425–449.

Hammond, W. R. (2003). Public health and child maltreatment prevention: The role of the Centers for Disease Control and Prevention. *Child Maltreatment, 8*(2), 81-83.

Haskett, M. E., Ahern, L. S., Ward, C. S., and Allaire, J. C. (2006). Factor structure and validity of the Parenting Stress Index-Short Form. *Journal of Clinical Child and Adolescent Psychology, 35*(2), 302–312.

Haskett, M. E., Allaire, J.C., Kreig, S., Hart, K. C. (2008). Protective and vulnerability factors for physically abused children: Effects of ethnicity and parenting context. *Child Abuse and Neglect, 32,* 567-576.

Hildyard, K. L., and Wolfe, D. A. (2002). Child neglect: Developmental issues and outcomes. *Child Abuse and Neglect, 26*(6–7), 679–695.

Hill, T. D., Kaplan, L. M., French, M. T., Johnson, R. J. (2010). Victimization in Early Life and Mental Health in Adulthood: An Examination of the Mediating and Moderating Influences of Psychosocial Resources. *American Sociological Association, 51,* 48-63.

Hofstra, M. B., Van der Ende, J., and Verhulst, F. C. (2000). Continuity and change of psychopathology from childhood into adulthood: A 14-year follow-up study. *Journal of the American Academy of Child and Adolescent Psychiatry, 39,* 850–858.

Hussey, J. M., Chang, J. J., and Kotch, J. B. (2006). Child maltreatment in the United States: Prevalence, risk factors, and adolescent health consequences. *Pediatrics, 118*(3), 933-942.

Iwaniec, D., Larkin, E., Higgins, S. (2006). Research Review: Risk and resilience in cases of emotional abuse. *Child and Family Social Work, 11,* 73-82.

Kairys, S. W., and Johnson, C. F. (2002). The psychological maltreatment of children—technical report. *American Academy of Pediatrics, 109,* 1-3.

Kaufman Kantor, G., Holt, M. K., Mebert, C., Straus, M. A., Drach, K. M., Ricci, L. R., MacAllum, C., and Brown, W. (2004). Development and psychometric properties of the Child Self-Report Multidimensional Neglectful Behavior Scale (MNBS-CR). *Child Maltreatment, 9*(4), 409–429.

Kendall-Tackett, K. A., Williams, L. M., and Finkelhor, D. (1993). Impact of sexual abuse on children: A review and synthesis of recent empirical studies. *Psychological Bulletin, 113,* 164-180.

Kilpatrick, D. G., Ruggerio, K. J., Acierno, R., Saunders, B. E., Resnick, H. S., and Best, C. L. (2003). Violence and risk of PTSD, major depression, substance abuse/dependence, and comorbidity: Results from the national survey of adolescents. *Journal of Consulting and Clinical Psychology, 71,* 692-700.

Kim, J. (2009). Type-specific intergenerational transmission of neglectful and physically abusive parenting behaviors among young parents. *Children and Youth Services Review, 31,* 761-767.

Kim, J. and Cicchetti, D. (2010). Longitudinal pathways linking child maltreatment, emotion regulation, peer relations, and psychopathology. *Journal of Child Psychology and Psychiatry, 51*(6), 706–716.

Knutson, J. F., DeGarmo, D. S., and Reid, J. B. (2004). Social disadvantage and neglectful parenting as precursors to the development of antisocial and aggressive child behavior: Testing a theoretical model. *Aggressive Behavior, 30,* 187–205.

Knutson, J. F., DeGarmo, S., Koeppl, G., and Reid, J. B. (2005). Care neglect, supervisory neglect, and harsh parenting in the development of children's aggression: A replication and extension. *Child Maltreatment, 10*(2), 92–107.

Knutson, J. F., Taber, S. M., Murray, A. J., Valles, N., and Koeppl, G. (2010). The role of care neglect and supervisory neglect in childhood obesity in a disadvantaged sample. *Journal of Pediatric Psychology, 35*(5), 523-532.

Kocher, M. S., Kasser, J. R. (2000). Orthopaedic aspects of child abuse. *American Academy of Orthopaedic Surgeons, 8,* 10-20.

Kohen, D. E., Leventhal, T., Dahinten, V. S., and McIntosh, C. N. (2005). Neighborhood disadvantage: Pathways of effects for young children. *Child Development, 79*(1), 156–169.

Kolko, D. J. (2002). Individual cognitive-behavioral treatment and family therapy for physically abused children and their offending parents: A comparison of clinical outcomes. *Child Maltreatment, 1,* 322-342.

Lee, S. J., Guterman, N. B., and Lee, Y. (2008). Risk factors for paternal physical child abuse. *Child Abuse and Neglect, 32,* 846-858.

Levy, K. N., and Blatt, S. J. (1999). Attachment theory and psychoanalysis: Further differentiation within insecure attachment patterns. *Psychoanalytic Inquiry, 19,* 541-575.

Loue, S. (2005). Redefining the emotional and psychological abuse and maltreatment of children. *The Journal of Legal Medicine, 26,* 311-337.

Lyon, T.D. and Ahern, E.C. (2011). Disclosure of child sexual abuse. In J. E. B. Myers (Ed.), *The APSAC* handbook on child maltreatment (3rd ed., pp. 233-252). Newbury Park, CA: Sage.

Maniglio, R. (2009). The impact of child sexual abuse on health: A systematic review of reviews. *Clinical Psychology Review, (29)*7, 647-657.

Mathews, B., and Kenny, M. C. (2008). Mandatory reporting legislation in the United States, Canada, and Australia: A cross-jurisdictional review of key features, differences, and issues. *Child Maltreatment, 13*(1), 50-63.

May-Chahal, C. and Cawson, P. (2005). Measuring child maltreatment in the United Kingdom: A study of the prevalence of child abuse and neglect. *Child Abuse and Neglect, 29,* 969-984.

McSherry, D. (2007). Understanding and addressing the "neglect of neglect": Why are we making a mole-hill out of a mountain? *Child Abuse and Neglect, 31*(6), 607–614.

Mennen, F.E. (1995). The relationship of race/ethnicity to symptoms in childhood sexual abuse. *Child Abuse and Neglect, 19,* 115-124.

Mennen, F. E., Kim, K., Sang, J., and Trickett, P. K. (2010). Child neglect: Definition and identification of youth's experiences in official reports of maltreatment. *Child Abuse and Neglect, 34,* 647-658.

Miller-Perrin, C. L. and Perrin, R. D. (2007). Child maltreatment: An introduction (2nd ed.). Thousand Oaks, CA: Sage.

Minnesota Department of Health (2007). Costs of Sexual Violence in Minnesota http://www.health.state.mn.us/svp.

Moran, P. B., Vuchinich, S., and Hall, N. K. (2004). Associations between types of maltreatment and substance use during adolescence. *Child Abuse and Neglect, 28,* 565–574.

Moran, P.M., Bifulco, A., Ball, C., Jacobs, C., and Benaim, K. (2002). Exploring psychological abuse in childhood: I. Developing a new interview scale. *Bulletin of the Menninger Clinic, 66,* 213-240.

Mustaine, E. E. (2011). Child abuse (sexual and physical). In Clifton D. Bryant (Ed.) *The Routledge handbook of deviant behavior.* (pp. 541-547). New York, NY: Routledge/Taylor and Francis Group.

Narang, D. S., Contreras, J. M. (2005). The relationships of dissociation and affective family environment with the intergenerational cycle of child abuse. *Child Abuse and Neglect, 29,* 683-699.

Noll, J. G., Trickett, P. K., and Putnam, F. W. (2003). A prospective investigation of the impact of childhood sexual abuse on the developmental of sexuality. *Journal of Consulting and Clinical Psychology, 71,* 575-586.

Paavilainen, E. and Tarkka, M. (2003). Definition and identification of child abuse by Finnish public health nurses. *Public Health Nursing, 20*(1), 49-55.

Paolucci, E. O., Genuis, M. L., and Violato, C. (2001). A meta-analysis of the published research on the effects of child sexual abuse. *The Journal of Psychology, 135,* 17-36.

Pereda, N., Guilera, G., Forns, M., and Gomez-Benito, J. (2009). The prevalence of child sexual abuse in community and student samples: A meta-analysis. *Clinical Psychology Review, 29*(4), 328-338.

Pires, P., and Jenkins, J. (2007). A growth curve analysis of the joint influences of parenting affect, child characteristics and deviant peers on adolescent illicit drug use. *Journal of Youth and Adolescence, 36,* 169–183.

Pitzer, L.M., and Fingerman, K.L. (2010). Psychosocial resources and associations between childhood physical abuse and adult well-being. *Journal of Gerontology: Psychological Sciences, 65B*(4), 425–433.

Pompili, M., Ilecito, P., Innamorati, M., Rihmer, Z., Lester, D., Akiskal, H.S., Girardi, P., Ferracuti, S., and Tatarelli, R. (2009). Suicide risk and personality traits in physically and/ or sexually abused acute psychiatric inpatients: a preliminary study. *Psychological Reports, 105,* 554–568.

Raghavan, R., Bogart, L. M., Elliott, M. N., Vestal, K. D., and Schuster, M. A. (2004). Sexual victimization among a national probability sample of adolescent women. *Perspectives on Sexual and Reproductive Health, 36,* 225-232.

Reinert, D. F. and Edwards, C. E. (2009). Childhood physical and verbal mistreatment, psychological symptoms, and substance use: Sex differences and the moderating role of attachment. *Journal of Family Violence, 24,* 589-596.

Repetti, R. L., Taylor, S. E., and Seeman, T. E. (2002). Risky families: Family social environments and the mental and physical health of offspring. *Psychological Bulletin, 128*(2), 330-366.

Roberts, R., O'Connor, T., Dunn, J., Golding, J., and The ALSPAC Study Team. (2004). The effects of child sexual abuse in later family life; mental health, parenting and adjustment of offspring. *Child Abuse and Neglect, 28,* 525-545.

Rodriguez, C. M., and Richardson, M. J. (2007). Stress and anger as contextual factors and preexisting cognitive schemas: Predicting parental child maltreatment risk. *Child Maltreatment, 12*(4), 325–337.

Satcher, D. (2001). The Surgeon General's call to action to promote sexual health and responsible sexual behavior. Washington, DC: U.S. Department of Health and Human Services. Retrieved from www.surgeongeneral.gov/library/sexualhealth/call.htm.

Saunders, B. (2012). Determining best practices for treating sexually victimized children. In Paris Goodyear-Brown (Ed.) *Handbook of Child Sexual Abuse: Identification, Assessment, and Treatment.* (pp. 173-197). Hoboken, NJ: Wiley Press.

Scannapieco, M. (2008). Developmental outcomes of child neglect. *APSAC Advisor, 20*(1), 7–13.

Schneider, R., Baumrind, N., and Kimerling, R. Exposure to child abuse and risk for mental health problems in women. *Violence and Victims, 22*(5), 620–31.

Sedlak, A.J. (1997). Risk factors for the occurrence of child abuse and neglect. *Journal of Aggression, Maltreatment and Trauma, 1*(1), 149-187.

Sedlak, A. J., Mettenburg, J., Basena, M., Petta, I., McPherson, K., Greene, A., et al. (2010). Fourth National Incidence Study of Child Abuse and Neglect (NIS-4): Report to Congress. Washington, DC: U.S. Department of Health and Human Services, Administration for Children and Families.

Shaw, J., Lewis, J. , Loeb, A., Rosado, J. and Rodriguez, R. (2011). A comparison of Hispanic and African-American sexually abused girls and their families. *Child Abuse and Neglect, 25*, 1363-1379.

Slack, K. S., Berger, L. M., DuMont, K., Yang, M., Kim, B., Ehrhard-Dietzel, S., and Holl, J.L. (2011). Risk and protective factors for child neglect during early childhood: A cross-study comparison. *Children and Youth Services Review, 33*, 1354-1363.

Slep, A. M., Heyman, R. E., and Snarr, J.D. (2011). Child emotional aggression and abuse: Definitions and prevalence. *Child Abuse and Neglect, 35*, 783-796.

Springer, K.W., Sheridan, J., Kuo, D., and Carne, M. (2007). Long-term physical and mental health consequences of childhood physical abuse: Results from a large population-based sample of men and women. *Child Abuse Neglect, 31*, 517-530.

Stith, S. M., Ting Liu, L., Davies, C., Boykin, E. L., Alder, M. C., Harris, J. M., Som, A., McPherson, M. and Dees, J. E. (2009). Risk factors in child maltreatment: A meta-analytic review of the literature. *Aggression and Violent Behavior, 14*, 13-29.

Svensson, B., Bornehag, C., Janson, S. (2011). Chronic conditions in children increase the risk for physical abuse – but vary with socio-economic circumstances. *Acta Paediatrica, 100*, 407-412.

Teague, R., Mazerolle, P., Legosz, M., and Sanderson, J. (2008). Linking childhood exposure to physical abuse and adult offending: Examining mediating factors and gendered relationships. *Justice Quarterly, 25*(2), 313-348.

Thompson, M. P., Arias, I., Basile, K. C., and Desai, S. (2002). The association between child- hood physical and sexual victimization and health problems in adulthood in a nationally representative sample of women. *Journal of Interpersonal Violence, 17*(10), 1115-1129.

Trocmé, N., MacMillan, H., Fallon, B., and De Marco, R. (2003). Nature and severity of physical harm caused by child abuse and neglect: Results from the Canadian Incidence Study. *Canadian Medical Association Journal, 169*(9), 911-915

Trocmé, N., Fallon, B., MacLaurin, B., Chamberland, C., Chabot, M., and Esposito, T. (2011). Shifting definitions of emotional maltreatment: An analysis child welfare investigation laws and practices in Canada. *Child Abuse and Neglect, 35*, 831-840.

Tyler, K. A. (2002). Social and emotional outcomes of childhood sexual abuse: A review of recent research. *Aggression and Violent Behavior, 7*, 567-589.

U. S. Department of Health and Human Services. (2003). Child maltreatment 2002: Reports from the states to the National Child Abuse and Neglect Data System. Washington, DC: U. S. Government Printing Office.

U. S. Department of Health and Human Services. (2006). Child neglect: A guide for prevention, assessment, and intervention. Washington, DC: U. S. Government Printing Office.

U. S. Department of Health and Human Services. (2010). Child maltreatment 2009: Reports from the states to the National Child Abuse and Neglect Data System. Washington, DC: U. S. Government Printing Office.

U. S. Department of Health and Human Services. (2011). *Child maltreatment 2010: Reports from the States to the National Child Abuse and Neglect Data System.* Washington, DC: U. S. Government Printing Office.

Vinchon, M., Defoort-Dhellemmes S., Desurmont M., and Dhellemmes P. (2005). Accidental and non-accidental head injuries in infants: a prospective study. *Journal of Neurosurgery, 102*, 380–84.

Vitale, M. A., Squires, J., Zuckerbraun, N. S., and Berger, R. P. (2010). Evaluation of the Siblings of Physically Abused Children: A Comparison of Child Protective Services Caseworkers and Child Abuse Physicians. *American Professional Society on the Abuse of Children, 15,* 144-151.

Vorrasi, J. A., de Lara, E., and Bradshaw, C. P. (2005). Psychological maltreatment. In A. Giadino and R. Alexander (Eds.), *Childhood maltreatment: A clinical guide and reference,* (3rd ed., pp. 315–341). St. Louis, MO: G.W. Medical Publishing.

Walsh, C. A., Jamieson, E., Macmillan, H., and Boyle, M. (2007). Child abuse and chronic pain in a community survey of women. *Journal of Interpersonal Violence, 22*(12), 1536-1554.

Whitaker, R. C., Phillips, S. M., Orzol, S. M., and Burdette, H. L. (2007). The association between maltreatment and obesity among preschool children. *Child Abuse and Neglect, 31*(11-12), 1187-1199.

Wilson, H. W. and Widom, C. S. (2011). Pathways from childhood abuse and neglect to HIV-risk sexual behavior in middle adulthood. *Journal of Consulting and Clinical Psychology, 79*(2), 236-246.

Wolfe, D. A., McIsaac, C. (2011). Distinguishing between poor/dysfunctional parenting and child emotional maltreatment. *Child Abuse and Neglect, 35,* 802-813.

Yates, T. M. (2009). The long-term consequences of childhood emotional maltreatment on development: (Mal)adaptation in adolescence and young adulthood. *Child Abuse and Neglect, 33,* 19-21.

Yonas, M. A., Lewis, T., Hussey, J. M., Thompson, R., Newton, R., English, D. and Dubowitz, H. (2010). Perceptions of neighborhood collective efficacy moderate the impact of maltreatment on aggression. *Child Maltreatment, 15*(1), 37-47.

Young, R., Lennie, S., and Minnis, H. (2011). Children's perceptions of parental emotional neglect and control and psychopathology. *The Journal of Child Psychology and Psychiatry, 52*(8): 889-897.

Ystgaard, M., Hestetun, I., Loeb, M., and Mehlum, L., (2004). Is there a specific relationship between childhood sexual and physical abuse and repeated suicidal behavior? *Child Abuse and Neglect, 28,* 863–875.

Zielinski, D. (2009). Child maltreatment and adult socioeconomic well-being. *Child Abuse and Neglect, 33,* 666–678.

In: Child Abuse
Editors: Raymond A. Turner and Henry O. Rogers

ISBN: 978-1-62257-113-0
© 2012 Nova Science Publishers, Inc.

Chapter 2

BONE DISEASE AND FRACTURES IN EARLY CHILDHOOD

Colin R. Paterson[1]

Formerly Department of Medicine
University of Dundee
Dundee, Scotland

ABSTRACT

It was, at one time, assumed that, when a child was found to have fractures that the parents could not explain, the cause was inevitably a non-accidental injury. In recent years however it has become increasingly clear that a wide variety of bone disorders may present with unexplained fractures in young children. These include osteogenesis imperfecta, vitamin D deficiency rickets, scurvy, copper deficiency, Menkes' syndrome, bone disease of prematurity and, more controversially, temporary brittle bone disease. The review outlines the various disorders that need to be considered in such cases. It also outlines the factors that have in the past played a part in contributing to the misdiagnosis of abuse and the avoidable damage to otherwise normal families.

INTRODUCTION

The child found to have fractures that the parents cannot explain presents an acute problem for paediatricians and orthopaedic surgeons. At one time it was accepted that, unless the evidence for some form of bone disease was obvious, the diagnosis was inevitably non-accidental injury. In recent years, it has become increasingly clear that a wide variety of bone disorders may present with unexplained fractures in young children. The purpose of this review is to summarise these reports and so to assist in the differential diagnosis of fractures in children.

---
[1] Correspondence: Dr Colin R Paterson, Temple Oxgates, Longforgan, Dundee DD2 5HS, Scotland, Tel: +44 1382 360240, e-mail: c.s.paterson@btinternet.com.

One hallmark of all these disorders is the discrepancy between the radiological evidence of injury and the clinical signs and symptoms of fractures. One early reference to this discrepancy was included in a paper by Feiss in the Journal of Bone and Joint Surgery in 1906 [1]. He commented on a four-year-old child seen at the Cleveland General Hospital. "I thought I had to deal with a most severe and malignant case of rickets, pure and simple. It being so severely malignant it seemed to be well worthwhile to take Röntgen pictures of the limbs. The results showed, to my surprise, three fractures in the arms which I would have overlooked completely if the pictures had not been taken."

In this context the best known bone disorder is osteogenesis imperfecta where fractures occur spontaneously or with normal handling. Parents frequently complain that, because of the lack of physical signs of injury, they have difficulty persuading emergency department doctors to arrange an x-ray. Similarly in the more controversial field of temporary brittle bone disease one striking finding is the discrepancy between the often huge numbers of fractures seen radiologically and the clinical features in the patient [2, 3].

Osteogenesis Imperfecta

Osteogenesis imperfecta is not a single disease but a large group of inborn disorders, the majority of which are thought to be caused by defects of collagen. Most cases appear to have a molecular cause in the genes coding for type I collagen but various other molecular disorders have been identified [4]. Collagen is the principal protein of bone and essential for its structural properties.

Collagen is found in tissues other than bone and many of the clinical features of osteogenesis imperfecta relate to this fact. These include blue or grey colouration of the sclerae, increased joint laxity, fragile discoloured teeth (dentinogenesis imperfecta) and an increased tendency to bruising and other bleeding problems, thought most commonly to be due to defective collagen of small blood vessels [5]. Few patients have all these clinical features and some individuals, undoubtedly affected on the basis of family history, have none.

The great variety of molecular causes is reflected in a very large range of clinical findings. At one extreme there are infants so severely affected that stillbirth or early neonatal death is inevitable. Equally, there are patients who have few or no fractures in childhood and who are only correctly identified in adult life; some are initially thought to have ordinary osteoporosis. Similarly, the fracture pattern can be very variable in the individual patient, sometimes with runs of fractures and long fracture-free periods (Figure 1). In both males and females, the rate of fracturing decreases markedly at about the time of puberty.

Osteogenesis imperfecta is the best known disorder to cause fractures leading to an incorrect diagnosis of non-accidental injury [6-8]. One factor contributing to the difficulty in differentiating osteogenesis imperfecta from non-accidental injury is the great variability in the clinical features of the condition. Scleral colour is normal in patients with the type IV variant [9]. Dentinogenesis imperfecta may be absent (or the teeth may not have erupted at the time of the acute need for a diagnosis). There may be no recognisable family history since new mutations of all types of osteogenesis imperfecta are well recognised. Many patients have no excess of wormian bones (but the Towne view essential for this evaluation is often not done). Osteopenia on ordinary radiographs is often not seen [8,10]. Even in adults a normal bone density is a common finding in many cases of osteogenesis imperfecta [11].

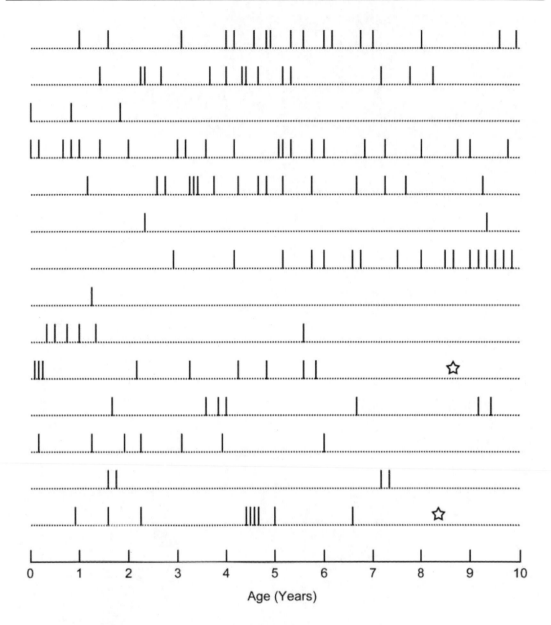

Figure 1. Incidence of fractures in 14 patients with osteogenesis imperfecta type IVA for whom complete records were available for at least eight years. In two cases details were not available for later than the point marked with a star. Data of Paterson et al 1987 [10].

In one study of 33 children with osteogenesis imperfecta initially misdiagnosed as cases of child abuse [8] the mean age at presentation was 7.1 months (range 1 to 23 months). The frequent lack of obvious signs of fracture is illustrated in this series; only 14 presented with pain, seven had swelling, five had diminished limb movement and two had unusual limb positions. Clinical findings pointing to osteogenesis imperfecta were found in only 23 patients and a relevant family history in only 18. Radiological findings consistent with osteogenesis imperfecta were found in only 19 patients.

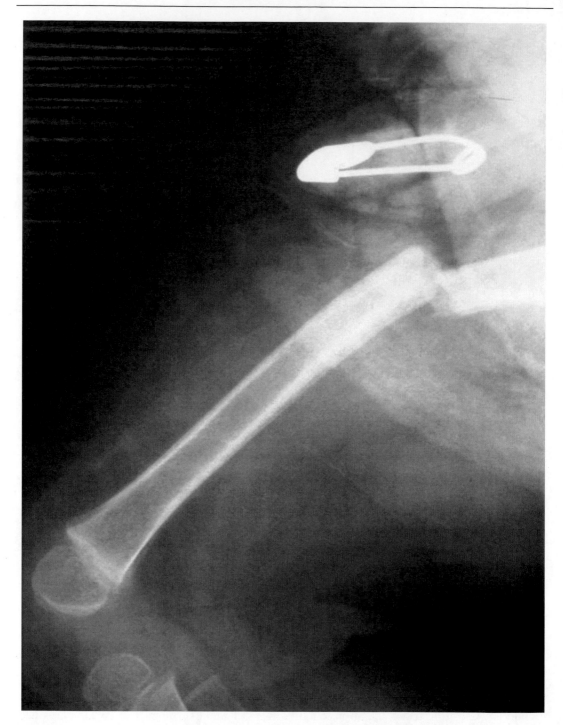

Figure 2. Spontaneous transverse fracture of right femur in a girl aged 10 months. She had normal sclerae but large numbers of wormian bones. The child was removed from the mother and placed into a series of foster homes with a view to adoption. A further spontaneous femur fracture 18 months later while in foster care led to a review of the diagnosis. She was returned to her mother soon afterwards.

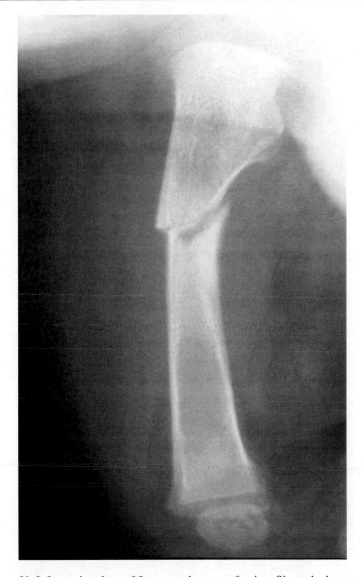

Figure 3. Fracture of left femur in a boy of four months, one of twins. Since the bone appeared normal radiologically it was assumed that considerable force was involved and a care order was sought for both boys. However it later became clear that his father, uncle and grandfather all had pale blue sclerae, dentinogenesis imperfecta and a typical history of osteogenesis imperfecta. By the time of the hearing the boy and his twin brother had obvious dentinogenesis imperfecta.

The difficulties are compounded by the fact that all types of fractures are recognised in osteogenesis imperfecta [12] including skull fractures, diaphyseal fractures (Figures 2 and 3), metaphyseal fractures (Figure 4) and rib fractures (Figure 5). Patients may have multiple fractures at the time of presentation and old fractures at various stages of healing may be found by accident when skeletal surveys are undertaken. These facts too may contribute to the danger of misdiagnosis.

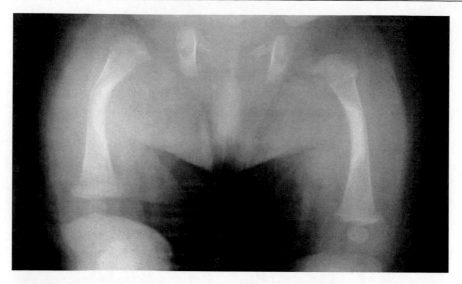

Figure 4. Metaphyseal fractures of both femora in a three day old child later recognised as having osteogenesis imperfecta type IVA.

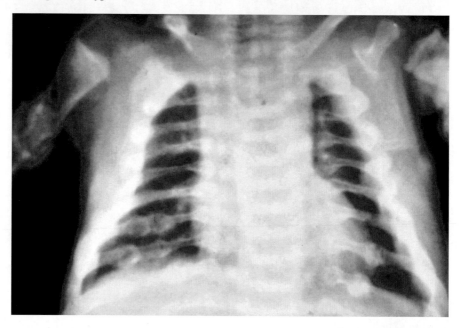

Figure 5. Chest x-ray of a boy on the day of birth showing multiple rib fractures of different ages all of which had occurred in utero. He was later thought to have osteogenesis imperfecta type III.

A variety of biochemical investigations have been used for the diagnosis of osteogenesis imperfecta. These fall into two main groups. Some tests examine the biochemistry of collagen from cultured fibroblasts derived from skin biopsies. Other tests search for mutations in the genes coding for type I collagen. While these tests are very useful, helping to make a diagnosis of osteogenesis imperfecta in some cases in which it is not obvious, there is no information on the likelihood of finding abnormalities in a large unselected group of patients with known osteogenesis imperfecta. We therefore have little insight into the frequency of false negatives. Table 1 shows the findings in two studies. Detailed examination of the figures indicates that false negatives are most common in the patients in whom there is the greatest diagnostic difficulty. It is clearly incorrect to say that the absence of a biochemical abnormality excludes osteogenesis imperfecta.

Table 1. Percentage of positive findings in known cases of osteogenesis imperfecta investigated by collagen analysis and by mutation detection

Type	Percentage	
	Collagen analysis[1]	Mutation detection[2]
Type 1 (generally mild, blue sclerae)	94%	94%
Type III (severe with progressive deformities)	84%	81%
Type IV (mild or moderate, normal sclerae)	84%	69%
Type unknown	50%	____

[1] Data of Wenstrup et al [13]
[2] Personal communication from Dr D Prockop 8 May 2000.

Vitamin D Deficiency Rickets

The availability of good biochemical investigations to demonstrate vitamin D deficiency has recently made it clear that subnutrition and frank deficiency are not at all uncommon in many populations including many in western countries [14,15]. There are no similar surveys of the incidence of radiological abnormalities indicative of rickets, not least because such a survey of asymptomatic young children would not be regarded as ethical. While the radiological abnormalities of rickets have been recognised for many years, it is important to note that biochemically severe deficiency may not be accompanied by any radiological abnormality [15-17].

Vitamin D is obtained in part from the diet and in part by its synthesis in the skin under the influence of ultraviolet B light. Most individuals in western countries obtain most of their vitamin D from the sunlight but many factors can diminish its effectiveness including pigmented skin, clothing and particularly veiling, sunscreens, atmospheric pollution, the obliquity of the sun's rays at high latitudes and the weather, as well as lifestyle factors [14,18]. At birth an infant's stores of vitamin D are entirely dependent on the nutritional status of the mother. Overt radiological evidence of rickets has been described in the unborn child of a vitamin D deficient mother [19]. Rickets is well recognised in newborn infants and studies in several countries including the United States have shown the correlation between the vitamin D status of infants and their mothers [20]. The discovery of vitamin D deficiency in a child should prompt the investigation of the mother. The intake of vitamin D in infancy depends partly on the manner of feeding; breast milk is a relatively poor source of vitamin D particularly if the mother is herself deficient.

Vitamin D deficiency rickets has been identified in a number of case reports of patients with fractures who were initially thought to be victims of non-accidental injury [15,21,22] (Figure 6). In nine of the ten patients in these reports the fractures were first found between the ages of 2 months and 5 months. In one the fractures were first found at 34 months. These reports have stimulated a lively response [23-25]. This has questioned the likelihood that fractures can occur in patients without overt radiological evidence of rickets. It has been suggested that, even if radiological evidence of rickets is visible, the fractures are still caused by non-accidental injury.

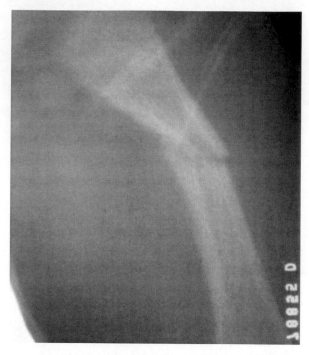

Figure 6. Oblique fracture of left femur in a boy of 4 months with widespread radiological evidence of rickets elsewhere in the skeleton.

However the literature has for many years been clear that rickets may not only cause fractures but also that some fractures, like those of osteogenesis imperfecta, can be asymptomatic. These are not identified unless a full skeletal survey is undertaken [1,26,27]. Over the last 50 years numerous case reports have described patients with vitamin D deficiency rickets and fractures [17]. In one recent retrospective study fractures were found in seven out of 40 children younger than 24 months with overt radiological evidence of rickets [28]. The classical physical signs of severe long-standing rickets such as genu valgus, genu varus, frontal bossing and the 'rachitic rosary' are not seen in many patients today. In infants enlargement or persistence of the anterior fontanelle is a useful pointer to bone abnormalities including rickets. On biochemical investigation low values for the serum calcium and serum inorganic phosphate may be found. The serum alkaline phosphatase is often raised but reference ranges for children are usually inadequate. It is generally better to relate the values in a child to the *adult* reference range for the laboratory involved; figures higher than 2.5 times the upper limit for adults should be regarded as abnormal in a child [29]. It should be noted the serum alkaline phosphatase may be inappropriately normal in children with rickets who are not growing [30]. The most useful biochemical investigations are the serum 25-hydroxyvitamin D and serum parathyroid hormone levels. 25-hydroxyvitamin D is the principal form of vitamin D in the blood; its level is generally regarded as the most appropriate measure of vitamin D status in an individual. One difficulty with the assessment of 25-hydroxyvitamin D levels is the uncertainty about the appropriate reference range.

Preparation of a range in the conventional manner as 95% of an apparently normal population is meaningless since much depends on the season, the habitual diets and the habitual exposure to sunlight within that population. The distribution of the results is not normal partly because of the inclusion of apparently normal individuals who are in fact deficient. In adults an approximate lower reference value can be obtained as the lowest level at which the serum parathyroid hormone level does not respond to the administration of vitamin D [31]. This is 20 ng/mL (50 nmol/L). However most patients with symptomatic rickets have figures lower than 10 ng/mL (25 nmol/L). The classical radiological appearances of rickets, particularly in the wrists and knees, have been known for many years. However it is important to recognise the limitations of radiology in that only a minority of children with significant vitamin D deficiency have any radiological abnormalities [32,33]. This discrepancy is particularly true in infants aged less than one year [15,16]. Even in older children there is no relationship between the radiological signs and the severity of the vitamin D deficiency as measured by the serum 25-hydroxyvitamin D [34]. One factor that contributes to the discrepancy between radiology and biochemistry is the 'paradox of rickets' familiar to earlier generations of paediatricians [35]. As the deficiency worsens the epiphyseal changes become less obvious. The classical radiological signs are not seen in a child who is not growing. As in adults with osteomalacia, pseudofractures (Looser zones, Milkman's fractures) do occur in vitamin D deficiency rickets (Figure 7). They are often mistaken for true fractures. They can be distinguished from fractures by the lack of associated clinical signs and by lack of changes in serial radiographs before vitamin D therapy is instituted.

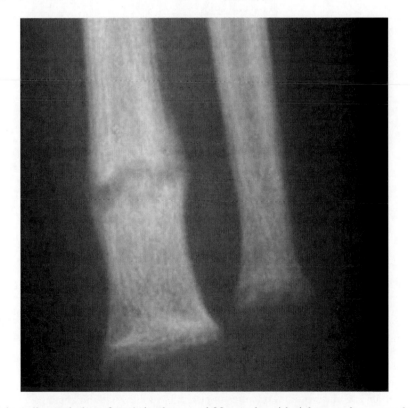

Figure 7. Right radius and ulna of an Asian boy aged 30 months with rickets to show pseudofracture.

Vitamin C Deficiency (Scurvy)

Ascorbic acid (vitamin C) is essential for the formation of mature collagen [36]. Many of the clinical findings in scurvy are explained by this fact. The abnormal collagen of small blood vessels leads to the well recognised problems of bleeding gums, bruising, subperiosteal bleeding and intracranial haemorrhage.

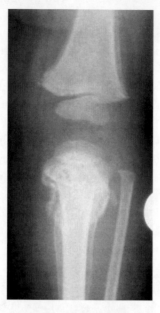

Figure 8. Left knee showing old fracture of upper tibia and periosteal reaction in a girl of 14 months with biochemical evidence of severe vitamin C deficiency. Courtesy of Dr M Fraser.

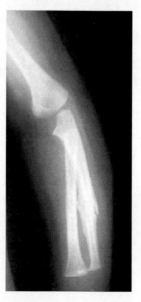

Figure 9. Left radius and ulna with old fractures in girl of 14 months with biochemical evidence of severe vitamin C deficiency. Courtesy of Dr. M. Fraser.

Fractures, including metaphyseal fractures, are described in scurvy [37,38]. Fractures are well recognised in laboratory animals with scurvy such as in macaque monkeys [39]. Metaphyseal fractures are common [40]. Multiple spontaneous fractures also occur in other animals with mutations affecting the synthesis of ascorbic acid, including rats, mice and pigs [41-43]. There are two reports of children with scurvy in whom an initial diagnosis of non-accidental injury was made. A boy of 32 months had a fracture of one humerus [44] and a girl of 14 months had multiple fractures [45] (Figures 8 and 9). There is also one report of a girl of 11 months who had a transverse fracture of the right femur and was thought to have both rickets and scurvy [46]. In the older literature the combination of rickets and scurvy was well recognised [47]. Vitamin C deficiency is said to be common at least in adults both in the western world and in developing countries [48]. The small number of case reports of children with fractures and scurvy might be taken to suggest that this disorder is rare. However the rarity might simply be a reflection of the infrequency with which the diagnosis of scurvy is considered. The biochemical investigation of vitamin C deficiency is difficult. Plasma levels of ascorbic acid are a limited reflection of the body pool. Low levels may point to a low intake but also occur in inflammatory episodes in which the vitamin is taken up by tissues. Leucocyte ascorbic acid assays are thought to be a better indication of body stores but the assays are technically difficult and need relatively large blood samples (2mL to 5mL).

The ascorbic acid saturation test is probably the most accurate indication of deficiency. In one form of this test, particularly valuable in children, a loading dose of 11mg ascorbic acid per kg body weight is given orally. The urinary excretion of ascorbic acid is measured in the two-hour period starting four hours later, when the maximum excretion would be expected if the patient had adequate tissue levels. Considerable attention to detail is needed for all these tests.

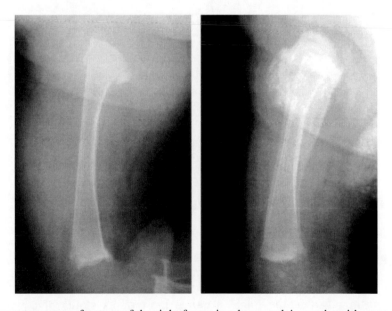

Figure 10. Recent transverse fracture of the right femur in a boy aged 4 months with copper deficiency. A metaphyseal lesion is also seen. The figure on the right shows the same femur four weeks later. Courtesy of Prof B Pontz.

Copper Deficiency

Copper is an essential component of several enzymes. One of them, lysyl oxidase, is needed for the formation of mature collagen [36,49]. Some of the clinical features of known cases of copper deficiency can therefore be attributed to defective collagen formation. These include fractures (Figure 10). Of 19 reported infants with copper deficiency and fractures, the fractures were symptomatic in only eight [50-53]. In two of these a spontaneous symptomatic fracture at one site led to the discovery of numerous previously unsuspected fractures elsewhere. The other eleven infants with asymptomatic fractures included two with multiple rib fractures. The fractures were found between the ages of 2 and 6 months in 17 patients and at 12 months and 22 months in the other two. Metaphyseal abnormalities were seen in 37 out of 41 infants with copper deficiency for whom x-rays were available [50-54]. These included concavity, flaring of the metaphyseal edges, irregularity of the metaphyses, spur formation and fractures through metaphyseal spurs (Figure 11). The abnormalities were often but not always symmetrical. The most common sites were the lower femur, the upper tibia, the lower tibia and the distal radius and ulna. Some of the metaphyseal abnormalities resembled those of scurvy. In two cases the appearances were thought to resemble those attributed to non-accidental injury [55,56]. As in scurvy subperiosteal bleeding is a common finding. Some patients appear to be osteopenic. Some patients have enlargement of the costo-chondral junctions similar to those seen in rickets due to vitamin D deficiency.

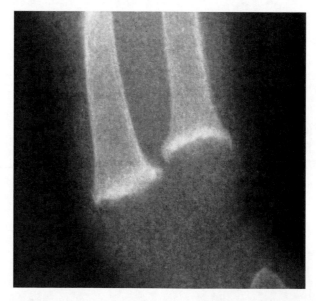

Figure 11. Metaphyseal abnormalities in the distal radius and ulna of a boy aged 4 months with copper deficiency. Courtesy of Prof B Pontz.

The most obvious risk factors for copper deficiency are pre-term birth and multiple pregnancy. It is thought that the infant acquires most of its stores of copper in the last trimester of pregnancy. Multiple pregnancy may be an independent risk factor since copper deficiency has been reported in twins born after 36 weeks gestation [50]. One additional risk factor for copper deficiency is the use of total parenteral nutrition with a fluid deficient in copper.

Most of the reported cases of copper deficiency have been formula fed; infant formulas may have a low copper content. Copper absorption is impaired by a high iron intake [57]. The iron content of infant formulas varies greatly but it is not yet known whether the high iron content of some is a cause of copper deficiency.

The most widely used investigations for the diagnosis of copper deficiency are the serum copper and the serum caeruloplasmin. However serum copper is a very small proportion of the body stores of copper and studies in animals have demonstrated that serum copper levels are an imperfect reflection of tissue stores [50,58]. Most of the copper in erythrocytes is as the enzyme superoxide dismutase; low values of erythrocyte superoxide dismutase have been found in copper deficient infants and were corrected after copper administration. Other methods for assessing copper status have been proposed but their value remains uncertain [59].

Menkes' Syndrome

Menkes' syndrome ('kinky hair disease') is an x-linked recessive disorder of copper metabolism. The major clinical findings are of developmental delay, often seen from the age of two months and a progressive neurological impairment leading to death, often from intracranial bleeding, by the age of three years. The characteristic sparse, tortuous hair may not be obvious before the age of three months.

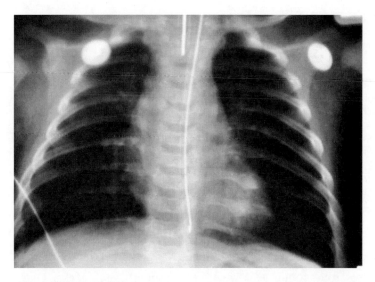

Figure 12. Old posterior rib fractures found in a boy at the age of 4 months. Initially the parents were investigated for child abuse but a diagnosis of Menkes' syndrome was made two weeks later. Courtesy of Dr R Allen.

As with copper deficiency, fractures, particularly rib fractures and metaphyseal abnormalities, do occur and can lead to a false diagnosis of non-accidental injury, particularly if intracranial bleeding is also present [60-64]. While spontaneous rib fractures may be present at birth, fractures first recognised later are particularly likely to lead to an initial misdiagnosis (Figure 12).

Biliary Atresia

Biliary atresia may be associated with bone disease and fractures, particularly rib fractures, diaphyseal and metaphyseal fractures [65,66]. These may lead to inappropriate investigation for non-accidental injury [66]. While in some cases vitamin D deficiency may be the underlying mechanism this is not true of all. The fracture rate decreases after liver transplantation [67].

Proprionic Acidemia

One case report describes a boy aged 16 months who sustained a fracture of the right radius after minimal trauma. Another report concerns a 6 year old boy with a spontaneous fracture of the right femur. Both were known to have proprionic acidemia [68,69].

Myofibromatosis

This rare mesenchymal disorder is characterised by the presence of small tumours in skin, subcutaneous tissue, muscle and bone. Spontaneous fractures including rib fractures and diaphyseal fractures have been reported in infants [70-72].

Congenital Syphilis

Fractures including metaphyseal fractures have long been recognised as complications of congenital syphilis [73,74]. While the well known radiological features of congenital syphilis, such as periostitis, are often also present in such cases this is not true of all. Six cases aged between 1 and 5 months have been reported recently in which fractures mimicked those of non-accidental injury [75-77]. In one there were multiple fractures in different stages of healing.

Congenital Cytomegalovirus Infection

Spontaneous fractures have been reported in two infants with cytomegalovirus infection [78]. The fractures were found at 4 weeks of age and at 11 weeks. One infant was born preterm; the other was a twin.

Immobility

Uncommon neuromuscular disorders present in intra-uterine life lead to diminished fetal movement and diminished bone formation. Multiple diaphyseal, metaphyseal and rib fractures have been found after birth [79]. Similarly older children with cerebral palsy or with neurological impairment of other causes have long been recognised as liable to sustain spontaneous fractures. For example Brunner and Doderlein [80] studied 37 cerebral palsy patients who sustained 54 fractures without any significant trauma.

Osteopathy of Prematurity

Spontaneous fractures have long been recognised in infants born preterm [81-85]. The most common fractures are asymptomatic rib fractures identified while the child is in a premature baby unit (Figure 13). Posterior rib fractures are not uncommon [85]. Metaphyseal abnormalities are also often described. Diaphyseal fractures as in Figure 14 are not uncommon and occur with normal handling.

The underlying bone disorder is often called rickets but there is no biochemical evidence in most cases that vitamin D deficiency is the cause. While the serum alkaline phosphatase is sometimes raised, the serum 25-dihydroxyvitamin D level is usually normal [86]. The serum 1, 25 hydroxyvitamin D level is higher in patients with fractures and/or radiological 'rickets' than in other preterm infants [79].

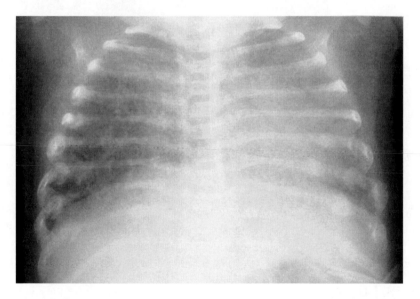

Figure 13. Multiple rib fractures of different ages in an 11 week old girl born preterm at 28 weeks gestation. All the rib fractures had occurred in hospital.

The significance of this finding remains unclear. Osteopenia is evident radiologically in some cases but this is a very inexact assessment. It may be that in the future bone densitometry, for example with quantitative ultrasound, will be helpful [87]. There is no relationship between the bone mineralisation and the biochemical findings for serum alkaline phosphatase and serum inorganic phosphate [88].

If this disorder is not caused by vitamin D deficiency what are the causes? Deficiencies of calcium and/or phosphorus have been postulated but there is no reliable evidence for these [89]. Copper deficiency has been considered; the levels of copper and of caeruloplasmin are lower in preterm infants than in full term infants but not different between preterm infants with fractures and those without [90]. However no assays were done in infants aged less than 3 months.

While fractures can be confidently attributed to this disorder in infants who are still in hospital, it is important to note that fractures associated with preterm birth are recognised up to the age of 6 months or more [82,84,91]. There is a real danger that, while the cause of fractures occurring in hospital is correctly identified, similar fractures occurring after discharge home may be attributed to child abuse, particularly if metaphyseal lesions are present [92].

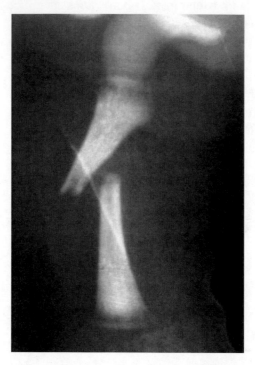

Figure 14. Transverse fracture of right femur found immediately after birth in a boy born at 31 weeks gestation by emergency caesarean section. Three weeks later spontaneous fractures of five ribs were found to have occurred. Courtesy of Dr H Barrie.

Temporary Brittle Bone Disease

From 1985 onwards I saw substantial numbers of infants who appeared to have a distinctive syndrome with multiple fractures. The patients were seen both in a clinical context and for medico-legal reasons. Ordinary osteogenesis imperfecta seemed unlikely because the often very numerous fractures in the first year of life were followed by no unexplained fractures in later years. Non-accidental injury seemed equally unlikely since the many fractures were never accompanied by commensurate clinical evidence of inflicted injury. Indeed the great majority of the fractures were asymptomatic. To this disorder we gave the provisional name 'temporary brittle bone disease' (TBBD) [2]. Others have reached similar conclusions [3, 93].

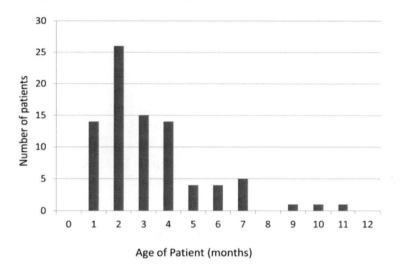

Figure 15. Age when first fracture found in 85 children with temporary brittle bone disease. All these patients had been the subject of civil proceedings [100].

These considerations were controversial since the fractures seen, including rib fractures and metaphyseal lesions, were those confidently ascribed to non-accidental injury over the last forty years [94,95]. However there are at least four lines of evidence indicating that these cases reflect real bone disease rather than misdiagnosed child abuse. First, the patients show striking clinical and radiological similarities to each other. The ages at which the fractures are found are illustrated in Figure 15. The distribution of fractures is similar with a preponderance of rib fractures and metaphyseal lesions. The metaphyseal lesions are sometimes symmetrical which is difficult to explain in terms of inflicted injury. Many patients are anaemic or neutropenic. Other authors have reported patients who are clearly similar but without using the term TBBD [96,97].

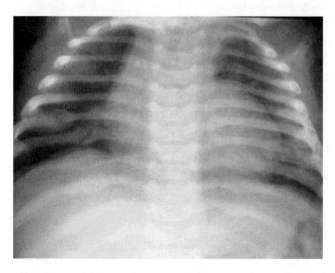

Figure 16. Chest x-ray showing multiple rib fractures of different ages in a boy, one of twins, born at 36 weeks gestation by elective caesarean section. At least six of these fractures had occurred while in hospital.

Second, there is often a gross discrepancy between the radiological evidence of fractures and the clinical reports made at the time that they were apparently sustained. Most of our patients had reliable evidence of independent examinations by doctors or nurses at relevant times. This discrepancy is particularly telling in relation to rib fractures. An infant's ribs are flexible and fractures seldom occur in accidental injury. When they do, for example in traffic accidents, more than about four rib fractures represents injury so severe that survival is unlikely [98]. In contrast patients appearing to have TBBD may have more than 20 rib fractures and be clinically asymptomatic. Similarly recent transverse fractures (implying local force) are found without superficial evidence of injury. Third, an identical clinical picture may be seen in children in whom there is reliable evidence that all or most of the fractures occurred whilst they were in hospital [99]. An example is shown in Figure 16. Fourth, subsequent non-accidental injury has not occurred in 61 children returned to their parents after a report specifying TBBD as the cause of fractures [100]. The mean follow-up period was 6.9 years. The patients in question had had an average of 9.1 fractures. Had these been caused by non-accidental injury it would have been severe and repeated. The lack of subsequent suspect injury contrasts with published recurrence rates of 20% to 50% in abused children returned to their parents [101,102]. It is consistent with the view that the original fractures were unlikely to have been caused by abuse. The cause of TBBD remains unclear. However some risk factors can be identified. Among patients with TBBD there are large numbers of infants born preterm so that the osteopathy of prematurity could well be the same disorder. Above average numbers of twins and triplets are found in all series [2,93]. Miller and Hangartner [103] reported the frequency of a history of decreased fetal movement. It is likely that this and intrauterine confinement are contributory factors as with diminished fetal movement of neurological causes [79]. Biochemical factors may play a part. There are similarities between TBBD patients and infants with copper deficiency [2]. The metaphyseal lesions of TBBD also resemble those of scurvy and healing rickets [104]. While few patients have been investigated systematically for these deficiencies (and none for scurvy), the finding of normal values for plasma copper or caeruloplasmin or for 25-hydroxyvitamin D after fractures are found does not exclude abnormalities causing bone disease during intra-uterine life at the time when the bones were being formed.

Heritable factors may contribute to the propensity to develop TBBD. In the course of evaluating individual cases of unexplained fractures, the family history was investigated as fully as possible. We found that of 81 children, both of whose parents had been examined personally, no less than 40 had at least one parent with significant joint laxity (a Beighton score of four or more) [105]. The difference from a control population was significant.

This disorder may be heterogeneous and multifactorial; much further work is needed to identify all its causes. However, in the meantime, it is important to recognise this distinctive bone disorder when it occurs.

DISCUSSION

Some of the disorders discussed in this article may be thought of as rare. There is however an important distinction between genuinely rare and 'rarely considered and therefore rarely diagnosed'. We sometimes encounter evidence for child abuse which can be paraphrased as an assertion that 'the disease postulated is rare and child abuse is common; therefore these fractures are due to abuse'.

Until very recently vitamin D deficiency was thought to be rare in the western world. It is now clear that whatever standards are applied significant vitamin D deficiency is widespread in many parts of society. Scurvy and copper deficiency are still thought to be rare but these are seldom looked for. There are no systematic studies of the incidence of either in unselected infants and these disorders, too, may be much more common than anticipated.

One further difficulty in this field is that a confident initial diagnosis of child abuse tends to inhibit any more than perfunctory investigation of alternative causes of fractures. In our experience of osteogenesis imperfecta we were surprised to find that in six out of twelve cases of initial misdiagnosis the family history was positive but had not been elicited [6]. In one recent study attempting to explore the significance of vitamin D deficiency [106] in fracture liability the authors reported 118 children with fractures, including 37 thought to have been abused. Just ten cases were referred for evaluation by the metabolic bone service.

One limitation of this review is that it summarises reports of fractures in various metabolic disorders. However the association may be unreliable. Some patients with temporary brittle bone disease could equally be regarded as cases of osteopathy of prematurity. Some could in fact be cases of vitamin D deficiency, copper deficiency or scurvy. Some patients reported as having copper deficiency could equally be cases of osteopathy of prematurity. The patients with biliary atresia could have vitamin D deficiency.

One feature common to all the bone disorders discussed here is that fractures occur spontaneously or with normal handling. Consequently the fractures are seldom accompanied by any clinical evidence of the external force that would have been required had the bones been normal. This discrepancy is a valuable pointer to the likelihood of bone disease.

One study is sometimes cited in this connection. Mathew et al [107] reported a series of children with fractures and commented that bruising was an uncommon feature. However the relevance of this study to most cases in which there is a differential diagnosis of bone disease is very uncertain. The majority of infants with unexplained fractures are aged less than one year and all Mathew's patients were older than one year.

Most patients in the Mathew study only had a single fracture whereas many of the patients we see with various bone disorders have much larger numbers of fractures at the time of presentation. The diagnosis in a child with a single fracture can be difficult. However, the more fractures that are found without commensurate clinical evidence of trauma, the more *unlikely* it is that the cause was inflicted injury.

A second study attempted to address this issue. Peters et al [108] reviewed the records of 192 children with fractures regarded as caused by inflicted injury. Bruising was uncommon at the fracture sites. However the authors did not recognise the circular argument at the heart of this study; there was no evidence in the paper that the patients had been routinely investigated for any form of bone disease.

One difficulty in this field is that there is a widely reported view that certain fractures are characteristic or even 'pathognomic' for child abuse [109]. This is particularly true of metaphyseal lesions. These are usually asymptomatic and are found with a full skeletal survey which is usually only carried out in children suspected of having been abused. These were originally assumed to be fractures caused by avulsion of small fragments of bone and adjacent cartilage by trauma [110]. It is no longer thought that all metaphyseal lesions are fractures and it is now more appropriate to describe them as 'metaphyseal lesions'[111].

It is important to recognise that these lesions have a substantial differential diagnosis. This includes osteogenesis imperfecta [12], hyperparathyroidism [112-114], copper deficiency [53,56], Menkes' syndrome [54,55], scurvy [115] and after fetal exposure to magnesium [116]. Metaphyseal lesions are recognised in infants born with congenital neurological problems [79]. They have been reported in the apparent absence of bone disease after an 'easy' delivery by caesarean section [117], with normal handling in an intensive care unit [118] and after physiotherapy [119,120]. Metaphyseal lesions often resemble the changes of rickets [15,111]. Others have commented on the limitations of the view that metaphyseal lesions represent non-accidental injury [121,122].

Families and not least the children concerned pay a heavy price for the failure to identify a medical cause of unexplained fractures. In a study of 33 children with osteogenesis imperfecta Kocher and Dichtel [8] found that 26 were removed from the parents before the correct diagnosis was made. In our experience of temporary brittle bone disease substantial numbers of children were removed permanently from their parents. They then grow up being told that when they were young their real parents hurt them badly. Unaffected older siblings are particularly likely to be permanently damaged by removal from their families. Long-term damage to the relationships between the parents is very common even after the children concerned are returned home [100]. It is vitally important to investigate these children with an open mind.

ACKNOWLEDGMENT

I am grateful to Mrs S Paterson for a critical review of this paper in draft, to Miss E Alexander for preparing several of the figures and to Ms K Bovill for excellent secretarial help.

REFERENCES

[1]   Feiss HO. Spontaneous fractures with rickets. *J Bone Joint Surg Am*, 1906;s2-3:271-8

[2]   Paterson CR, Burns J, McAllion SJ. Osteogenesis imperfecta: the distinction from child abuse and the recognition of a variant form. *Am J Med Genet* 1993;45:187-92

[3]   Miller ME. The lesson of temporary brittle bone disease: all bones are not created equal. *Bone* 2003;33:466-74

[4]   Roughley PJ, Rauch F, Glorieux FH. Osteogenesis imperfecta – clinical and molecular diversity. *Eur Cell Mater* 2003;5:41-7

[5]   Evensen SA, Myhre L, Stormorken H. Haemostatic studies in osteogenesis imperfecta. *Scand J Haematol* 1984;33:177-9

[6]   Paterson CR, McAllion SJ. Classical osteogenesis imperfecta and allegations of nonaccidental injury. *Clin Orthop Relat Res* 2006;452:260-4

[7]   Pandya NK, Baldwin K, Kamath AF, Wenger DR, Hosalkar HS. Unexplained fractures: child abuse or bone disease. *Clin Orthop Relat Res* 2011;469:805-12

[8]   Kocher MS, Dichtel L. Osteogenesis imperfecta misdiagnosed as child abuse. *J Pediatr Orthop B* 2011;20:440-3

[9]   Paterson CR, McAllion S, Miller R. Osteogenesis imperfecta with dominant inheritance and normal sclerae. *J Bone Joint Surg Br* 1983;65-B:35-9

[10]   Paterson CR, McAllion SJ, Shaw JW. Clinical and radiological features of osteogenesis imperfecta type IVA. *Acta Paediatr Scand* 1987; 76:548-52.

[11]   Paterson CR, Mole PA. Bone density in osteogenesis imperfecta may well be normal. *Postgrad Med J* 1994; 70:104-7.

[12]   Dent JA, Paterson CR. Fractures in early childhood: osteogenesis imperfecta or child abuse? *J Pediatr Orthop* 1991; 11:184-6.

[13]   Wenstrup RJ, Willing MC, Starman BJ, Byers PH. Distinct biochemical phenotypes predict clinical severity in nonlethal variants of osteogenesis imperfecta. *Am J Hum Genet* 1990;46:975-82

[14]   Holick MF. Resurrection of vitamin D deficiency and rickets. *J Clin Invest* 2006;116:2062-72

[15]   Keller KA, Barnes PD. Rickets vs abuse: a national and international epidemic. *Pediatr Radiol* 2008;38:1210-6

[16]   Pettifor JM, Isdale JM, Sahakian J, Hansen JDL. Diagnosis of subclinical rickets. *Arch Dis Child* 1980;55:155-7

[17]   Paterson CR. Vitamin D deficiency and fractures in childhood. *Pediatrics* 2011; 127:973- 4

[18]   Paterson CR. Vitamin D deficiency: a diagnosis often missed. *Br J Hosp Med* 2011;72:456-62

[19]   Russell JGB, Hill LF. True fetal rickets. *Br J Radiol* 1974;47:732-4

[20]   Bodnar LM, Simhan HN, Powers RW, Frank MP, Cooperstein E, Roberts JM. High prevalence of vitamin D insufficiency in black and white pregnant women residing in the northern United States and their neonates. *J Nutr* 2007;137: 447-52

[21]   Seniappan S, Elazabi A, Doughty I, Mughal MZ. Fractures in under 6-month old exclusively breast-fed infants born to immigrant parents: nonaccidental injury? *Acta Paediatr* 2008;97:836-7

[22]   Paterson CR. Vitamin D deficiency rickets and allegations of non-accidental injury. *Acta Paediatr* 2009;98:2008-12

[23]   Slovis TL, Chapman S. Evaluating the data concerning vitamin D insufficiency/deficiency and child abuse. *Pediatr Radiol* 2008; 38:1221-4

[24]   Feldman KW, Done S. Vitamin D deficiency rickets and allegations of non accidental injury. *Acta Paediatr* 2010; 99:486-7

[25]   Ayoub D, Plunkett J, Keller KA, Barnes PD. Are Paterson's critics too biased to recognize rickets? *Acta Paediatr* 2010;99:1282-3

[26]   Bevan R. Severe rickets with multiple spontaneous fractures. *Proc R Soc Med* 1938;31:361-4

[27]   Rossier A, Arvay N, Blanchet G, Martin H, Babok J. Les fractures des enfant rachitiques. *J Radiol Electrol Med Nucl* 1963;44:377-8

[28]   Chapman T, Sugar N, Done S, Marasigan J, Wambold N, Feldman K. Fractures in infants and toddlers with rickets. *Pediatr Radiol* 2010;40:1184-9

[29]   Kovar I, Mayne P. Plasma alkaline phosphatase activity in the preterm neonate. *Acta Paediatr Scand* 1981;70:501-6

[30]   Nagi NA. Vitamin D deficiency rickets in malnourished children. *J Trop Med Hyg* 1972;75:251-4

[31]   Malabanan A, Veronikis IE, Holick MF. Redefining vitamin D insufficiency. *Lancet* 1998;351:805-6

[32]   Root AW, Vargas A, Duckett GE, Hough G. Hypocalcemia and hypovitaminosis D in an infant from Florida, the sunshine state. *J Fla Med Assoc* 1980;67:933-4

[33]   Ahmed I, Atiq M, Iqbal J, Khurshid M, Whittaker P. Vitamin D deficiency rickets in breast-fed infants presenting with hypocalcaemic seizures. *Acta Paediatr* 1995;84:941-2

[34]   Abdul-Motaal A, Gettinby G, McIntosh WB, Sutherland GR, Dunnigan MG. Relationships between radiological and bicohemical evidence of rickets in Asian schoolchildren. *Postgrad Med J* 1985;61:307-12

[35]   Mankin HJ. Rickets, osteomalacia and renal osteodystrophy. *J Bone Joint Surg Am* 1974;56:352-86

[36]   Prockop JD. Collagens: Molecular biology, diseases and potentials for therapy. *Annu Rev Biochem* 1995;64:403-34

[37]   Silverman FN. An unusual osseous sequel to infantile scurvy. *J Bone Joint Surg Am* 1953;35:215-20

[38]   Swischuk LE. Metaphyseal corner fractures in infants: a review. *Emerg Radiol* 1998;5:103-7

[39]   Eisele PH, Morgan JP, Line AS, Anderson JH. Skeletal lesions and anemia associated with ascorbic acid deficiency in juvenile rhesus macaques. *Lab Anim Sci* 1992;42:245-9

[40]   Ratterree MS, Didier PJ, Blanchard JL, Clarke MR, Schaeffer D. Vitamin C deficiency in captive nonhuman primates fed commercial primate diet. *Lab Anim Sci* 1990;40: 165-8

[41]   Tsunenari T, Fukase M, Fujita T. Bone histomorphometric analysis for the cause of osteopenia in vitamin D deficient rat (ODS rat). *Calcif Tissue Int* 1991;48:18-27

[42]   Beamer et al. Spontaneous fracture (sfx): a mouse genetic model of defective peripubertal bone formation. *Bone* 2000;27:619-26

[43]   Hasan L, Vögeli P, Neuenschwander S, Stoll P, Meijerink E, Stricker C, Jörg H, Stranzinger G. The L-gulono-gamma-lactone oxidase gene (GULO) which is a candidate for vitamin C deficiency in pigs maps to chromosome 14. *Anim Genet* 1999;30:309-12

[44]   Berant M, Jacobs J. A "pseudo" battered child. *Clin Pediatr (Phila)* 1966;5:230-7

[45]   Paterson C R. Multiple fractures in infancy: scurvy or nonaccidental injury? *Orthop Res Rev* 2010;2:45-8

[46]   Lewis D, Carpenter C, Evans E, Thomas P. Rickets and scurvy presenting in a child as apparent non accidental injury. *Internet J Orthop Surg* 2007;4(2)

[47]   McLean S, McIntosh R. Healing in infantile scurvy as shown by x-ray. *Am J Dis Child* 1928;36:875-930

[48]   Fain O. Musculoskeletal manifestations of scurvy. *Joint Bone Spine* 2005;72:124-8

[49]   Uauy R, Olivares M, Gonzalez M. Essentiality of copper in humans. *Am J Clin Nutr* 1998;67:952s-9s

[50]   Paterson CR, Burns J. Copper deficiency in infancy. *J Clin Biochem Nutr* 1988;4:175-90

[51]   Pontz BF, Herwig J, Greinacher I. Cu-Mangel als Ursache einer Spontanfraktur bei einem Frühgeborenen. *Monatsschr Kinderheilkd* 1989;137:419-21

[52]   Velin P, Dupont D, Daoud A. La carence nutritionnelle en cuivre. *Ann Pédiatr (Paris)* 1989;36:269-74

[53]   Schmidt H, Herwig J, Greinacher I. Skelettveränderungen bei Frühgeborenen mit Kupfermangel. *Fortschr Röntgenstr* 1991;155:38-42

[54]   Hoyle GS, Schwartz RP, Auringer ST. Pseudoscurvy caused by copper deficiency. *J Pediatr* 1999;134:379

[55]   Bennani-Smires C, Medine J. Infantile nutritional copper deficiency. *Am J Dis Child* 1980;134:1155-6

[56]   Grünebaum M, Horodniceanu C, Steinherz R. The radiographic manifestations of bone changes in copper deficiency. *Pediatr Radiol* 1980;9:101-4

[57]   Arredondo M, Martinez R, Núñez MT, Ruz M, Olivares M. Inhibition of iron and copper uptake by iron, copper and zinc. *Biol Res* 2006;39:95-102

[58]   Olivares O, Araya M, Uauy R. Copper homeostasis in infant nutrition: deficit and excess. *J Pediatr Gastroenterol Nutr* 2000;31:102-11

[59]   Harvey LJ, Ashton K, Hooper L, Casgrain A, Fairweather-Tait SJ. Methods of assessment of copper status in humans: a systematic review. *Am J Clin Nutr* 2009;89:2009s-24s

[60]   Danks DM. Inborn errors of trace element metabolism. *Clin Endocrinol Metab* 1985;14:591-615

[61]   Adams PC, Strand RD, Bresnan MJ, Lucky AW. Kinky hair syndrome: serial study of radiological findings with emphasis on the similarity to the battered child syndrome. *Radiology* 1974;112: 401-7.

[62]   Stanley P, Gwinn JL, Sutcliffe J. The osseous abnormailities in Menkes' syndrome. *Ann Radiol* 1976;19:167-172

[63]   Bacopoulou F, Henderson L, Philip S G. Menkes' disease mimicking non-accidental injury. *Arch Dis Childh* 2006;91:919

[64]   Tümer Z, Møller LB. Menkes disease. *Eur J Hum Genet* 2010;18:511-8

[65]   Katayama H, Suruga K, Kurashige T, Kimoto T. Bone changes in congenital biliary atresia. *Am J Roentgenol Radium Ther Nucl Med* 1975;124:107-12

[66]   De Russo PA, Spevak MR, Schwarz KB. Fractures in biliary atresia misinterpreted as child abuse. *Pediatrics* 2003;112:185-8

[67]   Katsura S, Ogita K, Taguchi T, Suita S, Yoshizumi T, Soejima Y, Shimada M, Machara Y. Effect of liver transplantation on multiple bone fractures in an infant with end-stage biliary atresia: a case report. *Pediatr Surg Int* 2005;21:47-9

[68]   North KN, Korson MS, Gopal YR, Rohr FJ, Brazelton TB, Walsbren SE, Warman ML. Neonatal-onset proprionic acidemia: Neurologic and developmental profiles, and implications for management. *J Pediatr* 1995:916-22

[69]   Talbot JC, Gummerson NW, Kluge W, Shaw DL, Groves C, Lealman GT. Osteoporotic femoral fracture in a child with proprionic acidaemia presenting as non-accidental injury. *Eur J Pediatr* 2006;165:496-7

[70]   Zeller B, Storm-Mathisen I, Smevik B, Sund S, Danielsen K, Lie SO. Cure of infantile myofibromatosis with severe respiratory complications without antitumour therapy. *Eur J Pediatr* 1997;56:841-4

[71]   Wada H, Akiyama H, Seki H, Ichihara T, Ueno K, Miyawaki T, Koizumi S. Spinal canal involvement in infantile myofibromatosis. *J Pediatr Hematol Oncol* 1998;20:353-6

[72]   Buonuomo PS, Ruggiero A, Zampino G, Maurizi P, Attinà G, Riccardi R. A newborn with multiple fractures as first presentation of infantile myofibromatosis. *J Perinatol* 2006;26:653-5

[73]   Russo PE, Shryock LF. Bone lesions of congenital syphilis in infants and adolescents: report of 46 cases. *Radiology* 1945;44:477-84

[74]   Rasool MN, Govender S. The skeletal manifestations of congenital syphilis. *J Bone Joint Surg Br* 1989;71-B:752-5

[75]   Lee G, Ball C, Sellars M, Hannam S. Congenital syphilis as a differential diagnosis of non-accidental injury. *Eur J Pediatr* 2008;167:1071-2

[76]   Kim SJ, Lee SW, Rhim JW, Youn YS, Lee JS, Hwang JY. A case of congenital syphilis mistaken for possible child abuse. *Korean J Pediatr* 2009;52:710-2

[77]   Prince M, van Dijk J, van As AB. An unusual cause of humeral fracture. *SAJCH* 2008;2:30-1

[78]   Smith RK, Specht EE. Osseous lesions and pathologic fractures in congenital cytomegalic inclusion disease. *Clin Orthop Relat Res* 1979;144:280-3

[79]   Rodríguez JI, Garcia-Alix A, Palacios J, Paniagua R. Changes in the long bones due to fetal immobility caused by neuromuscular disease. *J Bone Joint Surg Am* 1988;70-A:1052-60

[80]   Brunner R, Doderlein L. Pathological fractures in patients with cerebral palsy. *J Pediatr Orthop B* 1996;5:232-8

[81]   Geggel RL, Pereira GR, Spackman TJ. Fractured ribs: unusual presentation of rickets in premature infants. *J Pediatr* 1978;93:680-2

[82]   Amir J, Katz K, Grunebaum M, Yosipovich Z, Wielunsky E, Reisner SH. Fractures in premature infants. *J Pediatr Orthop* 1988;8:41-4

[83]   Koo WWK, Sherman R, Succop P, Krug-Wispe S, Tsang RC, Steichen JJ, Crawford AH, Oestreich AE. Fractures and rickets in very low birth weight infants: conservative management and outcome. *J Pediatr Orthop* 1989;9:326-30

[84]   Dabezies EJ, Warren PD. Fractures in very low birth weight infants with rickets. *Clin Orthop Relat Res* 1997;335:233-9

[85]   Wei C, Stevens J, Harrison S, Mott A. Fractures in a tertiary neonatal intensive care unit in Wales. *Acta Paediatr* 2012 (in press)

[86]   Koo WWK, Sherman R, Succop P, Ho M, Buckley D, Tsang RC. Serum vitamin D metabolites in very low birth weight infants with and without rickets and fractures. *J Pediatr* 1989;114:1017-22

[87]   Rack B, Lochmüller EM, Janni W, Lipowsky G, Engelsberger I, Friese K, Küster H. Ultrasound for the assessment of bone quality in preterm and term infants. *J Perinatol* 2012;32:218-26

[88]   Faerk J, Peitersen B, Petersen S, Michaelsen KF. Bone mineralisation in premature infants cannot be predicted from serum alkaline phosphatase or serum phosphate. *Arch Dis Child Fetal Neonatal Ed* 2002;87:F133-6

[89]   Backström MC, Kuusela A, Mäki R. Metabolic bone disease of prematurity. *Ann Med* 1996;28:275-82

[90]   Koo WWK, Succop P, Hambidge KM. Sequential concentrations of copper and ceruloplasmin in serum from preterm infants with rickets and fractures. *Clin Chem* 1991;37:556-9

[91]   Noble R, McDevitt H, Herbison J, Butler S, Ahmed SF. The prevalence of rib fractures in ex-preterm infants. *Bone* 2009;45:S100

[92]   Carroll DM, Doria AS, Paul BS. Clinical-radiological features of fractures in premature infants – a review. *J Perinat Med* 2007;35:366-75

[93]   Miller ME. Temporary brittle bone disease: A true entity? *Semin Perinatol* 1999;23:174-82

[94]   Mendelson KL. Critical review of 'temporary brittle bone disease'. *Pediatr Radiol* 2005;35:1036-40

[95]   Carole J. Evaluating infants and young children with multiple fractures. *Pediatrics* 2006;118:1299-303

[96]   Tsujii M, Hirata H, Hasegawa M, Uchida A. An infant with unexplained multiple rib fractures occurring during treatment in a neonatal intensive care unit. *Turk J Pediatr* 2008;50:377-9

[97]   Hyman CJ. Response to Paterson. Temporary brittle bone disease: fractures in medical care. *Acta Paediatr* 2010;99:1281

[98]   Garcia VF, Gotschall CS, Eichelberger MR, Bowman LM. Rib fractures in children: a marker of severe trauma. *J Trauma* 1990;30:695-700

[99]   Paterson CR. Temporary brittle bone disease: fractures in medical care. *Acta Paediatr* 2009;98:1935-8

[100]   Paterson CR, Monk EA. Long-term follow-up of children thought to have temporary brittle bone disease. *Pediatr Health Med Therapeut* 2011;2:55-8

[101]   Galleno H, Oppenheim WL. The battered child syndrome revisited. *Clin Orthop Relat Res* 1982;162:11-9

[102]   Terling T. The efficacy of family reunification practices: Reentry rates and correlates of reentry for abused and neglected children reunited with their families. *Child Abuse Negl* 1999;23:1359-70

[103]   Miller ME, Hangartner TN. Temporary brittle bone disease: association with decreased fetal movement and osteopenia. *Calcif Tissue Int* 1999;64:137-43

[104]   Ayoub D, Miller ME, Hyman C. The forgotten signs of healing rickets in early infantile hypovitaminosis D. 2010.rsna2010.rsna.org/search/event_display.cfm?em_id=9016026andprintmode=Yand autoprint=N

[105]   Paterson CR, Mole PA. Joint laxity in the parents of children with temporary brittle bone disease. *Rheumatol Int* 2012 (in press)

[106]   Schilling S, Wood J, Levine MA, Langdon D, Christian CW. Vitamin D status in abused and nonabused children younger than 2 years old with fractures. *Pediatr* 2011;127:835-41

[107]   Mathew MO, Ramamohan N, Bennet GC. Importance of bruising associated with paediatric fractures: prospective observational study. *BMJ* 1998;317:1117-8

[108]   Peters ML, Starling SP, Barnes-Eley ML, Heisler KW. The presence of bruising associated with fractures. *Arch Pediat Adolesc Med* 2008;162:877-81

[109]   Ablin DS, Greenspan A, Reinhart M, Grix A. Differentiation of child abuse from osteogenesis imperfecta. *AJR* 1990;154:1035-46

[110]   Caffey J. Some traumatic lesions in growing bones other than fractures and dislocations: clinical and radiological features. *Br J Radiol* 1957;30:225-38

[111]   Offiah A, Van Rijn RR, Perez-Rossello JM, Kleinman PK. Skeletal imaging of child abuse (non-accidental injury). *Pediatr Radiol* 2009;39:461-70

[112]   Ch'ng JLC, Kaiser A, Lynn J, Joplin GF. Post-parathyroidectomy restoration of normal calcium homeostasis in neonatal primary hyperparathyroidism. *Acta Endocrinol* 1984;105:350-3

[113]   Wilkinson H, James J. Self limiting neonatal primary hyperparathyroidism associated with familial hypocalciuric hypercalcaemia. *Arch Dis Child* 1993;69:319-21

[114]   Bai M, Pearce SHS, Kifor O, Trivedi S, Stauffer UG, Thakker RV, Brown EM, Steinmann B. In vivo and in vitro characterization of neonatal hyperparathyroidism resulting from a de novo, heterozygous mutation in the Ca^{2+}- sensing receptor gene: normal maternal calcium homeostasis as a cause of secondary hyperparathyroidism in familial benign hypocalciuric hypercalacemia. *J Clin Invest* 1997;99:88-96

[115]   Caffey J. *Pediatric X-ray Diagnosis* 7th ed, Chicago: Year Book Medical Publishers 1978;

[116]   Wedig KE, Kogan J, Schorry EK, Whitsett JA. Skeletal demineralization and fractures caused by fetal magnesium toxicity. *J Perinatol* 2006;26:371-4

[117]   Alexander J, Gregg JEM, Quinn MW. Femoral fractures at caesarean section. *Br J Obstet Gynaecol* 1987;94:273

[118]   Phillips RR, Lee SH. Fractures of long bones occurring in neonatal intensive therapy units. *BMJ* 1990;301:225-6

[119]   Helfer RE, Scheurer SL, Alexander R, Reed J, Slovis TL. Trauma to the bones of small infants from passive exercise: a factor in the etiology of child abuse. *J Pediatr* 1984;104:47-50

[120]   Grayev AM, Boal DKB, Wallach DM, Segal LS. Metaphyseal fractures mimicking abuse during treatment for clubfoot. *Pediatr Radiol* 2001;31:559-63

[121]   Hiller HG. Battered or not – a reappraisal of metaphyseal fragility. *Am J Roentgenol* 1972;114:241-6

[122]   Miller M. Another perspective on the cause of metaphyseal fractures. *Pediatr Radiol* 2008;38:598-9

In: Child Abuse   ISBN: 978-1-62257-113-0
Editors: Raymond A. Turner and Henry O. Rogers   © 2012 Nova Science Publishers, Inc.

Chapter 3

CHILD SEXUAL ABUSE PREVENTION PROGRAMS FOR PARENTS: BEYOND PROTECTIVE BEHAVIOURS

Georgia Babatsikos
Deakin University, Burwood, Australia

ABSTRACT

While there are some child sexual abuse prevention programs for parents, these tend to focus solely on protective behaviours and urging parents to report abuse to authorities. The current focus of the majority of prevention programs on teaching children protective behaviours has been criticised for placing the burden of responsibility for prevention on children while overlooking the critical population of parents. Parents are responsible for the protection and care of children and are in a powerful position to make a difference in terms of prevention and early detection. There is a need for parents to take more responsibility for prevention given the extent of known sexual abuse of children, particularly by persons known to families, and there is a need for more prevention programs targeting parents due to the scarcity of such programs. This research was undertaken to better understand the knowledge, attitudes and behaviours of parents around child sexual abuse prevention and to inform the development of effective prevention programs for parents.

This study explored how parents manage the risk of child sexual abuse, including prevention as well as intervention strategies when sexual boundaries had been crossed with their children. Using a social constructivist philosophy and grounded theory methods, qualitative in-depth interviews were conducted with 28 parents (16 mothers and 12 fathers) from two cities in Australia, Cairns and Melbourne, between 2006 and 2008.

The findings from this primary research provide a range of prevention strategies that parents used to reduce the risk of sexual abuse to their children, including not only protective behaviours but also an array of important early intervention strategies. These include general communication skills with children to begin conversations on a range of challenging topics, including but not limited to child sexual abuse prevention, as well as specific communication strategies with children about child sexual abuse, including initiating conversations with children about sexual abuse. Other strategies included investigating social situations for safety, engaging with an extended support network to protect children and monitoring and respecting children's comfort levels with other persons within their social networks.

Early intervention strategies reported by parents once they believed sexual boundaries had been crossed included: making the person who had crossed the boundary aware, through verbal and non-verbal communication, that the parent was cognisant of what they were doing; limiting contact with that person; confidentially warning others in their social networks of potential boundary-crossing risks from that person and reporting boundary-crossing incidents to authorities. Each of these prevention and early intervention strategies are discussed in detail in this chapter.

Recommendations from this research include the need for further research to understand parental knowledge attitudes and behaviours relevant to child sexual abuse prevention, research to understand models of prevention from different countries on so as to expand and improve prevention education for parents and the development of appropriate and accessible prevention programs for parents.

OVERVIEW

Programs to prevent child sexual abuse are essential because of the extent of the problem (Australian Institute of Health and Welfare, 2010; Pereda, Guilera, Forns and Gómez-Benito, 2009) and the serious and long-term consequences of child sexual abuse (Andrews, Gould and Corry, 2002; Conway, Mendelson, Giannopoulos, Csank and Holm, 2004; Molnar, Berkman and Buka, 2001; Nelson, Heath, Madden, Cooper, Dinwiddie, Bucholz, Glowinski, McLaughlin, Dunne, Statham and Martin, 2002). The majority of prevention programs that have been carried out to date focus on teaching protective behaviours to children,[1] and there are limited programs targeting parents (Finkelhor, 2009).[2] This emphasis on programs for children has been criticised for placing undue burden for prevention on children, and there are calls for more programs targeting parents and other adults who have the responsibility for protecting children (Anderson, Mangels and Langsam, 2004; Reppucci, Haugaard and Antonishak, 2005; Resofsky, 2007; Stanley, 2010; Topping and Barron, 2009; Wurtele, 2009; Wurtele and Kenny, 2010).

A review of the literature reveals that the majority of prevention programs for parents are presented in schools in conjunction with programs targeting children (Kenny, Capri, Thakkar-Kolar, Ryan and Runyon, 2008). A review of prevention programs by MacIntyre and Carr (2000) found that programs targeting parents alone did not significantly increase parental knowledge about child sexual abuse prevention, while multi-systemic programs that targeted parents, children and teachers showed significant gains in knowledge and protective behaviours by parents. The content of prevention programs for parents generally includes teaching children protective behaviours, identifying characteristics of perpetrators and urging parents to report abuse to authorities (Burgess and Wurtele, 1998; Wurtele, Moreno and Kenny, 2008). While in many cases there are reported evaluations of these programs, it is often unclear in the literature how they are developed and exactly what material is presented; understanding program development and content is essential to conduct formative, process and outcome evaluation and replicate successful programs in other areas. Proper formative evaluation or needs assessment is an important step in program delivery, and research on the

---

[1] Protective behaviour programs teach children how to avoid unwanted sexual and physical advances and seek help if such advances occur; such programs are primarily carried out in schools (Tomison and Poole, 2000).

[2] The term 'parents' in this chapter includes primary caregivers of children.

experiences and concerns of parents about how they manage the risk of sexual abuse can assist in the development of effective programs. There is relatively little recent qualitative research explaining what the challenges are for parents when dealing with the risk of sexual abuse to their children and how to overcome these to develop effective prevention programs (Babatsikos, 2010). This research project was developed from this need for information on how parents manage the risk of sexual abuse so that programs targeting parents can be developed.

STUDY DESIGN

This study was designed to explore how Australian parents manage the risk of sexual abuse to their children, including prevention and early intervention strategies, as well as sources of support, information and education on the topic of child sexual abuse prevention to inform the development of child sexual abuse prevention programs for parents. Qualitative methods were used to understand the process and context in which these challenges took place. Using social constructivism and grounded theory, this research was carried out as part of a PhD at James Cook University in Cairns, Australia. In-depth interviews were conducted with 28 parents (16 mothers and 12 fathers) from two cities (Melbourne, a major city in the southern part of the country, and Cairns, a small city in the northern part of the country) from 2006 to 2008. Parents were asked how they perceived the risks of child sexual abuse and what measures were taken to prevent it, as well as their reactions and protective strategies used once sexually-related, boundary-crossing incidents had occurred. Parents who participated were generally from middle- to high-income families, with some representation from lower-income families. Participants had children from the ages of five to 15 years, and all parents had lived in Australia for at least five years or more. The cultural heritage of the parents included African, Australian, Chinese, Eastern European, English, Greek, Indian and Italian.

FINDINGS

Parents in this study reflected on two main issues related to the prevention of child sexual abuse. First, they discussed the challenge of providing appropriate prevention messages that were protective and empowering yet did not scare their children. They explained the importance of balancing this information with preserving the innocence of their children, especially when presenting information about the risk of persons known to the families, such as relatives or close acquaintances. This challenge of providing information without scaring children has been found to be a concern for parents in other studies on child sexual abuse prevention (Elrod and Rubin, 1993; Finkelhor, 1984).

Second, parents who had perceived that a boundary-crossing incident had occurred between their child and another person (adult or child) reported that when these incidents occurred with persons close to their family (relatives or good friends), they felt a substantial challenge in balancing the complex social relationships with taking action to protect their children from any further incidents. Parents were not comfortable reporting to authorities those incidents that occurred with uncles, cousins or friends because they were hesitant to upset the delicate social connections that their family had with those persons. When incidents occurred with distant acquaintances, such as child-care workers, or with complete strangers, parents were more likely to take action and report incidents to legal or organisational authorities. These findings are consistent with other research that shows parents are much less likely to report incidents that occur with persons close to their families (Finkelhor, 1984). Parents also reported the difficulty in proving the incidents, with many describing encountering actions that legally would be considered grooming activities. Grooming activities are notoriously subtle and difficult to prove, despite laws targeting these behaviours (Craven, Brown and Gilchrist, 2006). One parent demonstrated this when, after an incident had occurred between his teenage daughter and his brother-in-law, he explained:

> The thing is I couldn't prove anything directly. (Sam) [3]

This difficulty in finding proof was another reason why parents said they were hesitant to immediately report boundary-crossing incidents to authorities. Therefore, parents in this study reported other ways of dealing with their concerns and setting boundaries. The strategies used by parents in *prevention* and *early intervention* when incidents had occurred are described below.

STRATEGIES BEYOND PROTECTIVE BEHAVIOURS AND REPORTING

Parents in this study reported a number of strategies used to protect children from child sexual abuse beyond protective behaviours and reporting to authorities when intervening after boundary-crossing incidents. Before discussing these strategies, it is important to point out two important factors that parents reported had influenced the way in which they dealt with sexuality issues in general with their children, as well as the way they specifically managed the risk of sexual abuse to their children. The first factor was that their own parents had been conservative and had not spoken to them comfortably about sexuality issues; this was mentioned by nearly all of the parents in this study. As a result of this experience in their own childhood and the dramatic change in the way sexuality is now discussed when compared to previous generations, parents in this study made a concerted effort to speak more openly to their children about sexuality and wanted to be more present and communicative with their children on issues related to sexuality than their own parents had been.

> I always vowed that I would do it differently with mine because I thought I was just handed this stuff as if to say "you'll figure it out", and it's purely and simply because she [my mother] was never told ... my own mother, I couldn't talk to her about it, so I wanted [my daughter] to have the resources ... I'm just trying to do it better than it happened to me. (Judy)

The second factor was the experience of sexual abuse by parents in this study and its influence on their protectiveness towards their own children. Although parents in this study were recruited broadly and not because they had experienced sexual abuse, many of them voluntarily revealed in the interviews that they had been sexually abused as children or had

---

[3] The names of all participants and their family members have been changed for confidentiality.

known someone very close to them who had been sexually abused when they were growing up. As a result, these parents were aware of the reality of sexual abuse and were particularly vigilant about the safety of their own children, taking precautions based on what they believed would protect their children.

> I know my mum was sexually abused by her dad … she used to talk about that quite often … none of us in our wills will put her [Mum] down for the kids to go to her, because … there is the chance the children would be abused. (Lisanne)

This finding is consistent with other studies that show that parents who have been sexually abused or know of others who were sexually abused are more likely to discuss sexual abuse and in more depth than parents who have not experienced abuse (Deblinger, Thakkar-Kolar, Berry and Schroeder, 2010). These two factors provide an important generational and experiential context for understanding the actions and reactions to sexuality and sexual abuse issues of parents in this study.

STRATEGIES FOR PREVENTION

Parents in this study described a variety of communication methods and other strategies they used to prevent child sexual abuse. These strategies covered broad sexuality education for their children, as well as specific child sexual abuse prevention. Parents in this study discussed these areas as being intertwined, so they are discussed together in this section on prevention strategies.

Communication Strategies

The majority of prevention strategies described by parents in this study related to communication with their children. Parents described developing general communication strategies with children in order to make children comfortable speaking to them about a range of issues, including but not limited to child sexual abuse. These strategies included asking open-ended questions to children about their activities and their feeling about these, and reminding their children that, as parents, they were there to support their children, even if the children made mistakes.

> "If you need something and you want to know something, come to me or your dad. We're going to give you the best advice" … in general conversation I always reassure them that I love them, that everyone's got their strengths and [to] feel good about who they are. (Gabby)

Parents discussed common times when children tended to have conversations about experiences and concerns of the day, such as driving in the car, dinner time and bedtime. Parents used these opportunities to engage children and support them on any issues or concerns the children were having.

> I find there's times when, like my daughter, before she goes to bed, that's a good time …
> that's when she really opens up, so I find that I just sit on her bed and we just talk. (Mary)

Another communication strategy mentioned by parents was normalising sexuality for children. They wanted children to feel that their sexual development was normal and healthy and nothing to be ashamed of.

> Sexuality is part of being human, so I don't want to let him down … I said, "Anton, do you realise that all that's happening to you, I mean you've started to grow hair in places that you wouldn't of imagined, you *do* realise that's normal, don't you?" And he said, "Yes, Mum." [laughs] (Theresa)

Parents also wanted children to know that their parents' expressions of sexuality were healthy and acceptable expressions of love and affection.

> We just say, "Matt, that's just normal. When people like each other, that's how they show it, express it." I said, "Mum and Dad kiss." And he says, "Yeah, I know." (Mary)

Parents also described using teachable moments to explain sexuality and child sexual abuse with their children. These were times when either their children raised questions or there were other triggers, such as the media or family holidays, when conversations arose. These events provided opportunities to offer information and explanations to children that were protective or informative while the children were interested.

> [I talk to them] at that moment, because it's an opportune time, it's in their minds. And what I find with kids is they seem to just get over things … you just take that opportunity there and then, because if you try and do it later on or if they're focused on something else, they're not really going to take in what you are saying. (Gabby)

Parents also emphasised the importance of establishing family rules about safety in public places, such as shopping centres and festivals. These rules let children know where the boundaries lay in terms of who they would be allowed to be in the care of other than their parents, when they had to return to parents and how to communicate with parents (particularly with older children who might have access to mobile phones).

> [At] festivals and shopping centres, our boys are never allowed to go to the toilet by themselves, they always have to go with somebody else, even if it is with each other … we have our family rules about how we behave in those situations. (Alice)

Many parents also mentioned trying to provide age and developmentally appropriate information at regular intervals to their children throughout their growing years and gauging what was appropriate at the time by asking their children questions and assessing their response to determine their readiness to receive the information.

> I tried to approach her about things … I was trying to lead on to the fact of how your body changes and getting your period, and as soon as I started to go on about it, she said, "I'm

really tired now, Mum. I just want to go to sleep." So I said, "Ok," and I thought "She's not ready for it." That was two years ago, and I thought, "Ok, I'll leave it." (Gabby)

Parents discussed the importance of clarifying questions asked by children when having informative or protective discussions with them so that they did not provide excessive information that may have been too much for their child at that developmental stage.

I'll use my eight-year-old boy as an example. He has not as good a knowledge about sex and what it actually is, and he had seen two people on television kissing, and he's going "Well, they're having sex." We said to him, "Joel, you don't even know … do you know what sex is?" And he goes, "I do, it's kissing each other." We left it at that, we thought, "Oh that's good … he doesn't need to know the rest." So the conversation didn't go any further than that. (Lydia)

A number of parents described using humour to diffuse potentially uncomfortable or embarrassing topics with their children. This appeared to be useful with younger children as well as older children, such as the example below:

"If you wanna not get pregnant and have sex with lots of people, then you take the *pill and* you use a condom." And she said "Right, Mum." [laughter] She has a good laugh with me because I try to always make it serious but fun, and to not scare her, I suppose. That's probably why I did that. (Rita)

Many parents had reported discussing protective behaviours with their children, including asking children to tell their parents if anyone had touched them inappropriately.

My older one would have been at kinder, so she was probably four or five, and the other one would have been three … I just say, "Make sure nobody ever touches you there, that is private." (Karina)

An important child sexual abuse prevention strategy was discussing secret keeping with children and how children should tell adults if someone had asked them to keep a secret.

I've always said to them, "I don't care what anybody else has ever said to you, you never have secrets with Mum, *never*. You always tell Mum everything." (Judy)

Parents also mentioned discussing internet safety with children as a prevention strategy. Parents mentioned their fears of their children meeting persons in online chat rooms who might pretend to be other children but were in fact adults preying on children.

Our son is heavily into one of these online games called Dreamscape … we've talked very clearly about what stuff, what information, who is allowed to have, your friends some information through Runescape. (Wendy)

Some parents mentioned using teaching tools, namely books, with their children. They described using books usually from the children's schools or from local bookshops to discuss general sexuality issues with their children.

> [The book] was actually one of the school club things where they sell lots of books and some of the money goes to the school. I saw it in there and I thought because it's got little inserts with all kids writing things in and different age groups [that it would be useful]. They tell you the child, the age and something that they felt about a certain time in their life. And it's good because it's like her reading about her[self]. (Rita)

Only one parent mentioned using a book to specifically discuss sexual abuse with their children.

> I was quite shocked when I started reading [a book about sexual abuse], because I just didn't realise the level that paedophiles will go. Being in a park and someone comes to you and says, "I've got a puppy in the car, would you like to see?" I've gone through those stories … [I got these from] Family Planning.

Overall, parents in this study engaged in a range of communication strategies to prevent child sexual abuse and provide opportunities for their children to talk to them about potential incidents that the parents wanted to know about so that they could take protective action. These communication skills are helpful for parents to develop and can be incorporated into prevention programs, especially with the use of roleplaying techniques (Jackson and Dickinson, 2009).

Other Prevention Strategies

Beyond communication strategies, parents discussed other preventive strategies they used to protect their children from sexual abuse. These included investigating social situations for safety where their children were socialising, such as parties and children's sleepovers.

> When he goes to other kids' houses, I know the other parents fairly well, so I'm not too concerned, except sometimes at parties. Sometimes they get invited to parties of kids that they haven't necessarily been to the house of. I always go to drop him off and try to meet whatever adults are there and try to get a feel for their place and check out the house a bit without being too nosy. (Carol)

Another strategy mentioned was monitoring the comfort levels of children to see how they reacted around other people, especially looking for signs of discomfort.

> I've been watching and often thought to myself, sort of assessing the situation to see whether there is discomfort about being with a particular person, from the kids. If they seem uncomfortable being with that person or if there was any touching or physical contact that they don't seem to want, or they do not want to be in the same room or by themselves, be on the lookout for that. (Alice)

Parents also discussed relying on their social supports to protect their children in their absence.

It's more "I'll look after yours if you look after mine" because we recognise that letting kids go by themselves is not a good option … The idea is that we've known each other, therefore we trust each other with each other's kids. (Abe)

The results described above suggest that there are a variety of strategies that parents use and could use to protect their children from child sexual abuse beyond the protective behaviours emphasis. Many of these strategies are similar to those mentioned in programs targeting children, but are equally important to include in programs for parents.

STRATEGIES FOR EARLY INTERVENTION

When parents in this study made the decision that a sexual boundary had been crossed, either through observation or through the relaying of incidents by children and others, they reported a number of strategies used to intervene and protect their children. First, parents made a decision about whether the activities demonstrated normal or abnormal sexual behaviour. This was purely a subjective decision made by parents based on their knowledge, opinion and experience, although there are guidelines that can help parents make such decisions about normal and abnormal behaviour (Goldman and Bradley, 2001; Sexuality Information and Education Council of the United States, 2004). When parents decided that an incident was abnormal, meaning that it was no longer an innocent expression of sexual curiosity by the parties involved but had some intention to be clearly sexual in a way that parents believed was inappropriate for or harmful to their children, then parents made choices about how to respond. As discussed earlier, this response depended on their relationship with the person who had crossed the boundary with their child, and parents were hesitant to contact authorities when incidents occurred with persons close to their family (relatives or good friends); this constituted the majority of incidents described by parents. One parent captured this general sentiment:

Because if it's outside of the family, I think it gets reported quickly, that's what I have understood. But if it's within the family, it probably doesn't get reported. (Kumar)

Note that when parents were recruited for this study, they were not chosen because they had observed or experienced boundary-crossing incidents or sexual abuse between their child and another person because recruitment guidelines were very broad. However, it was revealed in the interviews that all of the parents reported what they would consider to be sexual boundary-crossing incidents with their children. They were clearly aware that this research was about child sexual abuse but, interestingly, as they described the incidents, almost none used the term 'child sexual abuse' (nor the term 'boundary-crossing incident'). They tended to use descriptions rather than labels for the incidents that had occurred.

Parents described a variety of strategies they used when boundary-crossing incidents had occurred between their child and another person. One strategy of detecting incidents mentioned by a number of parents was a clear instinctual or gut feeling that something was not right, especially when the incidents were subtle or difficult to prove. Parents then decided to take protective action without further evidence, or took action after further incidents took place confirming their suspicions. One parent explains his reaction when his three-year-old daughter came running out of the house crying, and his friend came out explaining that the girl had tried to break off his penis:

> My instinct told me that I believe that something nasty had happened … A lot of it is instinct, it's the way he reacted and the way he looked. (James)

Another strategy mentioned by parents was to provide specific but indirect warnings to children to protect themselves, such as this incident in which Sam's daughter had been photographed under the table by his brother-in-law:

> I saw him try and break away with her and the kids. I'd go down there and say, "Celina, come here for a minute." And I said, "You may not realise, but just be careful the way you sit or the way you are sitting down or lying on the bed there. Realise that you are a growing girl and you have to be a bit more careful about how you sit."(Sam)

A strategy described by Sam's wife, Theresa, was to reduce the social contact with her brother-in-law in order to reduce the possibility of another incident occurring.

> I would never allow her to be in the situation where she alone with him, ever, and even to go to their house, even if my sister was there. Without me there … I don't know, it's just an unspoken thing, and so that's fortunate. (Theresa)

The parents in this case, Sam and Theresa, also used the strategy of letting the person who had crossed the boundary with their daughter (the brother-in-law) know that they were watching him and were aware of what he was doing. Both parents explained how this worked at social functions:

> *Sam:* I know a couple of times when it was at its worst, when we were at these functions, when he was in a certain position near her, I was basically staring straight at him.

> *Theresa:* He was uncomfortable

> *Sam:* He picked up a couple of times. He thought, "What's wrong with Sam? He's giving me a bit of a dirty look, why is he doing that?" … I was thinking "What are you up to?" and he's looking at me.

In the incidents where the person crossing the boundary with their child was a distant acquaintance or stranger, parents were more likely to use the following strategies. Some parents reported direct confrontation with persons who were strangers and who the parents believed had crossed a boundary with their child. For example, Sam, who found it difficult to directly confront his brother-in-law who had been filming his daughter under the table and taking photos of her on the bed in suggestive poses, directly confronted a man who his daughter claimed had touched her in a public pool.

> I followed him; I went into the change room. I challenged him. I said, "What the hell do you think you're doing? My daughter told me you touched her in the pool." He said, "No, what are you talking about?" He totally denied it. I said, "I believe my daughter. If I catch you

or ever hear of you doing something like that, if you ever come near my daughter again, you'll be sorry." He said, "Don't carry on, don't carry on." I said, "Listen, mate. Just watch out, or I'll have the police onto you." And I just walked out.

Parents who explained that they had reported incidents to authorities generally did not know the person who had crossed the boundary well or at all. Karen, whose daughter had claimed that she had been touched by a fellow classmate at school, explains that she reported the incident to the school and the department of education because:

> I cannot have any sympathy. I've got none left for [the accused child], whereas if it was my friend's child, I might explore more with them, even if their child was the aggressor, the implications and how to deal with it and how the school system works, but I wasn't close enough friends. I wasn't the least bit interested in engaging in their situation.

Another mother in this study, whose child was in a daycare where several children disclosed that a male carer had touched them, reported that the staff and parents at the daycare immediately called the police.

> But what then happened, another child, unbeknownst to the crèche, another child said something in the car to their parents. The parents drove straight to the police … It subsequently went to court and he went to jail for a period.

As these results show, there are additional early intervention strategies that parents can use, particularly when identifying some of the grooming activities that are subtle yet are clearly unacceptable to parents. These strategies provide parents with additional protective tools and the power to intervene early and take action to protect their children, even if the evidence is subtle or hard to prove. Parents should feel comfortable erring on the side of caution rather than taking risks against their better judgement.

SOURCES OF SUPPORT, INFORMATION AND EDUCATION

When sources of support and information were discussed with parents in relation to how they managed the risk of child sexual abuse, many discussed their partners as their key support and the person to communicate with about how to manage prevention and early intervention strategies.

> I speak a lot to my husband. We often talk, especially at the end of the night and the kids are in bed and you're in bed yourself, and you get into those discussions. You might say, one of the kids did this, and then we'll discuss certain things. (Gabby)

Outside of intimate partners, parents also mentioned the importance of good friends and even siblings as sources of support.

> My sister and friends with children the same age … I've got friends with older children and that could be the sort of thing that we would talk about, particularly as we have younger

children and are busier, and theirs are older and it doesn't so much get easier as it changes as they get older. (Wendy)

In terms of organisations that parents turn to for information, many parents mentioned programs and literature from their children's schools.

I went to a parenting session, and it's something that the secondary school had, a session on how to parent adolescents, and anything that came up like that ... it did cover sexuality, it covered all sorts of things. (Gabby)

Only one parent discussed contacting a community-based organization (Family Planning) for information. One mentioned their family doctor, and none reported using hotlines or the internet. Parents who turned to authorities either went to their children's school (in the case where one child had crossed a boundary with another child while at school) or to the police (a child-care worker was reported when two children disclosed having been touched). No parents reported contacting child-protection authorities.

IMPLICATIONS OF THE FINDINGS FOR PREVENTION PROGRAMS

The most important finding of this study was that many parents were unlikely to report many of the more subtle or initial boundary-crossing incidents; therefore, many of the traditional child sexual abuse prevention messages that urge parents to immediately report when there is suspected abuse may not be effective in detecting some cases of abuse. Parents in this study described the use of various strategies beyond protective behaviours that might be considered for inclusion in prevention programs for parents. These strategies lie on a prevention continuum, where parents have a critical role at the beginning of the continuum in terms of their position as caregivers and protectors, their proximity to children and their responsibility for prevention and early detection. The strategies suggested here can be used to empower parents to take action before waiting for children to disclose abuse and can be used as preventative methods to stop grooming activities from escalating or continuing. These are summarised in the table below.

This study, and others, has found that parents are hesitant to call the authorities when incidents have occurred. Therefore, prevention programs within countries like Australia and the United States where victim advocacy is the focus of early detection and where the key message is to call the police could consider trialling alternative confidential family support services for parents to contact before going to the police or child protection. Such confidential support services are available in northern European countries in the form of family support models.[4] One example of this is the Child Protection Centre in Lubeck, Germany, which offers a 'non-punitive, self-help approach ... [and] a significant guarantee not to involve law enforcement agencies or to initiate court proceedings without the families' consent (Thyen,

---

[4] Family support models, which are frequently found in northern Europe, encourage a whole-family approach to intervening in cases of child sexual abuse. Confidential counselling is offered to the offender and the entire family as a step before legal action is taken, if the offender agrees. This is distinct from victim advocacy models in countries such as Australia, the United States and the United Kingdom, where counselling is usually made available primarily to victims and cases usually lead directly to legal action.

Thiessena and Heinsohn-Krugb, 1995, pp. 1337). Another example is the Confidential Doctor service in Sweden, where reports of child sexual abuse are addressed confidentially by a doctor-led team and aims to engage the whole family in treatment (Hill, Stafford and Green Lister, 2002). While the family support approach was trialled in Perth, Western Australia, by Safecare, a non-profit organisation providing treatment services to victims, offenders and their families (Grant, Thornton and Chamarette, 2006), there were many opponents to the program who believed that it was sympathetic to sex offenders (Movement Against Kindred Offenders, 2005). Despite some disagreement on this approach, such services could be trialled in Australia and the United States to ascertain whether parents are more successful in identifying and intervening early in boundary-crossing incidents and ultimately preventing child sexual abuse. Another strategy, recommended by Finkelhor (1984), is based on similar results of a study nearly 30 years ago in which most parents avoided calling authorities when sexual abuse was discovered. The strategy is to include education for parents about the benefits of reporting, including the roles of the different authorities, how they work and what can be achieved by contacting them.

Table 1. Child Sexual Abuse Prevention and Early Intervention Strategies for Parents

Prevention strategies	• developing general communication strategies with children • normalizing sexuality • using teachable moments • establishing family rules about safety • providing age and developmentally appropriate information • clarifying questions asked by children • using humour to diffuse potentially uncomfortable or embarrassing topics • discussing protective behaviours with children • discussing secret-keeping with children • discussing internet safety • investigating social situations for safety • monitoring comfort levels of children • relying on social supports to protect children • using teaching tools
Early intervention strategies	• parents using instinct and own discomfort as early warning signs • providing specific but indirect warnings to children • reducing social contact with person who had crossed boundary with child • letting person who had crossed the boundary know that parents were aware of what they were doing through indirect verbal communication and/or body language • using direct confrontation • reporting incidents to authorities

Based on the importance of good general communication with children, as mentioned by parents in this study, it is recommended that prevention programs for parents incorporate skill building around general communication with children. Good general communication has been successful in other programs that have reduced sexual assault in university students (Testa, Hoffman, Livingston and Turrisi, 2010). The findings that parents in this study rarely used the term 'child sexual abuse' to describe incidents that could legally be defined as child sexual abuse means that the language used in prevention programs may need to be updated to include other terms and descriptions to which parents can relate. Further research could explore the language parents might be comfortable using in prevention messages and test the use of this language in pilot interventions. Programs could also explain the legal definitions of child sexual abuse and grooming, as well as the legal punishment for these actions, so that parents are made aware of sexual activities with children that are illegal. This may provide parents with a greater understanding of what may be happening to their children and the social and legal prohibitions against such behaviour. Another important finding that parents discussed was trusting their own feelings if something wasn't right during an incident, even if hard evidence was not present. This suggests that programs could teach parents this concept of trusting their feelings, which is already a component of some protective behaviours programs that teach children to listen to their feelings if they are not comfortable in certain situations (MacIntyre and Carr, 2000).

The emphasis on partners and peers (friends and relatives) as key sources of personal support, both in prevention and early intervention, suggests the use of peer-education programs to reach parents. Other prevention programs have successfully used parents as peer educators, specifically around the topic of sexuality education for children (Green and Documét, 2005; So, 2002). This study shows that parents are more likely to get information on child sexuality and child sexual abuse from their local schools rather than from community-based organisations or the internet. This information is vital for community-based organisations that are primarily responsible for developing prevention initiatives. They could partner with and build lasting infrastructure within schools to regularly deliver prevention programs for parents in conjunction with programs targeted at children. Partnering with schools is highly recommended in other studies mentioned earlier, which show that programs that involve parents in schools are more effective than programs for children or parents alone (MacIntyre and Carr, 2000). Also, while there is an increased presence of prevention messages on the internet (Resofsky, 2007), it is unclear to what extent parents are accessing this information, as reflected by parents in this study. Further research could evaluate the reach and effectiveness of these innovative programs.

CONCLUSION

This research fills an important gap in understanding on the issues that affect parents' behaviour related to preventing child sexual abuse and intervening early when suspected incidents have taken place. Further research is needed to examine how prevention messages are developed for programs targeting parents and the effectiveness of these on the knowledge, attitudes and behaviours of parents. There is a need for even more research, both qualitative and quantitative, to understand the needs of parents in order to develop effective prevention messages. This includes updating previous quantitative research on how many parents are actually talking to their children about preventive messages, how they are intervening when they have concerns about incidents and who they are turning to for support (Babatsikos,

2010). The content of prevention programs should not be taken for granted; they need to be based on thorough needs assessment with target populations in order to be comprehensive and effective. Research with specific populations, such as rural, aboriginal and low-income populations, may help reveal specific issues related to prevention. Further research into the different prevention strategies carried out internationally can also provide ideas on best practices. A public-health, community-wide approach to prevention is essential, supplementing efforts directly targeted to children and affecting the traditions and systems within communities that affect the sexual abuse of children (Anderson et al., 2004; McMahon, 2000; Reynolds and Blackstock, 2007; Sanders and Cann, 2002). Professionals are encouraged to partner with parents to have a significant affect on the prevention of child sexual abuse and to take greater responsibility for protecting children from sexual abuse.

REFERENCES

Anderson, J., Mangels, N. and Langsam, A. (2004). Child sexual abuse: A public health issue. *Criminal Justice Studies, 17*(1), 107–126. doi: 10.1080/08884310420001679386

Andrews, G., Gould, B. and Corry, J. (2002). Child sexual abuse revisited. *Medical Journal of Australia, 176*(10), 458–459.

Australian Institute of Health and Welfare. (2010). *Child protection Australia 2008–2009: Child welfare series no. 47*. Canberra, Australia.

Babatsikos, G. (2010). Parents' knowledge, attitudes and practices about preventing child sexual abuse: A literature review. *Child Abuse Review, 19*, 107–129. doi: 10.1002/car.1102

Burgess, E. and Wurtele, S. (1998). Enhancing parent-child communication about sexual abuse: A pilot study. *Child Abuse and Neglect, 22*(11), 1167–1175.

Conway, M., Mendelson, M., Giannopoulos, C., Csank, P. and Holm, S. (2004). Childhood and adult sexual abuse, rumination on sadness, and dysphoria. *Child Abuse and Neglect, 28*(4), 393–410. doi: 10.1016/j.chiabu.2003.05.004

Craven, S., Brown, S. and Gilchrist, E. (2006). Sexual grooming of children: Review of literature and theoretical considerations. *Journal of Sexual Aggression, 12*(3), 287–299. doi: 10.1080/13552600601069414

Deblinger, E., Thakkar-Kolar, R., Berry, E. and Schroeder, C. (2010). Caregivers' efforts to educate their children about child sexual abuse: A replication study. *Child Maltreatment, 15*(1), 91–100. doi: 10.1177/1077559509337408

Elrod, J. and Rubin, R. (1993). Parental involvement in sexual abuse prevention education. *Child Abuse and Neglect, 17*, 527–538. doi: 10.1016/0145–2134(93)90027-3

Finkelhor, D. (1984). *Child sexual abuse: New theory and research*. New York: The Free Press.

Finkelhor, D. (2009). The prevention of childhood sexual abuse. *Future of Children, 19*(2), 169–194.

Goldman, J. and Bradley, G. (2001). Sexuality education across the lifecycle in the new millennium. *Sex Education, 1*(3), 197–217. doi: DOI: 10.1080/ 14681810120080613

Grant, J., Thornton, J. and Chamarette, C. (2006). Residential placement of intra-familial adolescent sex offenders. *Trends and Issues in Crime and Criminal Justice, 315*.

Retrieved April 27, 2011, from http://www.aic.gov.au/publications/current%20series/tandi/301–320/tandi315/view%20paper.aspx.

Green, H. and Documét, P. (2005). Parent peer education: Lessons learned from a community-based initiative for teen pregnancy prevention. *Journal of Adolescent Health, 37*(3), S100–S107. doi: 10.1016/j.jadohealth.2005.05.002

Hill, M., Stafford, A. and Green Lister, P. (2002). International perspectives on child protection; Part of the Scottish executive child protection review (Protecting children today and tomorrow). Glasgow: Centre for the Child and Society, University of Glasgow.

Jackson, C. and Dickinson, D. (2009). Developing parenting programs to prevent child health risk behaviors: A practice model. *Health Education Research, 24*(6), 1029–1042. doi: 10.1093/her/cyp039

Kenny, M., Capri, V., Thakkar-Kolar, R., Ryan, E. and Runyon, M. (2008). Child sexual abuse: From prevention to self-protection. *Child Abuse Review, 17*(1), 36–54. doi: 10.1002/car

MacIntyre, D. and Carr, A. (2000). Prevention of child sexual abuse: Implications of programme evaluation research. *Child Abuse Review, 9,* 183–199. doi: 10.1002/1099-0852(200005/06)9:3<183::AID-CAR595>3.0.CO;2-I

McMahon, P. (2000). The public health approach to the prevention of sexual violence. *Sexual Abuse: A Journal of Research and Treatment, 12*(1), 27–36. doi: 10.1023/A:1009559720231

Molnar, B., Berkman, L. and Buka, S. (2001). Psychopathology, childhood sexual abuse and other childhood adversities: relative links to subsequent suicidal behavior in the United States. *Psychological Medicine, 31,* 965–977. doi: 10.1017/S0033291701004329

Movement Against Kindred Offenders. (2005). *Safecare notification, WA, 2004.* Retrieved 8 April, 2005, from http://www.mako.org.au/mandatesafe.html.

Nelson, E., Heath, A., Madden, P., Cooper, L., Dinwiddie, S., Bucholz, K., Glowinski, W., McLaughlin, T., Dunne, M., Statham, D. and Martin, N. (2002). Association between self-reported childhood sexual abuse and adverse psychosocial outcomes: Results from a twin study. *Archives of General Psychiatry, 59,* 139–145.

Pereda, N., Guilera, G., Forns, M. and Gómez-Benito, J. (2009). The prevalence of child sexual abuse in community and student samples: A meta-analysis. *Clinical Psychology Review, 29*(4), 328–338. doi: 10.1016/j.cpr.2009.02.007

Reppucci, N., Haugaard, J. and Antonishak, J. (2005). Is there empirical evidence to support the effectiveness of child sexual abuse prevention programs? In D. Loseke, R. Gelles and M. Cavanaugh (Eds.), *Current controversies on family violence* (pp. 271–284). Thousand Oaks: Sage Publications.

Resofsky, V. (2007). Stewards of children: A primary prevention program for sexual abuse. *Australian Institute of Family Studies Newsletter, 15*(2), 12–16.

Reynolds, M. and Blackstock, P. (2007). A public health approach for preventing child sexual abuse. *Community Practitioner, 80*(2), 14–15.

Sanders, M. and Cann, W. (2002). Promoting positive parenting as an abuse prevention strategy. In K. Browne, H. Hanks, P. Stratton and C. Hamilton (Eds.), *Early prediction and prevention of child abuse: A handbook.* West Sussex: John Wiley and Sons.

Sexuality Information and Education Council of the United States. (2004). *Guidelines for comprehensive sexuality education: Kindergarten–12th grade.* Retrieved 12 August, 2010, from http://www.siecus.org/_data/global/images/guidelines.pdf.

So, O. (2002, July 7–12). *Using cultural leaders and parents as peer educators for HIV prevention among the rural Maasai youth of Kenya.* Paper presented at the International AIDS Conference, Barcelona.

Stanley, N. (2010). Engaging communities and parents in safeguarding. *Child Abuse Review, 19*(2), 77–81. doi: 10.1002/car.1114

Testa, M., Hoffman, J., Livingston, J. and Turrisi, R. (2010). Preventing college women's sexual victimization through parent based intervention: A randomized controlled trial. *Prevention Science, 11*(3), 308–318. doi: 10.1007/s11121-010-0168-3

Thyen, U., Thiessena, R. and Heinsohn-Krugb, M. (1995). Secondary prevention: Serving families at risk. *Child Abuse and Neglect, 19*(1), 1337–1347.

Tomison, A. and Poole, L. (2000). Preventing child abuse and neglect: Findings from an Australian audit of prevention programs. Melbourne: Australian Institute of Family Studies.

Topping, K. and Barron, I. (2009). School-based child sexual abuse prevention programs: A review of effectiveness. *Review of Educational Research, 79*(1), 431–463. doi: 10.3102/0034654308325582

Wurtele, S. (2009). Preventing sexual abuse of children in the twenty-first century: Preparing for challenges and opportunities. *Journal of Child Sexual Abuse, 18*(1), 1–18. doi: 10.1080/10538710802584650

Wurtele, S. and Kenny, M. (2010). Partnering with parents to prevent childhood sexual abuse. *Child Abuse Review, 19*(2), 130–152. doi: 10.1002/car.1112

Wurtele, S., Moreno, T. and Kenny, M. (2008). Evaluation of a sexual abuse prevention workshop for parents of young children. *Journal of Child and Adolescent Trauma, 1*(4), 331–340. doi: 10.1080/19361520802505768

In: Child Abuse   ISBN: 978-1-62257-113-0
Editors: Raymond A. Turner and Henry O. Rogers   © 2012 Nova Science Publishers, Inc.

Chapter 4

LINK BETWEEN MISTREATMENT AND OBESITY DURING THE CHILDHOOD

J. Foucart[1]

Universite Libre de Bruxelles, Brussels, Belgium

ABSTRACT

These past ten years, numerous studies have established a link between mistreatments (physical, sexual, or of type deficiency) in childhood and obesity. The risk of becoming obese would be multiplied by 9 in children living in situations of abuse or neglect. In order to verify and clarify the relationship which may exist between a failed family environment and obesity, we have conducted a study in three parts.

1° part: study of the demographic profile, medical, family, psychological and psycho-pathological perspective of a population of adolescents suffering from severe obesity. Those informations have been collected with the help of questionnaires and by observation of 164 adolescents satisfying the criteria of severe obesity. A pedo-psychiatric diagnosis according to the CFTMEA's R 2000 has been asked for each subject and included a study of the factors of ill-treatment. Our results of this first part stressed the multiple causes of the obesity of our subjects but especially have confirmed the importance of the factors of unfavourable family environment (deficiencies, neglect, maltreatment) such as described in the literature.

2° part: We have conducted a factor analysis on our data in order to clarify the links between the data that we collected. We have highlighted a correlational relationship between the presence of non favorable environmental factors (mental disorders in the family, deficiencies, child abuse), the severity of the obesity and the development of a psycho-pathological perspective profile in the child.

3° part: we wanted to identify the linkages between these different elements through a more thorough analysis of the psychological profile of our subjects. To do this, we have by means of case analysis and with the aid of a Rorschach, the questionnaire of the image of the body of Bruschon-Schweitzer, and from a drawing by itself, evaluated the presence of disorder of the body-image among 10 of our subjects and their evolution during the care taking in link with the loss of weight. Our results have highlighted the presence of

---

[1] jennifer.foucart@ulb.ac.be; Ph. D. (psychology).

disorder of the body-image with an image of itself uncertain, undifferentiated, the limits disseminated very specific to subjects suffering from obesity in comparison with a population with average weight.

We concluded that the severe obesity develops more particularly in the context of a cloudy psycho-pathological perspective including a disorder of the image of the body induced by the presence of environmental factors faulty for the child. Obesity installs itself in bodies with poor care, which can barely be changed imposing the necessary construction of barriers (obesity) between the "inside weakened" and the outside perceived as dangerous.

INTRODUCTION

Obesity During the Childhood in Question?

The prevalence of obesity is increasing at an alarming rate in our countries and in developing countries, regardless of socio-economic class, age, sex or origin [14]. Globally, it is estimated that about 30 to 45 million children and adolescents are obese [16]. More specifically, 19% pediatric population is considered obese [11]. With its growth, it is also the severity of pediatric obesity which is increasing.

But the prevalence is complex to assess accurately because of the lack of international agreement on the definition of pediatric obesity. By definition, obesity in adults is characterized by excess body fat associated with an increased risk of morbidity and mortality [10]. In this regard, as far as weight/height^2 is considered an indicator of body fat ('body mass index':BMI). A BMI above 30 is the threshold beyond which we consider an individual as obese. A BMI above 40 is severe or morbid obesity in adults. But in children and adolescents, this definition does not take place. The BMI changes with age and sex [8]. The International Obesity Task Force, under the aegis of the WHO (World Health Organization), has therefore drawn the curve "IOTF 30" founded on the risk of a child achieving a BMI of 30 at the age of 18. According to this, type II obesity in children is defined as BMI values above the IOTF curve 30 for a given age [21]. But this curve is unfortunately not widespread at clinical level.

Compared to adults, obesity in children and adolescents is not only defined by actual co-morbid conditions but also future ones. However, co-morbidities associated with obesity in children and adolescents are of all types and increase with the severity of obesity. Specifically, various studies focused on psychological factors show that the severity of obesity is related to increased co-morbidities and psychological distress [12].

Numerous endogenous and exogenous factors are indeed involved in the vulnerability, the development and the maintenance of this pathology. Among the exogenous factors, socio-cultural and socio-economic developments cannot be overlooked. Changes in eating habits and life style as well as food lobbying tend to favor the presence of an obesogenic environment. It can be defined as a social environment where access to food is facilitated, where travelling is essentially motorized and where games and entertainment are mostly sedentary [22]. Among the endogenous factors to be considered, overeating and the breakdown of dietary patterns are pointed as key factors. Genetic factors may play a fostering role as part of a genetic predisposition but also as a crucial multigenic disease apart from a few cases of monogenic diseases [2]. But it would be the lack of energy consumption related to physical inactivity which would be mostly to blame in the current increase of obesity in children [4]. In addition, reflection on psychological factors also occupies an important place in the understanding of this issue and is not challenged in the obesity medicine.

Psychology has focused on the conscious and unconscious determinants of this problem through to its various theoretical models. Regardless of the model studied, despite the different levels at which the models are situated, there are two principal problems which are put in tension: the influence of family environment on the development of obesity and the involvement and understanding of the body.

The issue of parental food patterns likely to promote the development of obesity in children is, in fact, raised by Wardle and Carnell [23]. While other studies show that the risk factor for a child to develop obesity is in the presence of parental psychopathology or child abuse [12]. These past ten years, numerous studies have established a link between mistreatement (physical, sexual, or of type deficiency) in childhood and obesity. The risk of becoming obese would be multiplied by 9 in children living in situations of abuse or neglect [1, 15].

These descriptive studies do not allow, however, to explain the relationship between the presence of ill-treatment and the development of obesity in the child.

The Ill-Treatment Questioned?

In the abuse, there are various forms such as physical violence, sexual abuse, mental cruelty and/or gross negligence. The most affected are infants and young children. Those most abusive are usually the father and/or the mother. But, it is not easy to distinguish the "evil" and the "good" treatement, this must be analysed "on a case-by-case basis" in times of crisis or present during a long period [3].

It is well known, the abuse has a strong impact on the physical and psychological development of the child. If a child is deprived of a healthy family environment, particularly that of a satisfying maternal image, it causes adverse consequences to its development. These effects persist from childhood and adolescence to adult life.

The traumatic event is not like a disease, therefore not at a specific time but rather "a process with a before, a time of child abuse and a after " [7]. These consequences must therefore be assessed on the long term.

Some children seem to be more qualified than others to defend himself against defective conditions of the existence [17]. As quoted by different authors: "In front of abuse, humans are definitely not equal to each other!"[3].

In defective socio-affective conditions, children with a poor self-identity can experience delays in the acquisition of motor skills and body scheme. Such delays are not limited to the period of abuse, but often persist over a long period in their life. These children with a "lack of physical rooting" are impeded in different aspects of their psychomotor development, such as balance, overall coordination, etc. [17]. More broadly, these phenomena suggest deficiencies of body-image.

The Body-Image?

The body-image represents the body's psychic concept. This complex concept, with multiple acceptances cannot be limited to the study of body satisfaction, something that seems to be the most studied in literature. We think the body-image must be conceived more like "a global configuration formed by the cohesion of representations, perceptions, feelings and attitudes that the individual has developed towards his body during his life and through various experiences" [6].

This means that when one considers the question of the body-image, that is to be situated in a developmental perspective which includes perception aspects, and also representations of subjective aspects (in terms of subjectivity), where the final synthesis of the body-image consists in perceiving his body as unique, different and as "his" (the understanding of oneself as object and subject). However, if we refer to Bruch [5], the early trauma as well as the influence of the first food experiences gives way to the question of consideration of obesity as a disorder of the body-image.

STUDY CONTEXT

Considering these works, we thought it essential to consider obesity as a multifactorial etiology syndrome which cannot do without a multiaxial assessment phase with a multidisciplinary biological, social and especially psychological dimension. Given the number of young people suffering from obesity Type II and failure of primary and secondary pediatric obesity prevention, centers offering multidisciplinary treatment to residential care for mental and physical complications of 'severe' obesity infant and child were created.

But the time taken to care in these centers has frequently helped to bring out many family background and complaints related to the mental health of young people who put obesity and somatic aspects in second place. In addition, weight loss was accompanied, in some cases, with the emergence of new psychological symptoms centered on the body (suicidal attempt or mutilation). Working in the clinical context as a researcher, we have been led to question ourselves about the interaction between obesity and severe mental health problems associated with both the development of obesity and its treatment.

It seemed therefore essential to objectify the psychological suffering of these young people who consult with a request that they declare, at first, as a principal request, that of somatic weight loss. These mainly clinical observations find little support in literature that focuses only rarely on the specificity of mental health of this adolescent population with severe obesity. Yet these are the problems which the therapeutic field teams have to face in the management of obesity and particularly in severe obesity and which we wish to study.

The purpose here is to highlight the importance of traumatic factors in the development of the severe obesity of children and more particularly of the factors of abuse. We will study their importance by looking more particularly into the disturbances of the image of the body among these young people. This work has a clinical foundation which will influence the way of reflection but also the methodology used due to the specific clinical institution in which we conducted our study.

OBJECTIVES

To better understand this problem and in order to objectify our clinical findings, as we said earlier, we have had to use two experimental strategies. The first is descriptive and aims at an objectification of characteristics bio-psycho-social issues associated with severe obesity through the construction of a tool-making multiaxial data. It will help to organize an inventory of bio-psycho-social characteristics, but also to search for specific associations between severe obesity and psychosocial factors. The second step is more transverse and aims to assess the management of severe obesity in adolescents in the treatment that questions the psychological variables associated with severe obesity, especially body-image. It will highlight some psychological and emotional components which are not resolved even if we treat obesity. To do this, we organized our work into three parts. In each part, we will always question the following two objectives, what characterizes these severe obesities but also everything which concerns its management and thus its evolution. Therefore the object of our work is to meet the needs of clinical problems that arise with these patients in order to ultimately improve models of care for severely obese adolescents.

HYPOTHESIS

To meet the objectives of our work, we raised various assumptions. First, to highlight this characteristic, beyond or should we say "below this obesity", these young adolescents with severe obesity, we hypothesized that there are multiple co-morbidities related with morbid obesity in adolescents, but where the psychological and psychopathological factors in connection with ill-treatment take an important part, despite a request that does not concern these aspects. In a second step, we wanted to clarify our first hypothesis by attempting to demonstrate the association of these aspects with the severity of obesity. Assuming that there is a specificity of severe obesity in adolescents, we want to highlight the involvement of certain variables (in the presence of obesity and its morbidity but also in its evolution during weight loss management). So our assumptions here concern the idea that adverse psychological and psychopathological factors as personal experience of ill-treatment determine the morbidity of obesity. But also the fact that most participants with severe obesity are those who are the less compliant to treatment for weight loss because of the involvement of psychopathological variables in the development of their obesity.

Finally, it seemed important to illustrate our work with clinical situations but it seemed also important to explore the question of the place of body-image in obese adolescents during the development of their severe obesity. Our hypotheses for this more clinical part are that there exists a disorder of body-image in adolescents with severe obesity, and that weight loss or more specifically the disappearance of severe obesity will not change these body-image disorders, as they are not only related to weight as such but most of all as personal experience of ill-treatment. Hypothesis which will lead us to approach these body-image disorders in the development of severe obesity but also in its management.

METHOD

Selection of Participants

The study concerns all obese adolescents hospitalized at the Pediatric Medical Center of Clairs-Vallons, at Ottignies in Belgium during five academic years (September 2003-September 2008). The expected duration of hospitalization is a whole school year. Hospitalization is initiated by medical prescription and the objectives are not only weight control, prevention and treatment of complications related to obesity, but also quality of life improvement and through these mechanisms understanding what caused eating disorders. All participants follow the same treatment protocol, which is a multidisciplinary management of obesity including medical check-ups, dietary appointments (individual and family), physical therapists, individual and family psychological, social and educational work if necessary.

Inclusion criteria : They are closely linked to the admission criteria of the institution. In order to fill in these inclusion criteria and in accordance with the definition of severe infantile obesity, our subjects have a B.M.I. greater than the 97 percentile (curve IOTF 25).

They are sent by their pediatric specialist or family physician, school medical centers, or a physician from an ambulatory hospital department where the management of obesity was not successful. The only criteria which is our own concerns the age of the participants. Our study is centered on adolescents suffering from severe obesity. We have, therefore, selected subjects aged 12 to 18 years old.

Exclusion criteria: All children suffering from secondary obesity as a result of a treatment or a disease such as endocrine, neurological, or genetic disorders, have been excluded from the study. Furthermore, none of the subjects were submitted during or before their hospitalization, to a medical or surgical treatment with the intention of losing weight. The study concerns all the obese children and adolescents hospitalized at "Centre Médical Pédiatrique de Clairs-Vallons" in Belgium from July 2003 till July 2008. The selection criteria of the subjects depend only on the admission criteria of the institution. In our population, exclusion criteria did not take into account the subjects suffering from secondary obesity due to a treatment or an organic pathology.

METHODOLOGY

Part 1 of the Research

In order to collect the different bio-psycho-social information, we put in place a multidisciplinary questionnaire concerning demographic, family and medical information, as well as data linked to progression during hospitalization (compliance with the treatment and weight loss). The psychological profile was evaluated through an I.Q. evaluation and a psychopathological diagnosis CFTMEA-R-2000, axis 1 and 2. These different questionnaires were filled in by practitioners relative to the numerous disciplines evaluated and were reviewed by the researcher, mainly with regard to diagnosis, in order to insure a relative coherence in the evaluation. These results were subjected to a descriptive statistical analysis and analyzed using SPSS software (version 16.0).At the end of the stay, so that we could evaluate the evolution of the different parameters, we carried out tests on comparison of averages.

Part 2 of the Research

To highlight the connexions that may be contained in our elements and more particularly the association between different psychological et psychopathological variables, we carried out a « Multiple correspondence factoral analysis » (MCFA). This type of statistical processing is based on the research of principal axes. It will be necessary to analyze all the elements linked to the problems studied together and not only in isolation as it was done in the first part. The software used was the SPAD-N (Portable Systeme for Numerical Data Analysis) version 7.0.

Part 3 of the Research

In order to comprehend all ties with our default environmental factors (ill-treatment), mental health problems, severe obesity, and compliance with the treatment, we have evaluated through the analysis of case studies, the presence of body-image disorder and its evolution during management of weight loss. As regards this last clinical approach, it takes in account the evolution of our conception concerning the problems of severe obesity in adolescents. 10 subjects were recruited amongst the primary cohort. They were hospitalized during the last year of our data collection and they accepted to participate in greater detail in this study. To achieve this objective, we have set out a plural evaluation of body-image by considering both its conscious and unconscious elements. We have therefore had to use: The questionnaire of body-image from Bruchon-Schweitzer [6]. The Rorschach, stripped with the help of a psychogram and the grid self-representation of Rausch de Trauenberg, a drawing of oneself evaluated on both quantitative and qualitative criteria of Machover. Given that this methodology is original and non-calibrated, we compared our data with a control population to whom we submitted the same test. This evaluation was managed by the researcher at the beginning and at the end of the stay and results were analyzed qualitatively using clinical data and quantitatively using a comparison test with the SPSS software (version 16.0).

RESULTS

Part 1

Our study focused on 164 subjects with an average age of 14 years (standard deviation = 1.56). With an average weight of 105 kg (standard deviation: 21), the average weight excess of our population is from 198% 1 at their entry. This is the double of what they should weigh to be considered as normal weight. The girls are overrepresented (66.5 %). The age of height and weight disconnect is located in the vicinity of an average age of 5 years (standard deviation= 2.9). Our results reveal the importance of medical, dietetic and morphological morbidities (75.3 % of subjects), actually current among our subjects. More than 32.2 % of the subjects do not have a family dinner sitting down at the table and they spend more than 4H (4.67, standard deviation = 2.6) per day in front of a screen. The family composition is similar to the general population while the sociological situation of parents is less than the population in spite of a higher level of education. The family data underline the omnipresence of the family history of obesity (83.7 %) and mainly affecting the parents. Half of the parents, mothers and fathers alike (51.5 %), submit or have submitted a mental health problem under care or in any case diagnosed by a doctor. The psychological and psychopathological data of our subjects highlight, in parallel, the presence of 74.1 % of adolescents with a diagnosis of pathology limit. The family environment appears as very precarious with 61% of mental disorders in the family (parents and siblings), 36.6 % of various deficiencies, 15.9 % of child abuse and 47.6 % of events leading to the breakdown of emotional ties. At the end of the stay, the weight, the somatic, dietetic, and morphological factors, are significantly reduced as well.

Part 2 of the Research

The results provided by the AFCM concerning the construction of the axis, show that the modalities that provide the largest contributions to the construction of axes in opposing are respectively and classified according to their contribution to the axis1:

The study has highlighted the fact that a greater severity of the obesity is associated with environmental pathological family factors (mental disorders in the family, deficiencies, abuse) and the presence of a psychopathological diagnosis in adolescents. In addition, these same terms are associated with less important family and individual compliance. In parallel, a less severe obesity and a better compliance to treatment are associated with a lack of psychopathological diagnosis and with an absence of factors of family pathological environment.

Negative side of the axis	Positive side of the axis
Absence of mental disorder among parents (7.11)	No family compliance (7.64)
Very good family compliance (4.45)	Deficiencies (6.63)
Absence of deficiency (3.86)	Ill-treatment (6.26)
Q. I. higher (3.77)	Compliance individual low (4.94)
B. M. I. entry lower average (3.69)	Evolution B. M. I missing data (4.3)
Lack of specific family environment (3.17)	B. M. I entry superior (3.99)
Lack of diagnosis (2.78)	Mental family disorders (3.47)
Absence of rupture of link (2.77)	Rupture of link (3.00)
Neurotic pathology (2.52)	No individual compliance (2.6)

(1)Corresponds to the percentage of excess body weight evaluated using the BMI reported on the curves for reference weight (here the French curves of distribution of weight). BMI on allows you to compare the BMI of children between them, taking account of the age.

Part 3 of the Research

The case study focusing on the particular question of the body-image, has highlighted the questionnaire of the body-image of Bruchon-Schweitzer [6], the below average results with a body-image characterized mainly by the fact of the dissatisfaction and the fact that it is uncertain. With the Rorschach, our results have highlighted the presence of body-image disorder with development difficulties and uncertain self-image, undifferentiated, the limits disseminated. Obesity is projected as the concrete guarantor facing a not much unified body-image. On the drawing of oneself, one can observe on the quantitative level, a substantial over-representation on both levels, that is the width and length of the body contours. At the qualitative level, we observed a significant number of body deformations (absence of hands, feet, ..) and a body which is undifferentiated. This over-representation and these distortions are not found in subjects with normal ponderal index. These results do not evolve in a significant way at the end of the stay when the subject has lost weight. The body-image does therefore not change with the loss of weight.

DISCUSSION

Our various results lead to consider that the obesity of our subjects is a result of many factors and is accompanied by multiple current existing comorbidities. It appears furthermore to be complicated by the psychopathological factors associated to a greater severity of the obesity and to a lesser compliance to treatment. These results, however, need to be moderated because they are not representative of the population as a whole. It is, indeed, composed of adolescents suffering from severe obesity who are hospitalized for a long time for weight loss. It is important to consider, in this context, that when one performs a search on subjects suffering from a disease, the choice of a clinical population is often due to the accessibility to a greater number of subjects.

As regards the pediatric obesity, we must also note that those who seek treatment are more severely obese than those who do not [19]. Despite these reservations, these different results have nevertheless led, to consider that the severe obesity in adolescents must be re-conceptualised in considering the place of multiple existing comorbidities and not only future. Our results indicate, in effect, the particularly high prevalence of medical pathologies associated with obesity (hypertension, hyperinsulinisme,...). Our results also stress their significant decrease at the time of a loss of weight. This leads us to talk about morbid obesity in adolescents, even young, because it is directly linked to a series of morbidities. Therefore, in our opinion, the definition of severe obesity in children and adolescents needs to be more than just considering the BMI as a criterion of distinction but much more considering the whole of the comorbidities presented.

Beyond the medical morbidities, we also emphasized the place of the psycho-social comorbidities, psychological and psycho-pathological. The psychosocial and psychological morbidities refer to all the factors of failed environment (neglect, ill-treatment) and the morbidities are related to the psychopathological diagnosis. These different comorbidities were clearly associated with the severity of the obesity. This finding is essential because it is the very essence of our work and responds to our first hypothesis. We, as a reminder, are interested in a population hospitalized not for psychological difficulties but for a weight loss. This is essential because 'in fine', what we are putting in evidence is the psychopathological nature of this population. Through our results, we can say that there is a multiple comorbidity linked to the severe obesity among adolescents where the psychopathological factors take such an important place, despite a request that is in no way based on those aspects. These elements are rarely mentioned in the literature concerning obesity in adolescents. The psychosocial problems are described as the psychological suffering of young obese but less mentioned is the occurrence of the psychopathology which is associated. When the latter is envisaged, it is mainly in the context of eating disorders. Yet several research indicate significant differences between the psychiatric comorbidity in obese children and non-obese. Some studies indicate that severe obesity is associated with a greater psychological suffering [15]. Our work addresses clearly the issue among adolescents suffering from severe obesity in confirming the link between the presence of psychopathological comorbidity and severe obesity. Psychopathology that is far from being specific, needs to be considered as linked with the presence of factors of deleterious environment such as indicated by our results in the correlational study, second part of our research. Therefore, the presence of deleterious environment factors such as deficiencies and ill-treatment seem linked to the occurrence of severe obesity.

We can therefore respond to our second hypothesis by speaking of unfavourable psychological factors which are associated with the most severe obesities. However, we cannot assert that there is a determinism of these factors on the severity of obesity but we assume that obesity is entered in a psychological complex dynamic where it found its place in the framework of a fragility of identity leading to behaviors that promote its development, its maintenance and its severity. Once the obesity installed, it continues, moreover, to influence the psychological components of the topic. One cannot consider any more that the psychological problems associated with obesity were only caused by the rejection that the adolescent has lived, but much more consider that it associates with the vulnerability already present in the subject, as described by Bruch [5]. Severe obesity in adolescents could therefore be found in a broader psychic problematic, that it would then maintain or strengthen by its presence.

We have tried to clarify this identity fragility by focusing our interest on the body-image of these adolescents. We put forward the idea that there is among these young people a breach of the body-image which could open the way toward the development of obesity. Our cases analysis dealing specifically with the body-image were emphasized through the various tests, the presence of a low level of elaboration, a dependence on the object and a difficulty in resorting to emotions. The psychodynamic analysis which may be made from these results is the presence of a defensive attitude that designates a fight against the emergence of the internal reality. It appears like a building of barriers between "the inside and the outside". Barrier between the inside and the outside that leads us to the concept of obesity" carapace" which protects the young obese subject from the external environment while assuring him an integrity and a value in the image of the body [18]. Dumet [13] speaks of the acquisition through obesity of a clean skin, forged of all parts by the subject and away from the spectrum of fusional infringement. Our cases analysis tends to support the idea of this place of obesity as a guarantor of an image of the unified body face to the confused limits of the identity [5]. The loss of weight is not accompanied by a profound change to the body-image as such, but by the emergence of more content deteriorated to different tests as if the body-image was, on the contrary, been weakened by the loss of weight. This weakening has been described by Clerici et al. [9] among the adult subject suffering from morbid obesity following a loss of weight related to a surgical intervention. He speaks of the change in the physical appearance which will not correspond to the ability of the subject to represent himself differently, with on the contrary, a disturbed perception by the body-image which may appear. This consideration of the obesity carapace allows to reconsider our results and to interpret the association found between a lesser individual compliance to treatment and the severity of obesity. By losing its obesity, the subject runs the risk of losing its defense mechanism, which had allowed him to keep until now, a unity of his body-image. Obesity is projected as the concrete guarantor versus a body-image poorly unified and hardly constructed.

Considering the whole of our results as well as the evolution of our research, we can put forward that our results, although they allow us to refine the profile of the teenager suffering from severe obesity, do not allow us to uniquely identify the etiologic factors. We have, on the other hand, tried to highlight that the development of obesity in our subjects was in processes that put in interaction of psychosocial problems and a fragility of identity more precisely a degradation of the body-image which are mutually reinforcing. The supported must therefore aim to break this type of vicious circle and no longer needs to dwell only on the resolution of the dietary errors and the rehabilitation movement but much more on the lived positive experiences through the body so far manhandled. We are led, just as we reviewed the disorder of the body-image as a psychopathological entity, to reconsider the therapeutic work with the subject adolescents suffering from severe obesity. Few studies, currently, have focused on attempts to direct changes in the body-image. However, if the body-image is not amended, there is a high risk of relapse even for other of psychopathology developments mentioned by Clerici et al. [9] and Raich [20].

Beyond the psychotherapeutic work, our results indicate the perceptual component involved in the body map. Therefore psychomotor activities and also motor activities must improved with those subjects. To be able to relive rewarding and global experiences with a body in motion which can be lived, finally, as a vector of pleasure, appears to us as essential for these subjects.

CONCLUSION

The main objective of this research was to understand better the profile of young adolescents suffering from severe obesity and to have a special interest in their mental health and family environment and its influence on the development of obesity, but also on the care taking. Our results have shown that obesity of our subjects is multi-factor and is accompanied by multiple morbidities and more particularly of the bio-psycho-social comorbodities. Using a factor analysis, we have highlighted the fact that a greater severity of obesity is associated with a handicapping environmental factors (mental disorders in the family, deficiencies, abuse) and to the presence of a psychopathological profile. In addition, these same terms were associated with a less important family and individual compliance.

In the last part, we wanted to identify the links between these different elements. To do this, we have by the means of cases analysis and with the help of a Rorschach, plus the questionnaire of the body-image of Bruchon-Schweitzer [6], and from a drawing by the subject itself, evaluated the presence of disorder of the body-image among 10 of our subjects and their evolution during their care taking in regard with weight loss. Our results have highlighted the presence of body-image disorder with uncertain self image, undifferentiated, the limits disseminated.

These elements do not allow us to define in a precise manner the determinants of severe obesity but they allow us to understand that severe obesity installs itself in a non- invested body, little mobilisable in link with the factors of deleterious environment imposing the need to build a barrier (obesity) between the "inside weakened" and the outside lived as dangerous. We can therefore understand the difficulty of the subject matter to accept to lose weight which would then prevent him from resorting to this type of operation. This body image cannot be designed without considering its links with the development of the body schema.

Our results have also stressed that the hospitalization of these subjects and the therapeutic model proposed allowed the improvement of many physical and physiological parameters linked to a loss of weight and this while taking into account for the first time the psychic suffering of these young people. But we have also highlighted the fact that it was done in part to improve the body-image disorders of these young people which we have emphasized as non-negligible in this population. The therapeutic model linked to the support of severe obesity must therefore take these elements into account.

REFERENCES

[1]   Amstrong J., Dorosty A.R., Reilly J.J, Child Health Information Team, Emmet P.M. (2003). Coexistence of social inequalities in undernutrition and obesity in preschool children: population based cross sectional study. Archives of Disease in Childhood, 88 (8), 671-675.

[2]   Basdevant A. (2004) Définitions et classification des obésités, In Ed. Flammarion Médecine-Sciences, Médecine de l'obésité. Basdevant A. et Guy-Grand B. Paris. De Becker E. And Leurquin F. (2010). L'impact des maltraitances physiques infantiles. Annales Medico-psychologiques, 168 (10), 746-751.

[3]   Borys J.-M. (2004) L'obésité de l'enfant. Paris : Ed. Masson.

[4]   Bruch H. (1971) (1994) Les yeux et le ventre. Pais : Payot and Rivage.

[5]   Bruschon-Schweitzer M. (1990), Une psychologie du corps. Paris: PUF.

[6]   Charritat J-L., Legrain D., Mingot V. et al. (2006) Enfants maltraités et victimes de violences : fonctionnement de l'Unité d'Accueil des Jeunes Victimes de l'hôpital Armand Trousseau, Journal de Pédiatrie et de Puériculture, 3, 93-96.

[7]   Chiolero A., Lasserre A.M., Paccaud F., Bovet P. (2007) Childhood obesity: definition, consequences and prevalence. Revue Med. Suisse 16;3 (111). 1262-1269.

[8]   Clerici M., Papa R., Basile R., Invernizzi G. (1991) Le vécu de soi corporel et le test de Rorschach dans l'obésité grave en traitement médico-chirurgical. Ann. Méd-psychol. 148 (5). 483-494.

[9]   Cole T.J., Bellizzi M.C., Flegal K., Dietz W.H. (2000) Establishing a standard definition of child overweight and obesity worldwide: international survey. Br Med Journal. vol.320. 1-6.

[10]   De Bandt J.P. (2004) Nutrition et obésité. Nutrition Clinique et Métabolisme. 18. 147-155.

[11]   Decaluwe V., Braet C., Moens E., Van Vlierberghe L. (2006). The association of parental characteristics and psychological problems in obese youngsters. International Journal of Obesity. 30 (12). 1766-74.

[12] Dumet N. (2002) La différence incarnée. Réflexions psychosomatiques sur un phénomène étrangement familier : l'obésité. Cahiers de psychologie clinique .18. 31-43.

[13] Inserm (2000) Obésité, dépistage et prévention chez l'enfant. Ed. Inserm. Isnard P. (2007) La psychopathologie de l'enfant et de l'adolescent obèses in Solal editeur. Les troubles des conduites alimentaires chez l'enfant et l'adolescent. 65-112. Marseille : Solal.

[14] Kosti Ri, Panagiotakos Db. (2006) The epidemic of obesity in children and adolescents in the world, Central European *Journal of Public Health*. 14 (4). 151-9.

[15] Lemay M. (1993) J'ai mal à ma mère: approche thérapeutique du carencé relationnel, Paris : Ed. Fleurus.

[16] Marcelli D., Braconnier A. (1981) Psychopathologie de l'adolescent. Paris : Masson, Paris.

[17] Pierce J.W., Wardle J. (1997) Cause and effects beliefs and self-esteem of overweight children. *Journal of Child Psychology and Psychiatry*. 38 (6). 645-650.

[18] Raich R.M., (2007) L'image du corps dans les troubles du comportement alimentaire : développement d'une image corporelle négative chez l'enfant et l'adolescent, in Solal editeur, Les troubles des conduites alimentaires chez l'enfant et l'adolescent. 113-140. Marseille : Solal.

[19] Tounian P., Girardet J.-P. (2004) Prise en charge de l'enfant obèse, in Ed. Flammarion Médecine-Sciences, Médecine de l'obésité, Paris : Basdevant A. et Guy-Grand B. TOUNIAN P. (2007), Obésité infantile : bousculons les idées reçues. Réalités en Nutrition. 2. 31-36.

[20] Wardle J., Carnell S. (2007) Parental feeding and children's weight. Actae Paediatric Suppl. 96 (454), 5-11.

In: Child Abuse
Editors: Raymond A. Turner and Henry O. Rogers

ISBN: 978-1-62257-113-0
© 2012 Nova Science Publishers, Inc.

Chapter 5

A CONSPIRACY OF SILENCE? ADDRESSING CHILDHOOD TRAUMA IN MALTA: AN EMPIRICAL REVIEW

Michael Galea
University of Malta, Malta

ABSTRACT

Childhood maltreatment is a heterogeneous domain, full of complexities. It occurs in all socioeconomic, religious and ethnic groups. Child abuse carries one universal denominator: abuse of power. Childhood maltreatment consists of sexual, emotional, and physical abuse, and neglect. The purpose of this review was to underline the potential effects of childhood maltreatment on the holistic development and well-being of victims. More specifically, these studies looked at key psycho-social variables which directly and indirectly affect victims of childhood maltreatment among a relatively new culture: Malta. Results suggested that this phenomenon is well present in Malta, which is uniform to related studies done elsewhere. A total of 11% in these studies qualified as 'severely' abused and neglected. Maltreatment may have a sequential effect on individuals' lives, impacting directly their personality and cognitive evaluation of life, which in turn influences other variables, such as the participants' emotional sense of well-being. This review intends first to foster greater social awareness of maltreatment in Malta in the hope it may spur more research. Such research should contribute to serious discussions around how best to develop public policies and laws to protect children. Furthermore, these studies suggest that the healing process has to be holistic in scope to be true to its name, including other variables in the equation that could have been sidelined for various reasons in the past.

CHILD ABUSE (CA)

Childhood abuse is a heterogeneous domain, full of complexities (Childhelp USA, 2011). It occurs in all socioeconomic, religious and ethnic groups. Perpetrators are most often ordinary people trapped in a stressful life situation with which they cannot cope properly.

Finkelhor (1984, 1993) opined that child abusers are usually persons closely related to the child (parent-figure, older siblings, etc.) and seldom a total stranger. Child abuse carries one universal denominator: abuse of power. This power could be either naturally created (e.g. family-system) or socially held (e.g. professional capacity).

DEFINITION OF CHILD ABUSE

According to the Child Abuse Prevention and Treatment Act (CAPTA – 2011), child abuse (CA) and neglect at a minimum means any act or failure to act on the part of parents/caretaker, which results in death, serious physical or emotional harm, sexual abuse or exploitation or an act or failure to act which presents an imminent risk of serious harm to a child. Child physical abuse (CPA) is defined as an act that results in physical injury to a child. Punching, beating, kicking, biting, burning, breaking bones, hair pulling, and shaking a baby are examples of physical abuse. Child sexual abuse (CSA) is defined as any misuse of a child for sexual pleasure or gratification. It is the involvement of children in sexual activities that they do not fully comprehend, that they are unable to give informed consent to and/or that violates societal taboos. It involves non-touching activities (exhibitionism, exposure to pornographic material or any sexual act), touching (fondling, penetration or any other sexual act with a child), and sexual exploitation (engaging a child for the purposes of prostitution or using a child to film pornographically). Child emotional abuse (CEA) is understood as a pattern of behavior that can seriously interfere with a child's positive development, psyche and self-concept. It is hard to identify due to no physical evidence. It includes rejection, ignoring, shaming and humiliating, terrorizing, isolating, or corrupting (CAPTA, 2011).

Although research on child abuse has often focused on sexual trauma, Lawson, Drebing, Berg, Vincellette, and Penk (1998) found that the inclusion of all forms of CA is necessary for a more realistic appraisal of trauma. Thus, CA has been defined as any act of commission or omission that endangers or impairs a child's physical or emotional health and development (Childhelp USA, 2001).

IMPACT AND PREVALENCE OF CA

Studies examining the consequences of child abuse document a broad spectrum of symptomatology affecting the psycho-spiritual status of individuals. These include depression, anxiety, low self-image, negative self-respect, violence, mistrust, shame, guilt, identity problems, sexual difficulties, adult personality disorders, delayed cognitive development, behavioral problems, and self-destructive behavior (Andrews, 2000; Childhelp, USA, 2001; Finkelhor, 1984; Grubman-Black, 1990; Kamsner and McCabe, 2000). Regarding the impact of CSA, Finkelhor and Browne (1985) described four basic dynamics concerning its traumatic impact, namely: traumatic sexuality, violation of trust, powerlessness, and stigmatization. The relevance and consequences of CA become more important in considering that the actual incidence is estimated to be three times higher than the number of cases reported (Childhelp, USA, 2001). Of those reported in the US for the year 1999, 55% were neglect cases, 23% child physical abuse (CPA), 12% child sexual abuse

(CSA), and around 12% child emotional abuse (CEA). However, it must be noted that the severity of each abuse was not verified. Finkelhor (1984) noticed a tendency through many studies among males to underreport sexual trauma. Eliciting retrospective abuse reports could be a problem. Silvern, Waelde, Baughan, Karyl, and Kaersvang (2000) found much less abuse reported on self- versus researcher- defined questionnaire formats. This may imply the probability of victims' reluctance to think of their past as abusive. Because no abuse occurs in a vacuum, Finkelhor (1998) cautioned retrospective research to take account of the environment in which the abuse takes place for better therapeutic measures. Other traumas may also be involved.

PERSONALITY

More specifically to this review, personality has been found to be a robust predictor of subjective well-being. It accounts for the largest portion of variance over other psychosocial variables (DeNeve and Cooper, 1998). One particular personality domain that is increasingly gaining attention due to its beneficial effects is extraversion. Research has indicated three main reasons why we should study extraversion, namely a) it's importance to personality (Costa and McCrae, 1992a), b) it predicts well-being across a broad domain including cognitive and social well-being (Eaton and Funder, 2003), and c) extraversion predicts risks and resilience for other forms of psychotherapy (Widiger and Samuel, 2005). Hans Eysenck modernized our understanding of extraversion. He long argued that our major personality dimensions have biological basis. The now famous arousal hypothesis of extraversion postulated extraverted behavior as arousal seeking (Eysenck, 1967). Therefore, it is interesting to highlight the personality profile of those with high extraversion. It seems that such people are highly motivated for social contact, power, and status (Olson and Weber, 2004). Extraversion relates to a relatively positive view of the world (Uziel, 2006). Extraverts may act more socially than introverts because they may have some traits not present in introverts (Liebermann and Rosenthal, 2001). Moreover, extraverts feel higher levels of positive affect than introverts (Costa and McCrae, 1980). The literature on child abuse suggests that a reported history of such events would be related to decreased positive aspects of subjective well-being and increased negative affect. We presumed that such would be the case and predicted that this effect would occur in a cross-cultural study. The design chosen here will help determine whether personality variables, particularly extraversion could overcome, as it were, the negative impact of child abuse. The final research question, therefore, is whether reported abuse in childhood will totally attenuate the relationship between personality variables with subjective well-being.

FAMILY ENVIRONMENT AND PSYCHO-SOCIAL DEVELOPMENT

Studies suggest that a key variable for a child's normal development is family environment. Family environment is not just the physical aspect under which children live and grow, but also other relevant factors that affect one's developmental process, such as parental styles and dynamics. Finkelhor and Browne (1985) found that the family environment was the context where most of the reported child abuse cases occur. Moreover, Finkelhor (1984, 1998) showed that not only is the family context part of such trauma, but that the perpetrator is often known to the victims.

Scarr (1996) stressed that except in extreme cases of abused and at-risk children, environmental experiences play a minimal role in influencing children's cognitive and socio-emotional development. To the contrary, Baumrind (1971) found that the environment does have an important role in children's development.

Thus parents should not be punitive or aloof, but promote their children with consistent rules along with considerable affection. Baumrind's argument is credible in light of attachment research.

Bowlby (1969, 1989) and Ainsworth (1979) spoke of the importance of secure attachment in infancy for normal development. Staying in physical proximity to the primary caregiver helps the child satisfy essentials for survival, such as nourishment and self-defense.

They further characterized the importance of reliable care-givers during infancy in two respects: a safe haven in times of distress and a secure base for exploring one's environment. This safety zone helps the child to develop and face life's challenges positively.

The contact comfort received from such a secure environment helps the child to develop the resiliency that is critical for survival (Harlow and Zimmerman, 1959). Darling and Steinberg (1993) also stressed the important implications of parenting styles. Research classifies parenting styles in two directions: (a) a combination of warmth, nurturance, acceptance and responsiveness, defined by parental empathy and closeness, and (b) a demand and control family dynamic, defined by parental neglect and indifference (Baumrind, 1971). The first parenting style is the optimal one (Darling and Steinberg, 1993).

CHILD ABUSE AND RELATED VARIABLES

Abuse may lead to people engaging in various defense mechanisms, repressing the trauma for example so that life can move on. Dickie et al. (1997) found that worse effects seem to occur when the abuser is the primary care-giver/parent. Children need to find ways to make sense of their trauma. They may internalize their guilt and feel rejected, sinful, unclean, or even ignored by a deity.

Using Bowlby's attachment theory (1969) in which individuals are not passive but active in constructing and maintaining close relationships, Kirkpatrick and Shaver (1990, 1992) indicated that God may serve as a 'perfect' substitute attachment figure for people with histories of avoidant attachment. Child abuse may be a potential reason for such avoidance. They speculated that the need for attachment is life-long. Kane, Cheston and Greer (1993) considered this element important in that "transference might easily occur in a child's mind from father the abuser to God the Father" (p. 229). In related studies, spirituality but not religiosity predicted subjective well-being (Ciarrocchi and Deneke, 2004; Galea, 2008).

Besides attachment and spirituality, two key and related variables are family conflict and cohesion. Meyerson, Long, Miranda, and Marx (2002) found that family conflict and cohesion are risk factors for the development of psychological distress and depression in adolescence, and therefore they suggest the particular study of these two variables for a more holistic appreciation and better understanding. Various researchers suggest the inclusion of other important variables when focusing on childhood maltreatment, as it never occurs in a vacuum (Bramblett, 1998; Margolin, 1994).

Moreover, patriarchal family systems, which are prevalent in Western countries including Malta, are positively correlated to childhood maltreatment (Asher, 1988). Other studies suggested the negative prediction of patriarchal systems on the well-being of family members (Morales, 1996; Whealin et al., 2002). This is more important in a small country like Malta, with its closely-knit family systems, and under a strong influence by a dominant Catholic faith (Galea et al., 2007).

CHILD ABUSE IN MALTA

The situation of CA in Malta was highlighted by the UN convention on the Rights of the Child (2000), which called for the urgent need of a comprehensive assessment and public policy decisions regarding this problem. Galea (1999) found that Malta still has no structures or means to successfully fight CA. Although the legal system generally covers CA, there still is a case for introducing more specific legislation in this regard. Recent developments are a significant breakthrough, even if still limited.

A confounding factor in establishing, assessing, and creating awareness against CA is culture. Cultural context provides the limitations for what is deemed appropriate versus inappropriate child care. Action in one culture may be seen as 'healthy' but 'perverted' in another.

THE REALITY IN MALTA

This review focused on the experience of childhood trauma in Malta, specifically among a sample of university students. Malta, a tiny republic island in the Mediterranean Sea, with a rich history dating back to thousands of years, has been highlighted in a recent document by the United Nations on children's welfare. The U.N. document (2000) called for the urgent need for a comprehensive assessment and public policy decisions regarding this problem. Malta does not have the necessary resources to protect children from child abuse, nor any mandatory reporting laws. Galea reiterates that statistics are scarce, and child protective services are still in their infancy (2008). More awareness and research is required for better and timely response.

Galea et al. (2007) surveyed Maltese university students on various aspects of childhood trauma and found that almost 11% qualified as severely abused. Interestingly, he indicated that spirituality may serve also as a potential resource in treating victims of childhood maltreatment.

To help further clarify the reality of childhood trauma, this review has analyzed research articles which sought to know how this reality impacts its victims, in view of key psycho-social variables. More poignantly, this review was interested whether family environment gives any additional value to well-being, after controlling other key variables, among Maltese students. Another objective was to clarify the input of personality variables to the whole equation. Finally, this review sought also any interactions or mediations, if any, among the key variables, in predicting subjective well-being.

Given the lack of relevant studies on this reality in Malta, these studies covered here could serve to further related studies among the general population, intended to highlight the incidences and relationships among such important variables to one's psycho-social well-being after trauma. As an overall summary therefore, this chapter looked at research findings on the potential implications of early attachment and family dynamics on the psycho-social well-being of young individuals.

PREVALENCE OF CHILD ABUSE IN MALTA FROM THIS SAMPLE

This review looked at a number of studies among Maltese university students. The student population from which these studies were randomly selected (by computer) represents 13% of the Maltese general population between the ages of 18 and 25 years old (Mean = 20.45, $\underline{SD}$ = 2.37). Various results were highlighted, and which are detailed below.

First of all, 11% of the Maltese students who participated in this research qualified as 'severely' abused and neglected across the five childhood maltreatment categories.

The first study sought to understand the correlation between child abuse and key variables usually related closely to this realm, particularly family environment, personality and well-being (Galea, 2008). How does child abuse relate to subjective well-being?

Well-being was measured through both the cognitive (SWLS) and the emotional components (ABS). The overall abuse index score (TOTCTQ) strongly correlated with cognitive well-being (r (310) = -.36, $p<$ .001), and with Affect Balance of the emotional well-being scale (r (310) = -.22, $p<$ .001). Abuse correlated also with low positive affect and high negative affect. Therefore, CA influences individuals to have negative self-perceptions and feelings.

When considering the correlation between abuse and personality, the following resulted: the composite abuse index score correlated significantly to lower Extraversion (r (310) = -.24, $p<$ .001), Agreeableness (r (310) = -.24, $p<$ .001), and Conscientiousness (r (310) = -.40, $p<$ .001), and to higher Neuroticism (r (310) = .22, $p<$. 001). Results seem to indicate a withdrawn, passive and temperamental personality. No interaction effects were found, in predicting the victims' well-being.

PATH ANALYSIS

In examining the patterns of correlations noted above, a sequential pattern of relationships appeared to emerge (Galea, 2008). This pattern was clarified through a series of regression analysis in which key variables were tested to determine their predictions by CA. The resulting pattern suggested that CA has both direct and indirect effects on these outcome variables. These are shown in three steps. First, the composite abuse index score (TOTCTQ) served as a single 'predictor' of these outcome variables: personality, and cognitive well-being. In the second step, the outcome variables predicted by abuse in step one, served as predictors of spirituality. In step three, spirituality predicted positive affect of emotional well-being. It should be also noted that the path model proposed was clearly post hoc in nature; it was developed after the pattern correlations among these variables were already examined.

Abuse was directly related to personality, religious practice, and cognitive well-being. Individuals who were abused tended to have a personality profile that was high in Openness to Experience, and low on Conscientiousness, which could be interpreted as a tendency to be escapist and withdrawn. Abuse related also to lower religious practice, indicating poorer level of public worship and prayerful life. Finally, CA correlated with lower levels of life satisfaction (cognitive well-being). Thus, an abuse victim has a high risk of low self-esteem, and self-respect. Although childhood maltreatment had no impact on levels of spirituality, the first layer of outcome variables themselves impacted spirituality. There are three points of interest here. First, high levels of spirituality are associated with higher levels of conscientiousness, religiosity, and life satisfaction. Furthermore, thinking (cognitive well-being) directly influences one's spiritual motivations. This may indicate that positive thinking augurs well to one's mature spirituality. Secondly, abuse had an indirect effect on spirituality. Finally, spirituality has a direct impact on positive affect, but not on negative affect, which is an important therapeutic issue. It should be noted that abuse was not directly related to this outcome, nor were the other variables, except cognitive well-being. Results therefore suggest that CA may have a sequential effect on an individual's life, impacting directly the adaptive orientation and cognitive evaluation of life, then spirituality, and finally emotional well-being.

In the second study reviewed (Galea, 2009), it was hypothesized that personality, especially extraversion would have unique variance in predicting the components of well-being over and above the contribution of family environment and history of child abuse. To determine this possibility, a series of hierarchical regressions were performed for all predictor variables with subjective well-being as the criterion variable. For each model, total child abuse history was entered in step one, family variables in step two, and the five personality variables entered separately in step three. Of the three family environment dimensions, only the relationship domain was used, due to its acceptable alpha reliability. Reported history of child abuse was related to subjective well-being. Personality was strongly related to subjective well-being as predicted, particularly Extraversion, Conscientiousness, Neuroticism and Openness to experience. Agreeableness did not significantly predict well-being. Even after controlling for child abuse and family environment, personality explained from 17 to 26% of the variance for the subjective well-being component. Extraversion, conscientiousness and neuroticism carried the majority of the predictive variance for the outcomes. In summary, these variables rounded out the importance of personality in its myriad facets as related to subjective well-being.

FAMILY PROFILE OF VICTIMS

Pearson correlations suggested that abusive families tend to be low on cohesion, expressiveness, intellectual-cultural emphasis, organization, and on moral-religiousness (Galea, 2012). These family environments seem also to be exposed to high conflict, as was hypothesized.

What about the family profile of a person with a history of child abuse? Abuse negatively correlated with cohesion (r (310) = -.40, p < .001), expressiveness (r (310) = -.30, p < .001), intellectual-cultural orientation (r (310) = -.20, p < .001), moral-religious emphasis (r (310) = -.22, p < .001), and a sense of organization (r (310) = -.23, p < .001). As expected, abuse correlated positively with conflict (r (310) = .41, p < .001). Therefore, results suggest a family profile with a history of child abuse as being: low in cohesion and expressiveness, and high in conflict. These indicate a family dysfunction which evidently is not a promising and positive environment for the normal psycho-emotional development of children, let alone for those already scarred by abuse (Galea, 2012).

It was hypothesized that family environment would have unique variance in predicting psychological well-being over and above the contribution of personality and history of mental trauma, focusing specifically on childhood maltreatment. To determine this possibility, a series of hierarchical regressions were performed for all predictor variables with subjective well-being as the criterion variable.

For each model, abuse (total score) was entered in step one, the five personality variables entered separately in step two, and family environment entered in step three. Of the three family environment dimensions, only the Relationship domain was used, due to its acceptable alpha reliability.

Reported history of mental trauma was related to Subjective Well-being. Personality was strongly related to Subjective Well-being, particularly Neuroticism, Conscientiousness, and Extraversion (Galea, 2012). Openness did not significantly predict well-being. Even after controlling for childhood maltreatment and personality, family environment as highlighted through the relationship dimension, explained 35% of the variance for the Subjective Well-being component. This is more critical when one considers the significant personality variables (explaining from 17 to 26% of variance) input into the equation.

Conscientiousness and the relationship dimension of family environment carried the majority of the predictive variance for the outcomes. The negative beta weight for relationship is logical when taking into account that environments of victims of abuse are usually conflicted and unhealthy for the required healthy psycho-emotional development of such individuals. Overall, these results rounded up the importance of family environment in its myriad facets towards subjective well-being of participants (Galea, 2012).

MEDIATOR VARIABLE EFFECT

The next step in our analysis concerned another key hypothesis of this review, that of the possibility of a mediator variable effect (Galea, 2010). One typically looks for mediators if there already is a strong relation between a predictor and an outcome and one wishes to explore the mechanisms behind that relation. More specifically, a mediator is defined as a variable that explains the relation between a predictor and an outcome (Baron and Kenny, 1986) variable. The mediator is the mechanism through which a predictor influences an outcome variable. According to this method, there are four steps (performed with three regression equations) in establishing that a variable (e.g., child abuse) mediates the relation between a predictor variable (e.g., family) and an outcome variable (e.g., well-being).

Baron and Kenny (1986) explain that a variable functions as a mediator when it meets certain conditions, namely: (a) the independent variable (IV) impacts the mediator variable (MV) in the first equation (path a), (b) the IV impacts the dependent variable (DV) in the second equation (path c), (c) the MV impacts the DV in the third equation (path b), (d) if (a), (b), and (c) all hold in the predicted direction, then the effect of the IV on the DV must be less in the third equation than in the second (path c'). A perfect mediation is said to occur when this is reduced to zero. Otherwise, it is a partial mediation. The mediator variable, then, serves to clarify the nature of the relationship between the independent and dependent variables.

In the first equation, the independent variable (family environment) affected the mediator variable (child abuse): r (310) = .18, p < .001. In the second equation, family environment impacted the outcome or dependent variable (cognitive well-being): r (310) = -.28, p < .001. Child abuse impacted the outcome variable (cognitive well-being): r (310) = -.23, p < .001. Results thus indicated only a partial mediation. The partial drop from -.19 to -.16 (i.e. from path c to c') could explain that child abuse partially mediates the relation between well-being and family. In terms of causation, a fairly strong argument can be made that family environment (predictor variable) preceded both child abuse (mediator variable) and well-being (outcome variable). However, it could be the case that individuals who are suffering from poor well-being (outcome variable) symptoms are more likely to be abused (i.e., that the outcome causes the mediator). In fact, in testing this alternative model, well-being also was a significant mediator of the relation between family and child abuse. Thus, there are alternative models that are consistent with the data. This study also did not control for other factors that may be related to or cause both family environment and child abuse, such as key personality traits like neuroticism. Thus, all we can say at this point is that our data are consistent with models in which child abuse causes poor well-being, and poor well-being causes abuse. We also must acknowledge that the mediation relations we found might not have been evident if other variables that cause both family environment and child abuse had been included in the model. In conclusion, these results continue to indicate the relevance of family variables to well-being.

IMPACT OF CHILD ABUSE

CA significantly correlated with personality. Results suggest that abuse influences victims with withdrawn and detached tendencies, indications that may need to be kept in mind by therapists helping victims of CA. Furthermore, CA influenced negatively the psycho-spiritual status of individuals. Empirical studies have shown both immediate and long-term negative effects on well-being.

The current study extends these findings by showing the impact of CA on the positive side of well-being and not just on symptoms of distress. This finding is noteworthy because subjective well-being or happiness is multi-layered, made up of low negative affect and high positive affect along with cognitive ratings of life satisfaction. CA impacts not only negative affect, but positive affect as well – a double-barreled assault on happiness with lasting implications.

MODELING THE IMPACT OF CHILD ABUSE

When adjusting for redundancies among the other variables, CA was found to have both direct and indirect effects on the psycho-spiritual status of participants. A developmental hypothesis was therefore proposed, presenting the sequential effects of trauma on well-being.

The Structural Equation used in the study reviewed (Galea, 2008) is particularly important for two reasons. First, it presents a more organized pattern of the unique relationships within the complex realm of childhood trauma. It explains the fact that CA impacts young individuals in a sequential and cumulative manner, through direct and indirect effects. Secondly, it provides an empirical model of child abuse impact that can be tested in future research.

From the standpoint of positive psychology, these results extend the concept of human flourishing in the face of potentially traumatic childhood experiences. Roughly, the same statistics of university students with a history of childhood maltreatment in this sample compare well with that in the United States (Bernstein and Fink, 1998).

This finding is noteworthy in that it controlled for a highly salient predictor of happiness. For positive psychology to continue to progress as a science as well as to develop scientifically derived applications for everyday life, it must address the issue of resilience. Given that tragedy and setbacks are intimately associated to human life, what we learn from positive psychology must have application to coping with such events if it is to have credibility in the larger social world. Childhood trauma, such as abuse, is a particularly good platform from which to study variables related to positive psychology. Society's concern for victims of child abuse is well-intentioned and necessary. It is equally important that victims themselves discard notions that they can never recover from its effects. Positive psychology can have a most useful role in directing people towards their hidden strengths, rather than the ever-conscious deficits and vulnerabilities.

In particular, key personality variables are increasingly found to be a beacon in the positive psychology movement. This is clearer in human resiliency. This study highlighted the positive contribution of particularly two such domains: extraversion and conscientiousness.

Extroverts, for example, find social situations more rewarding than introverts, not because they are more sociable but because they are more sensitive to the rewards inherent in most situations (Lucas and Diener, 2008). Stambor (2006) found that even though orangutans are semi-solitary apes, those with high extraversion, high agreeableness and low neuroticism tended to be rated as happier. Moreover, the author suggests that the study could bolster the use of human-provided ratings to assess animals' well-being.

These studies have several limitations. They were a sample of convenience in university students. The pool of participants was randomly selected by computer thus containing at least one aspect of participants' self-selection. More importantly, the cross-sectional nature of the design limits causal inferences. Obviously, longitudinal research with child abuse victims will permit stronger conclusions. Similarly, all the measures were self-report, thus raising questions as to the accuracy of the participants' memory.

As noted above, however, the fact that students in a different culture reported similar rates of child abuse as in the United States at least provides some face validity for the veracity of the child abuse history. The study's strengths include its relatively large sample size and the measure of control that was utilized to rule out some plausible alternative explanations. Lastly, one strength that has to be also mentioned is the fact that this study is a cross-culture study which confirms the benefit of such personality variables, as extraversion and conscientiousness, to cognitive well-being and happiness.

CONCLUSION

Results from this review continue to add to the existing literature on the importance that family variables have on the psycho-emotional well-being and development of young people. This becomes clearer in view of a history of child abuse and neglect. More specifically, cohesion, emotional self-expressiveness and conflict require particular assessment, when evaluating persons with child abuse history, and when planning therapeutic programs and strategies. Galea (2008) strongly suggests that the inclusion of family environment offers a better and more holistic perspective on the reality of child abuse and its consequences.

This is the next step in the Maltese scenario. Malta has long been grounded on cohesive families, supported by strong traditional and religious past. However, the effects of globalization are fast gaining pace, with not so positive consequences on such a vital cell within society. Moreover, lack of awareness of the scope of child abuse may further the weakening of the family structure, creating with it a conspiracy of silence that prevents timely action and prevention (Zammit, 2001). Hopefully, studies such as these may encourage more social alertness, backed up by an appropriate legal framework to help protect victims while preventing perpetrators from pursuing their evil pursuits. It is therefore hoped that this review encourages a drive towards a deeper and more rigorous look into the aftermath of childhood trauma in a culture, which has long been overshadowed by complacency and silence. Specifically, stronger and clearer legislation, mandatory reporting laws, and availability of professional assistance and education are areas that require serious consideration. The present review can assist in educating people as to the extent, nature, and impact of child abuse in Malta. Besides protecting children, related research will continue to shed more light on the reasons and profiles of perpetrators, who should not be ignored in order to evaluate a more objective appraisal of the reality of child abuse. Focusing the research among university students may have been the easiest to reach and study as a start. However, this review opens up an immediate requirement to further it among the general population for more appraisal of this painful reality. Child abuse is a social evil, with dire effects that shroud one's personality and emotional development. Such future research furthermore requests the inclusion of key variables such as family environment and subjective-well being, in light of their close affinity to the trauma in focus.

REFERENCES

Ainsworth, M.D.S. (1979). Infant-mother attachment.*American Psychologist*, 34, 932-937.
Andrews, B., Brewin, C. R., Rose, S., and Kirk, M. (2000). Predicting PTSD symptoms in victims of violent crime: The role of shame, anger and childhood abuse.*Journal of Abnormality Psychology, 109*(1), 69-73.

Asher, S.J. (1988). The effects of childhood sexual abuse: A review of the issues and evidence. In Handbook on sexual abuse of children. Walker L. E.A. (Ed.) NY: *Springer Publishing,* Co. 203-215.

Baron, R.M., and Kenny, D.A. (1986).The Moderator-Mediator Variable Distinction in Social Psychological Research Conceptual, Strategic, and Statistical Considerations.*Journal of Personality and Social Psychology*, 51/6, 1173-1182.

Baumrind, D. (1971). Current patterns of parental authority.*Developmental Psychology Monographs*, *4*(1), 2.

Bernstein, D. P., and Fink, L. (1998).Childhood Trauma Questionnaire*: A* retrospective self-report manual. San Antonio: Harcourt Brace and Co.

Bowlby, J. (1969). Attachment and loss: Attachment. NY: Basic Books.

Bowlby, J. (1989). Secure and insecure attachment. NY: Basic Books.

Bramblett, J.R. (1998). A qualitative study of family dynamics and coping resources among adult male survivors of childhood sexual abuse.*Dissertation abstracts International Section A*: *Humanities and Social Sciences*, *59*, 5A, 1787.

Ciarrocchi, J.W. and Deneke, E. (2004). Happiness and the varieties of religious experience: Religious support, practices, and spirituality as predictors of well-being. *Research in the Social Scientific Study of Religion*, *15*, 204-233.

Childhelp USA. 2001. Retrieved August 8, 2001, from http://www. childhelpusa.org /child/abuse.htm.

Childhelp USA, 2011. Retrieved December 20, 2011, from http://www.childhelp. org/index. php/content/search-results/.

Costa, P. T. Jr., and McCrae, R. R. (1980). Inuence of extraversión and neuroticis monsubjectivewell-being: Happy and unhappypeople. *Journal of Personality and Social Psychology*, 38(4), 668-678.

Costa, P. T. Jr., and McCrae, R. R. (1992). The five-factor model of personality and its relevance to personality disorders.*Journal of Personality Disorders*, *6*(4), 343-359.

Darling, N. and Steinberg, L. (1993).Parenting style as context: An integrative model.*Psychological Bulletin*, *113*(3), 487-496.

DeNeve, K. M., and Cooper, H. (1998). The happy personality: A meta-analysis of 137 personality traits and subjective well-being. *Psychological Bulletin, 124*, 197-229.

Dickie, J.R., Esleman, A.K., Merasco, D.M., Shepard, A., Vander W.M., and Johnson, W. (1997).Parent-child relation-ships and children's images of God.*Journal for the Scientific Study of Religion*, *36*(1), 25- 43.

Eaton, L.G. and Funder, D.C. (2003). The creation and consequences of the social world: An interactional analysis of extraversion. *European Journal of Personality*, 17(5), 375-395.

Eysenck, H.J. (1967). The biological basis of personality. Springfield: Thomas.

Finkelhor, D. (1984). Childsexual abuse: New theory and research. NY: Free Press.

Finkelhor, D., and Browne, A. (1985). The traumatic impact of child sexual abuse: A conceptualization. *American Journal of Orthopsychiatry, 55*, 530-541.

Finkelhor, D. (1998). Improving research, policy, and practice to understand child sexual abuse [Electronic Version].*Journal of the American Medical Association, 280*(21).

Galea, M., Ciarrocchi, J.W., Piedmont, R.L., and Wicks, R.J. (2007).Child abuse, personality, and spirituality as predictors of happiness in Maltese college students.*Research in the SocialScientific Study of Religion*, *18*, 141-154.

Galea, M. (2008).The impact of child abuse on the psycho-spiritual and religious status of Maltese college students.*Pastoral Psychology*, *57*(3-4), 147-159.

Galea, M. (2009).Personality, child abuse, and family environment as predictors of happiness and well-being among Maltese university students.*Advances in Psychology Research*, *65*(15), 1-10.

Galea, M. (2010). Does child maltreatment mediate family environment and psychological well-being? *Psychology,10*(1), 144-151.

Galea, M. (2012).Studying the Incremental Validity of Family Environment among Maltese university students with past Mental Trauma.*Pastoral Psychology,*61/1, 211-220.

Grubman-Black, S. D. (1990). Broken boys/mending men: Recovery fromchildhood sexual abuse. Pa. Tab Books.

Harlow, H.F., and Zimmerman, R.R. (1959).Affectional responses in Infant Monkey.*Science,130* (3373), 421-432.

Kamsner, S., and McCabe, M.P. (2000).The relationship between adult psychological adjustment and childhood sexual abuse, childhood physical abuse, and family-of-origin characteristics.*Journal of Interpersonal Violence,* 15*(12),* 1243-121.

Kane, D., Cheston, S.E., and Greer, J. (1993). Perceptions of God by survivors of childhood sexual abuse: An exploratory study in an under researched area. *Journal of Psychology and Theology, 21*(3),228-237.

Kirkpatrick, L.A., and Shaver, P.R. (1992).An attachment-theoretical approach to romantic love and religious belief.*Personality and Social Psychology Bulletin*, 18(3) 266-275.

Kirkpatrick, L.A., and Shaver, P.R. (1990). Attachment theory and religion: Childhood attachments, religious beliefs and conversion. *Journal for the Scientific Study*, *29*(3), 315-323.

Lawson, R., Drebing, C., Berg, G., Vincellette, A., and Penk, W. (1998).The long term impact of child abuse on religious behavior and spirituality in men.*Child Abuse and Neglect, 22*(5),369-380.

Lieberman, M.D., and Rosenthal, R. (2001). Why introverts can't always tell who likes them: multitasking and nonverbal decoding. *Journal of Personality and Social Psychology*, 90, 3, 157-169.

Lucas, R.E. and Diener, E. (2008). What can we learn about national differences in happiness from individual responses? A multilevel approach. In F.J.R. van de Vijver, D.A. van Hemert, and Y.H. Poortinga (Eds.). Psychological Data at Individual and Country Level: Issues ofAggregation and Disaggregation, (223-248). New York: Lawrence Erlbaum Associates.

Margolin, L. (1994). Child sexual abuse by uncles.*Child Abuse and Neglect, 18*, 215-224.

Meyerson, L.A., Long, P.J., Miranda, R., Marx, B.P. (2002). The influence of childhood sexual abuse, physical abuse, family environment, and gender on the psychological adjustment of adolescents.*Child Abuse and Neglect*, *26*(4), 387-406.

Morales, J.V. (1996).The relative contribution of family environment, social support, patriarchal values and coping in sexual abuse recovery.*Dissertation Abstract International B: Sciences and Engineering*, 57, 1-B, 0704.

Olson, K.R., and Weber, D.A. (2004).Relations between big five traits and fundamental motives.*Psychological Reports*, 95(3), 795-802.

Scar, S. (1996). Best of human genetics.*Contemporary Psychology*, *41*, 149-150.

Silvern, L., Waelde, L.C., Baughan, B.M., Karyl, J., and Kaersvang, L.L. (2000). Two formats for eliciting retrospective reports of child sexual and physical abuse: Effects on apparent prevalence and relationships to adjustment, *Child Maltreatment, 5*(3), 236-251.

Stambor, Z. (2006). Extraversion, agreeableness, linked to happiness in Urangutans. *Monitor on Psychology*, 37/4, 10.

UN Convention on the Rights of the Child. (2000).Resolution: 44/25;Articles: 19, and 37. Retrieved August 10, 2001, from http://www.unhchr.ch/html /menu3/b/k2crc.htm

Uziel, L. (2006). The extraverted and neurotic glasses are of different colors. *Personality and Individual Differences,* 41(4), 745-754.

Widiger, T.A. and Samuel, D.B. (2005).Diagnostic categories or dimensions? A question for the Diagnostic and Statistical Manual of Mental Disorders – Fifth Edition, *Journal of Abnormal Psychology,* 114, 494-504.

Whealin, J.M., Davies, S., Shaffer, J., Love, L. (2002). Family context and childhood adjustment associated with intra-familial unwanted sexual attentions. *Journal of Family Violence*, *17*(2), 151-165.

Zammit, C. (1998). Children at risk: Paper presented for discussion at theseminar on child care. Department of Family Welfare, Malta. Retrieved October 11, 2001, from http://www.geocities.com/Athens/ 4185/CarmZammit.

In: Child Abuse
Editors: Raymond A. Turner and Henry O. Rogers

ISBN: 978-1-62257-113-0
© 2012 Nova Science Publishers, Inc.

Chapter 6

THE ROLE OF CHILD SEXUAL ABUSE IN THE DEVELOPMENT OF PSYCHOPATHOLOGY

Roberto Maniglio[*]

Department of Pedagogic, Psychological and Didactic Sciences,
University of Salento, Lecce, Italy

ABSTRACT

Child sexual abuse is a primary focus of research investigating the development of psychopathology. Indeed, a growing number of studies and literature reviews investigating the potential link between child sexual abuse and a large variety of psychological problems have been published over the past twenty years. The largest number of these studies and literature reviews have suggested that child sexual abuse is related to a variety of mental disorders. However, there are fundamental questions regarding the nature of the relationship between early sexual abuse and subsequent psychological problems that remain unanswered. To prevent interpretative difficulties, mistaken beliefs, or confusion among all professionals who turn to this literature for guidance, this chapter aims to clarify the nature of the associations between child sexual abuse and the most commonly reported forms of psychological problems by estimating the significance and strength of such associations as well as the potential effects of third variables, such as moderators, mediators, or confounders. In addition, this chapters addresses the results of a number of reviews that have investigated the etiology and risk factors of those psychiatric disorders that are most commonly reported as potential outcomes in survivors of child sexual abuse. Evidence to date suggests that child sexual abuse is a significant risk factor for a variety of psychiatric disorders, but not the only important one. There is emerging evidence that child sexual abuse might promote other biological or psychological conditions, such as alterations in brain structure or function, information processing biases, and painful internal states, which, in turn, might predispose to the onset of psychopathology. Further evidence suggests that in some cases, certain biological and psychosocial factors, especially genes and the adverse

[*] Corresponding author:Roberto Maniglio,Department of Pedagogic, Psychological, and Didactic Sciences, University of Salento, Via Stampacchia 45/47, 73100 Lecce, Italy. Tel.: +39 0832 294723. E-mail address: robertomaniglio@virgilio.it.

environmental factors that might accompany child sexual abuse, such as other forms of child maltreatment and dysfunctional family relationships and climate, may contribute to the onset of psychopathology in people with a history of child sexual abuse.

AUTHOR CONTRIBUTIONS

Dr Maniglio had full access to all of the data in the study and takes responsibility for the integrity of the data and the accuracy of the data analysis. Financial disclosures: None reported. Funding/Support: None reported. Role of the sponsors: None reported. Disclaimer: The views expressed are those of the author. This study has no external funding source and was not financial supported. The author reports no financial interests, affiliations, conflicts of interest, or other relationship relevant to the subject matter of this paper.

INTRODUCTION

Child sexual abuse is a major topic in the scientific literature. A search of seven internet-based databases (AMED, Cochrane Reviews, EBSCO, ERIC, MEDLINE, PsycINFO, and ScienceDirect) for the keywords "child(hood) sexual abuse" and "child(hood) sexual maltreatment" has identified about 20,000 articles, published between January 1966 and December 2008 (Maniglio, 2009).

Child sexual abuse is a primary focus of research investigating the development of psychopathology. In fact, child sexual abuse is among the environmental factors potentially involved in the etiology of many psychiatric disorders and deviant behaviors that have received much attention from researchers and practitioners on the field. Indeed, a growing number of studies investigating the potential link between child sexual abuse and a large variety of psychological problems have been published over the past twenty years. Efforts to summarize the findings of such large amount of studies have resulted in several qualitative and quantitative reviews.

The largest number of these studies and literature reviews have suggested that child sexual abuse is related to a variety of mental disorders. However, such large body of research has not been unanimous in its conclusions. Indeed, there is a considerable lack of clarity about the relationship between child sexual abuse and later negative outcomes. In fact, there are fundamental questions regarding the nature of the relationship between early sexual abuse and subsequent psychological problems that remain unanswered. More specifically, while many studies and reviews have concluded that survivors of childhood sexual abuse are highly likely to experience several adverse effects, strongly implying a causal relationship between child sexual abuse and the later development of psychopathology, others have been more cautious, arguing that outcomes are variable, rather than being consistently and intensely negative (see Maniglio, 2009).

Therefore, although studies and reviews on the effects of child sexual abuse abound, the inconsistency in the conclusions of such large amount of research may create interpretative difficulties, mistaken beliefs, or confusion among all individuals who turn to this literature for guidance, including policymakers, physicians, psychologists, other professionals who treat children, and other individuals responsible for the welfare of children.

In response to these difficulties and with the current high level of societal interest in child sexual abuse, it seems evident that, despite a large amount of literature addressing the potential effects of child sexual abuse, the issue needs further careful consideration. More specifically, an analysis of what is currently known about the role of child sexual abuse in the etiology of psychopathology is required in order to implement research and health policy. In addition, the nature of the relationship between child sexual abuse and psychopathology needs to be clarified.

In order to address the best available scientific evidence on the topic, this chapter analyzes the findings of the several reviews that have addressed the literature on the short- and long-term effects of child sexual abuse. More precisely, the aim of the present chapter is to clarify the nature of the associations between child sexual abuse and the most commonly reported forms of psychological problems by estimating the significance and strength of such associations as well as the potential effects of third variables, such as moderators, mediators, or confounders. In addition, this chapter addresses the results of a number of reviews that have investigated the etiology and risk factors of those psychiatric disorders that are most commonly reported as potential outcomes in survivors of child sexual abuse. In doing so, this chapter expands on the findings of a series of systematic reviews of reviews on the role of child sexual abuse in the etiology of a variety of psychiatric disorders (Maniglio, 2009; 2010; in press; submitted, a; submitted, b).

THE RELATIONSHIP BETWEEN CHILD SEXUAL ABUSE AND PSYCHOPATHOLOGY

Empirical Evidence

As described above, a large amount of empirical research addressing the potential relationship between child sexual abuse and later psychological problems has been published. Efforts to summarize the findings of these studies have resulted in several qualitative and quantitative reviews.

The vast majority of these studies and literature reviews have found evidence for a relationship between child sexual abuse and psychopathology. For instance, many quantitative reviews have stated that survivors of child sexual abuse show higher levels of psychological problems — or, alternatively, that people with psychological problems show higher rates of child sexual abuse. In these reviews, child sexual abuse has been associated with a wide range of psychiatric disorders, such as psychotic symptoms or disorders, depression, anxiety symptoms or disorders, eating disorders, dissociation, somatization, personality disorders, self-esteem and self-concept impairment, suicide, non-suicidal self-injury, substance abuse, sexual dysfunction, and intelligence or learning impairment. However, the following are the most commonly reported outcomes:

- depressive symptoms or disorders (e.g., Alloy, Abramson, Smith, Gibb, & Neeren, 2006; Bagley, 1991; Beitchman, Zucker, Hood, daCosta, & Akman, 1991; Beitchman et al., 1992; Black & DeBlassie, 1993; Briere & Elliot, 1994; Browne &Finkelhor, 1986; Holmes & Slap, 1998; Kendall-Tackett, Williams, & Finkelhor,

1993; Kuyken, 1995; Leeners, Richter-Appelt, Imthurn, & Rath, 2006; Nielsen, 1983; Nurcombe, 2000; Polusny & Follette, 1995; Putnam, 2003; Weiss, Longhurst, & Mazure, 1999);

- anxiety symptoms or disorders (e.g., Black & DeBlassie, 1993; Beitchman et al., 1992; Bohn & Holz, 1996; Briere & Elliot, 1994; Browne & Finkelhor, 1986; Fine, 1990; Green, 1988; Kaysen, Resick, & Wise, 2003; Kendall-Tackett et al., 1993; Kuyken, 1995; Nurcombe, 2000; Polusny & Follette, 1995; Terr, 1991; Valente, 2005), especially posttraumatic stress disorder (e.g., Briere & Elliot, 1994; Bohn & Holz, 1996; Briere & Runtz, 1993; Holmes & Slap, 1998; Murray, 1993; Rowan & Foy, 1993);
- suicide and non-suicidal self-injury (Bagley, 1991; Beitchman et al., 1991; 1992; Briere & Elliot, 1994; Briere &Runtz, 1991; 1993; Brodsky & Stanley, 2008; Browne & Finkelhor, 1986; Evans, Hawton, & Rodham, 2004; 2005; Gould, Greenberg, Velting, & Shaffer, 2003; Holmes & Slap, 1998; Kendall-Tackett et al., 1993; Mulvihill, 2005; Nurcombe, 2000; Polusny & Follette, 1995; Putnam, 2003; Santa Mina & Gallop, 1998; Spirito & Esposito-Smythers, 2006; Valente, 2005; Wagner, 1997; Yang &Clum, 1996; Yates, 2004);
- alcohol or drugs use or abuse (Arellano, 1996; Arnow, 2004; Black & DeBlassie, 1993; Bollerud, 1990; Briere & Elliot, 1994; Browne & Finkelhor, 1986; Cicchetti & Toth, 2005; Downs & Harrison, 1998; Hecht & Hansen, 1999; Hans, 1999; Holmes & Slap, 1998; Hurley, 1991; Johnson, 2004; Kendall-Tackett et al., 1993; Langeland & Hartgers, 1998; Liebschutz et al., 2002; Margolin & Gordis, 2000; Miller & Downs, 1995; Moncrieff&Farmer,1998; Mulvihill, 2005; Murray, 1993; Nielsen, 1983; Nurcombe, 2000; Pilkington & Kremer, 1995; Polusny & Follette, 1995; Prosser & Corso, 2007; Putnam, 2003; Sartor, Agrawal, McCutcheon, Duncan, & Lynskey, 2008; Simpson & Miller, 2002; Springer, Sheridan, Kuo, & Carnes, 2003; Trickett & Putnam, 1993; Valente, 2005).

Depressive symptoms and disorders have been considered the most common (Browne & Finkelhor, 1986; Nielsen, 1983) and the best documented (Putnam, 2003) outcomes in survivors of child sexual abuse.

Anxiety symptoms and disorders, including panic, fear, phobias, and especially posttraumatic stress disorder, have been suggested to be some of the most common responses to child sexual abuse (Bohn & Holz, 1996; Browne & Finkelhor, 1986; Valente, 2005), perhaps second only to depression as the most common sequelae of incest (Fine, 1990). Among the various forms of anxiety disorders, posttraumatic stress disorder has been considered the most prevalent psychological problem in child sexual abuse survivors (Briere & Elliot, 1994). Posttraumatic stress disorder has been indicated as the diagnosis which best fits the syndrome commonly seen in victims of early sexual victimization (see Rowan & Foy, 1993). It has also been suggested that sexual abuse constitutes an acute traumatic event for the child, generating immediate phobic responses and anxiety-related symptoms, including posttraumatic stress symptoms, as well as long-term, chronic sequelae, especially posttraumatic stress disorder (Bohn & Holz, 1996; Briere & Elliot, 1994; Briere & Runtz, 1993; Murray, 1993).

In regard to suicidal and non-suicidal forms of self-injury, these have been often considered together as another common outcome in survivors of child abuse (Yates, 2004; Santa Mina & Gallop, 1998). For instance, both suicidal behavior and non-suicidal self-injurious behavior have been seen as deliberate self-damaging acts in which abuse victims engage in order to reduce abuse-related distress (see, e.g., Briere, 1992a).

However, it should be noted that many of these literature reviews are characterized by imprecision and subjectivity, given that most of them are not systematic reviews of the literature and many of their assumptions on the effects of child sexual abuse are mainly based on study findings indicating harmful effects.

Strength of the Association

A more objective process has been provided by some meta-analytic reviews, which have attempted to infer whether child sexual abuse is significantly associated with specific outcomes and to estimate the strength of this association. Based on the transformation of the results of all the relevant studies to a common statistical metric, which are then combined into one overall statistic, these reviews have used a more rigorous and transparent approach to reduce the potential for bias, avoiding imprecision and subjectivity. These meta-analytic reviews have detailed the data sources used to identify studies, the criteria used to select studies for inclusion in the review, and the methods used to obtain these results. Furthermore, they have described the main results in an objective fashion, considering the strength of evidence, exploring whether any observed effects were consistent across studies, and investigating possible reasons for any inconsistencies.

Taken as a whole, these meta-analytic reviews found a statistically significant, although modest, relationship between child sexual abuse and psychopathology (see Maniglio, 2009). In these reviews, child sexual abuse has been associated with a wide range of psychological problems, such as depression, anxiety, eating disorders, dissociation, somatization, paranoid ideation, personality disorders, self-esteem and self-concept impairment, suicide, non-suicidal self-injury, substance abuse, sexual dysfunction, hostility, anger, and intelligence or learning impairment (Maniglio, 2009). However, depression, anxiety symptoms and disorders, suicide, and non-suicidal self-injury are the most commonly reported outcomes (Maniglio, 2009; 2010; in press; submitted, a; submitted, b). More specifically, an association between child sexual abuse and depression was found by four meta-analyses (Jumper, 1995; Neumann, Houskamp, Pollock, & Briere, 1996; Paolucci, Genuis, & Violato, 2001; Rind, Tromovitch, & Bauserman, 1998), including about 60,000 subjects from 160 studies, with magnitudes ranging from small to medium (for a review and a critical discussion, see Maniglio, 2010). Seven meta-analyses undertaken by three reviews (Neumann et al., 1996; Paolucci et al., 2001; Rind et al., 1998), including 52,164 subjects from 134 studies, revealed a significant relationship between child sexual abuse and anxiety problems, such as generic anxiety symptoms and obsessive-compulsive, phobic, and posttraumatic stress symptomatology, with magnitudes ranging from small to medium (for a review and a critical discussion, see Maniglio, sumitted, a). An association between child sexual abuse and suicidal or nonsuicidal self-injurious behaviors was found by five meta-analyses undertaken by four reviews (Klonsky & Moyer, 2008; Neumann et al., 1996; Paolucci et al., 2001; Rind et al., 1998), including about 60,000 subjects from 160 studies, with magnitudes ranging from small to medium (for a review and a critical discussion, see Maniglio, in press). A modest relationship between child sexual abuse and drug and alcohol problems was found by two meta-analyses (Neumann et al., 1996; Rind et al., 1998), including 26,797 subjects from 97 studies (for a review and a critical discussion, see Maniglio, submitted, b). Child sexual abuse was also found to be significantly related to eating disorders (Rind et al., 1998; Smolak & Murnen, 2002), dissociation (Neumann et al., 1996; Rind et al., 1998), somatization (Neumann et al., 1996; Rind et al., 1998), borderline personality disorder (Fossati, Madeddu, & Maffei, 1999), and psychotic symptoms (Rind et al., 1998), with magnitudes ranging from small to medium (see Maniglio, 2009).

In conclusion, there is evidence that across methodologies, samples, and measures child sexual abuse is associated with a wide range of psychological problems, especially depression, anxious, obsessive-compulsive, phobic, and posttraumatic stress symptommatology, suicidal and non-suicidal self-injurious behaviors, and substance abuse. Therefore, it is apparent that child sexual abuse may be considered as a general, nonspecific risk factor for psychopathology. In regards to its strength, child sexual abuse appears to be a modest, although statistically significant, risk factor.

Moderators

Theoretical models of how child sexual abuse affects children's development have proposed certain factors that might moderate the relationship between child sexual abuse and psychopathology (for reviews see Freeman & Morris, 2001; Hulme, 2004).

It has been hypothesized that severity of child sexual abuse influences a person's reaction to such traumatic event and often leads to the development of posttraumatic stress disorders (Wolfe et al., 1989). According to theoretical models based on the posttraumatic stress disorder, moderating or mediating variables that can contribute to the development of chronic posttraumatic stress symptomatology include degree of physical injury (e.g., vaginal or anal intercourse), pain, or danger resulting from child sexual abuse (see Browne & Finkelhor, 1986; Spaccarelli, 1994; Rodriguez, Vande Kemp, & Foy, 1998).

Although efforts to conceptualize those factors that have the potential to moderate the relationship between child sexual abuse and psychopathology, empirical research has not led to unanimous conclusions, given that different studies and reviews have highlighted different moderators and mediators.

Much empirical research (see, e.g., Beitchman et al., 1992; Briere & Elliot, 1994; Browne & Finkelhor, 1986; Kendall-Tackett et al., 1993; Leserman, 2005; Polusny & Follette, 1995) has revealed that more severe and traumatic forms of sexual victimization, such as those involving force, violence, penetration, and multiple perpetrators, appear to be the most harmful. For example, many reviews (see, e.g., Beitchman et al., 1991; 1992; Santa Mina & Gallop, 1998) have suggested higher risk of suicide and non-suicidal self-injury for more severe and traumatic forms of sexual victimization, such as those involving force, violence, penetration, longer duration, and high frequency of sexual contact. In the same way, a number of studies (e.g., Briere, 1988b; Fergusson, Horwood, & Lynskey, 1996; Miller, Downs, & Testa, 1993; Mullen, Martin, Anderson, Romans, & Herbison, 1993) have suggested that the association between severe substance problems and child sexual abuse seems to be greater for longer periods or more severe and traumatic forms of sexual victimization, such as those involving violence, penetration, or multiple perpetrators. Furthermore, a number of narrative reviews have suggested that increased anxiety symptoms and disorders are associated with genital contact (Browne & Finkelhor, 1986), penetration (Beitchman et al., 1992; Kendall-Tackett et al., 1993; Polusny & Follette, 1995), use of force (Beitchman et al., 1992; Briere & Elliot, 1994; Browne & Finkelhor, 1986; Kendall-Tackett et al., 1993), abuse involving a parent (Beitchman et al., 1992; Briere & Elliot, 1994; Browne & Finkelhor, 1986; Kendall-Tackett et al., 1993), longer duration (Beitchman et al., 1992; Kendall-Tackett et al., 1993), or high frequency of sexual contact (Briere & Elliot, 1994; Kendall-Tackett et al., 1993). Moreover, while some narrative reviews have revealed that increased rates of depression are related to both the frequency and duration of sexual abuse experiences (Polusny & Follette, 1995), others have suggested that higher levels of depression are associated with contact sexual abuse (Kuyken, 1995; Putnam, 2003; Weiss et al., 1999) or abuse by a primary caregiver (Kuyken, 1995; Polusny & Follette, 1995; Putnam, 2003).

Nevertheless, the results of moderator analysis conducted by a number of meta-analytic reviews do not confirm suspicions that some variables concerning aspects of the abuse experience, such as age when abused, incestuous forms of abuse, contact, use of force, frequency, duration of abuse, and number of perpetrators, increase the likelihood of psychological problems in survivors of child sexual abuse, given that these moderators generated conflicting or nonsignificant results (Maniglio, 2009; 2010; in press; submitted, a; submitted, b).

The relationship between gender of the victim and outcomes is even more equivocal. Indeed, some narrative reviews have concluded that girls and women react more negatively than boys and men, whereas others have implied that sexual abuse is an equivalent experience for males and females in terms of its negative effects.

For example, most narrative reviews that focused on female samples have found great evidence of psychological problems, such as depression (Beitchman et al., 1992; Leeners et al., 2006; Bachmann, Moeller, & Benett, 1988; McGrath, Keita, Strickland, & Russo, 1990), anxiety symptoms or disorders (Bachmann et al., 1988; Beitchman et al., 1992), and substance abuse (e.g., Browne & Finkelhor, 1986; Hans, 1999; Kendall-Tackett et al., 1993; Miller & Downs, 1995) in women who have been victims of early sexual victimization, suggesting that female survivors of child sexual abuse are more likely to develop symptoms or disorders than male victims of early sexual victimization (e.g., Putnam, 2003; Weiss et al., 1999). Conversely, a number of narrative reviews that focused on male samples (Black & DeBlassie, 1993; Holmes & Slap, 1998; Nielsen, 1983; Valente, 2005) have shown high levels of psychopathology also in male subjects with a history of child sexual abuse, with some individual studies (e.g., Garnefski & Diekstra, 1997; Gold, Lucenko, Elhai, Swingle, & Sellers, 1999) revealing that sexually abused boys have worse outcomes.

Narrative reviews including both male and female samples have provided conflicting results. For instance, although some reviews (e.g., Moncrieff&Farmer,1998) have revealed a higher likelihood of alcohol problems among females who have been sexually abused as children, stating that there is less evidence from which to draw conclusions in men, a review (Downs & Harrison, 1998) has shown an association between child sexual abuse and later alcohol and drug problems for both males and females and another review (Black & DeBlassie, 1993) has concluded that the experience of being sexually abused as a child may be an important etiologic factor in the development of substance problems among women but not men.

However, gender has been found to be not significantly related to outcomes in a number of meta-analytic reviews (Maniglio, 2009; 2010; in press; submitted, a; submitted, b). Furthermore, a recent meta-analysis of studies yielding sex-specific risk of potentially traumatic events and posttraumatic stress disorder (Tolin & Foa, 2006) has shown no significant difference in prevalence and severity of posttraumatic stress disorder between male and female victims of child sexual abuse. Thus, the greater risk of psychopathology among female subjects seems to be not true for victims of child sexual abuse, although, in general, females appear to be more likely than males to experience both adult sexual assault and child sexual abuse (see Tolin & Foa, 2006).

Importantly, these meta-analyses have revealed that the source of the samples is a significant moderator of the relationship between child sexual abuse and psychopathology (Maniglio, 2009; 2010; in press; submitted, a; submitted, b). More precisely, samples drawn from nonclinical populations, especially samples drawn from college population, yielded smaller effect size estimates than did clinical samples, although in both groups outcomes were significant. In other words, psychiatric patients with a history of early sexual abuse showed greater evidence of psychological problems than did survivors of child abuse among community, student, or other populations. This result suggests that psychiatric samples tend to exclude well adjusted survivors of child abuse because these samples are likely to constitute the negative extreme of abuse outcomes (Neumann et al., 1996; Okami, 1991). Conversely, nonclinical samples tend to include more well adjusted abuse survivors, because a certain level of wellness is required to perform daily activities, such as occupational tasks, school obligations, family responsibilities, or household activities (Jumper, 1995; Roodman & Clum, 2001). Furthermore, in regards to college samples, it has been suggested that some negative long-term sequelae of child abuse may have not yet manifested at college age (Rind et al., 1998).

In conclusion, there is evidence that the association between child sexual abuse and psychopathology is moderated by the type of population from which the sample is drawn, with abuse survivors seeking or receiving psychiatric treatment experiencing more psychological problems. Therefore, it is apparent that survivors of child sexual abuse among nonclinical populations may experience fewer psychological problems than do survivors of child sexual abuse among clinical populations. It is noteworthy that, in the meta-analytic reviews, variables concerning aspects of the abuse experience, such as age when abused, relationship to the perpetrator, and type and severity of abuse (i.e., contact, use of force, frequency, and duration of abuse), did not moderate the association between child sexual abuse and psychopathology. Therefore, evidence today does not confirm many clinical impressions and theoretical explanations of the impact of child abuse suggesting worse outcomes for victim of more traumatic forms of abuse, such as those involving violence, penetration, multiple perpetrators, incestuous forms of abuse, higher frequency and longer duration of abuse, and younger age when abused.

Mediators

There is little research on those variables that may mediate, rather than moderate, the relationship between child sexual abuse and psychopathology. Nevertheless, it is possible that the effects of child sexual abuse on later psychological adjustment may operate through the mediating influences of other variables. In other words, it is possible that an early traumatic experience, such as child sexual abuse, may lead in later life to the development of other psychological (such as dysfunctional personality traits) or biological (such as neurobiological alterations) conditions which, in turn, might promote psychological problems. In these cases, child sexual abuse would not have a direct pathway to psychological adjustment but instead would have a direct relationship with another condition, which in turn would have a direct pathway to psychopathology.

There is emerging evidence that a number of neurobiological and psychosocial factors, such as dysregulation of the hypothalamic-pituitary-adrenocortical axis, alterations in brain development, and certain cognitive or personality characteristics of the victim (e.g., dysfunctional beliefs, impulsivity, or antisocial personality) that might follow the abuse experience might mediate the relationship between child sexual abuse and psychopathology. More specifically, it is possible that child sexual abuse may influence psychological adjustment by negatively affecting neurobiological or personality development.

A first important mechanism by which child sexual abuse may contribute to psychopathology might be through neurobiological system. For example, both animal and human studies have shown that early stress and adversity may result in both acute and chronic changes in the activity and regulation of the hypothalamic-pituitary-adrenocortical axis, similar to those believed to be important in the pathophysiology of depression (see Thase, 2006; Weiss et al., 1999). The pathophysiological similarities observed in both the stress response and depressive illness lend support to the hypothesis that an adverse event during childhood may contribute to adult-onset of depression by means of chronic dysregulation of the hypothalamic-pituitary-adrenocortical axis. Furthermore, both preclinical and clinical studies suggest that childhood trauma and early stressful events, such as child sexual abuse, may produce a cascade of neurobiological events that have the potential to cause persistent sensitization of central nervous system circuits, including long-lived hyper(re)activity of corticotropin-releasing factor systems and alterations in other neurotransmitter systems (Heim & Nemeroff, 2001), as well as enduring changes in brain structure or function, including reduced size of the mid-portions of the corpus callosum, attenuated development of the left neocortex, hippocampus, and amygdala, abnormal frontotemporal electrical activity, and reduced functional activity of the cerebellar vermis (Teicher, Andersen, Polcari, Anderson, & Navalta, 2002; Teicher, Andersen, Polcari, Anderson, Navalta, & Kim, 2003). These neurobiological sequelae, in turn, provide the neurobiological framework through which early abuse might increase the risk of developing a number of psychiatric disorders, such as anxiety disorders and substance-related disorders. It has been also hypothesized that sexual abuse in childhood may set serotonergic function at a lower level (Mann, 2003). This effect might persist into adolescence or adulthood, contributing to the increased risk for suicidal and non-suicidal self-injurious behaviors.

Another mechanism by which child sexual abuse may contribute to psychiatric symptoms or disorders might be through certain personality and cognitive variables.

The role of personality traits in the etiology of some psychiatric disorders is well known. For example, several reviews have found an increased risk of substance-related disorders in people with certain personality characteristics, such as high levels of openness to experience (Gorman & Derzon, 2002) and sensation-seeking (i.e., the willingness to take physical, social, legal, and financial risks for the sake of varied, novel, complex, and intense sensations and experiences; Bardo et al., 2007; Hawkins, Catalano, & Miller, 1992; Hittner & Swickert,

2005; Kuntsche, Knibbe, Gmel, & Engels, 2006), disinhibition (Iacono, Malone, & McGue, 2008; Ivanov, Schulz, London, & Newcorn, 2008; Sher & Trull, 1994), impulsivity (Bornovalova, Lejuez, Daughters, Zachary Rosenthal, & Lynch, 2005; Hawkins et al., 1992; Sher, Grekin, & Williams, 2005; Verdejo-García, Lawrence, & Clark, 2008), extraversion (Kuntsche et al., 2006; Sher et al., 2005), neuroticism/negative emotionality (Hawkins et al., 1992; Gorman & Derzon, 2002; Malouff, Thorsteinsson, Rooke, & Schutte, 2007; Sher et al., 2005; Sher & Trull, 1994). Similarly, other reviews have shown that aggression (Conner, Duberstein, Conwell, & Caine, 2003; Gould et al., 2003; Joiner, Brown, & Wingate, 2005; Mann, Waternaux, Haas, & Malone, 1999; Spirito & Esposito-Smythers, 2006) and impulsivity (Gould et al., 2003; Mann et al., 1999; Spirito & Esposito-Smythers, 2006), as well as other personality variables, especially hopelessness (Brezo, Paris, & Turecki, 2006; Evans et al., 2004; Glanz, Haas, & Sweeney, 1995; Gould et al., 2003; Joiner et al., 2005; Spirito & Esposito-Smythers, 2006) and ineffective problem-solving ability (Gould et al., 2003; Spirito & Esposito-Smythers, 2006), are related to self-injurious and suicidal behavior.

Thus, it is possible that child sexual abuse might contribute to psychopathology through the development of certain personality variables. For instance, there is some evidence that the relationship between child sexual abuse and self-injurious and suicidal behavior might be mediated by some personality variables, such as impulsivity (Baud, 2005), aggression (Baud, 2005), poor problem-solving skills (Yang & Clum, 1996), and hopelessness (Yang & Clum, 1996). Furthermore, in a meta-analytic review addressing the relationship between child sexual abuse and non-suicidal self-injury (Klonsky & Moyer, 2008), those studies that controlled for hopelessness revealed that the relationship between child sexual abuse and self-injury became minimal or negligible.

In addition, certain cognitive factors have also an important role in the etiology of other psychiatric disorders. For example, according to the major cognitive theories of depression, individuals' characteristic ways of interpreting relevant experiences in their lives may increase individuals' likelihood of developing depressive symptoms or disorders, in particular, a cognitively mediated subtype of endogenous depression, when they encounter negative life events (see, for example, Abramson, Metalsky, & Alloy 1989; Clark, Beck, & Alford, 1999). Several reviews (e.g., Alloy, Abramson, Walshaw, & Neeren 2006; Clark et al., 1999; Ingram, Miranda, & Segal, 1998; Joiner & Wagner, 1995) have shown that a set of maladaptive cognitive patterns (e.g., negative inferential or attributional style, information processing biases, maladaptive self-schemas, and dysfunctional beliefs, attitudes, or self-worth contingencies) may increase vulnerability to depression. Several studies have suggested that information processing biases, i.e., the tendency to preferentially process threatening information, intervening in cognitive processes such as attention, memory, and interpretation are also involved in the development and maintenance of anxiety disorders (see Alfano, Beidel, & Turner, 2002; Bar-Haim, Lamy, Pergamin, Bakermans-Kranenburg, & van IJzendoorn, 2007; Cisler & Koster, 2010; Daleiden & Vasey, 1997; Ehrenreich & Gross, 2002; Hadwin, Garner, & Perez-Olivas, 2006; Musa & Lépine, 2000; Ouimet, Gawronski, & Dozois, 2009). More precisely, a large amount of studies shows that anxious subjects pay more attention to potentially threatening stimuli (Bar-Haim et al., 2007; Cisler & Koster, 2010; Musa & Lépine, 2000; Ouimet et al., 2009) and more frequently interpret ambiguous events or situations as threatening than do nonanxious controls (Musa & Lépine, 2000; Ouimet et al., 2009). Further reviews have found an increased risk of substance-related disorders in people with low resistance or refusal self-efficacy (i.e. little belief in the ability to refuse drugs: Hasking & Oei, 2008; Oei & Baldwin, 1994), and dysfunctional automatic cognitions, especially implicit associations for substance use and attentional bias for substance-related cues (Field, Schoenmakers, & Wiers, 2008; McCusker, 2001; Rooke, Hine, & Thorsteinsson, 2008; Zucker, Donovan, Masten, Mattson, & Moss, 2008), and positive outcome expectancies for substance use (i.e., the positive consequences an individual expects to gain from substance use; Beck, Wright, Newman, & Liese, 1993; Sher et al., 2005; Hasking & Oei, 2008; Oei & Baldwin, 1994; Field et al., 2008; Zucker et al., 2008; Jones, Corbin, & Fromme, 2001).

Consequently, it is possible that the relationship between child sexual abuse and psychopathology might be mediated by certain cognitive factors. For example, it has been shown that one mechanism by which child sexual abuse contributes to depressive symptoms or disorders is through the development of negative cognitive styles and information processing biases (Alloy, Abramson, Smith, Gibb, & Neeren, 2006). Similarly, child sexual abuse might contribute to psychopathology through the development of certain cognitive or personality characteristics, such as cognitive biases, that fit the view of the world as dangerous or threatening. In other words, it is possible that child sexual abuse might promote in children a hypervigilant information processing style for the detection of threat (see Hadwin et al., 2006). Although such an increased vigilance for threat reflects effective adaptation to avoid danger, it may, in turn, predispose to the development of anxiety disorders.

In the case of substance-related disorders or suicidal behaviors, it is also possible that the relationship between child sexual abuse and negative outcomes might be mediated by painful feelings, affects, or memories resulting from child sexual abuse.

A number of studies (e.g., Epstein, Saunders, Kilpatrick, & Resnick, 1998; Kilpatrick et al., 2000; Mezzich et al., 1997) have suggested that child sexual abuse might be related to pathological substance use via an indirect pathway through a number of psychiatric symptoms or disorders, especially posttraumatic stress symptomatology and antisocial personality. Since many substance-addicted individuals use drugs or alcohol as a coping strategy or self-medication mechanism to separate psychologically from the environment and avoid or alleviate painful internal states (Beck et al., 1993; Evans & Sullivan, 1995; Herman, 1992; Khantzian, 1997; Leonard & Blane, 1999; Stewart, 1996), it is possible that child abuse survivors experiencing psychological problems resulting from child sexual abuse, including psychiatric symptoms or disorders as well as negative internal states (such as painful feelings, affects, memories, and cognitions), and lacking adequate self-regulatory processes, particularly regulation of affect, emotion coping strategies, or social skills, might use certain drugs and/or alcohol as an attempt to deal with or anesthetize uncomfortable symptoms in order to achieve an illusory sense of self-regulation of their intense internal states or self-control in interpersonal functioning. For example, specific substances might be used by people with social anxiety, posttraumatic stress, or depressive symptoms resulting from child sexual abuse as an attempt to modulate affects, gain feelings of relaxation, enhance self-esteem or self-efficacy, increase energy or feelings of euphoria, decrease anhedonia or inhibitions, and avoid or alleviate negative feelings (such as feelings of powerlessness, helplessness, or personal inadequacy), intrusive symptoms (e.g., flashbacks, nightmares), or persistent memories associated with the victimization experience. Thus, the relationship between child sexual abuse and substance problems might be mediated by psychiatric symptoms or disorders that might result from the victimization experience and lead the abuse victim to use alcohol or drugs to deal with or self-medicate painful internal states or to cope with adverse environmental conditions or stressful life events. Nevertheless, since alcohol and other drugs merely cover, rather than cure, psychiatric disorders, as most substances are short-acting and only provide a temporary illusion of immediate, short-term relief of some symptoms such as anxiety or depression, the need for substance use in child abuse survivors may persist or even increase over time, enhancing the likelihood of developing substance misuse for prolonged periods of time. Therefore, in these cases, whether early abuse victims go on to develop subsequent substance-related disorders would be contingent on whether they develop psychiatric symptoms or disorders, including negative internal states (such as painful feelings, affects, memories, and cognitions), associated with childhood sexual victimization.

In other cases, psychological disturbance, in terms of dysfunctional personality traits or psychiatric disorders following child abuse, may lead child sexual abuse survivors to self-injury, rather than to use drugs or alcohol, in order to reduce painful abuse-related internal states. A literature review has shown that most non-suicidal self-injurers identify the desire to alleviate negative affect as a reason for self-injuring and present decreased negative affect and relief after self-injury (Klonsky, 2007). It has been hypothesized that suicidal and non-suicidal self-injurious behaviors may be seen as emotionally avoidant coping activities, i.e. behavioral strategies employed to temporarily avoid, reduce, anesthetize, interrupt, or alleviate unpleasant internal states, such as, thoughts, memories, feelings, or affects, associated with an abuse history, in order to provide survivors with a temporary sense of calm and relief, at least for some period of time (Baud, 2005; Briere, 1992a; Briere & Elliot, 1994; Briere & Runtz, 1993; Briere & Runtz, 1991; Connors, 1996; Klonsky, 2007; Polusny & Follette, 1995; Spirito & Esposito-Smythers, 2006; Stanley, Winchel, Molcho, Simeon, & Stanley, 1992; Suyemoto, 1998; Yates, 2004). In other words, it is possible that child sexual abuse might lead to psychic distress, in terms of dysfunctional personality traits, psychiatric disorders, or painful abuse-related internal states, which in turn might lead child abuse victims to employ emotionally avoidant coping behaviors, such as self-inflicted injuries, to achieve temporary relief, especially when these individuals also have concurrent problem-solving deficiencies or poor coping skills. Although often effective in the short term, emotionally avoidant coping strategies are rarely adaptive in the long term, leading to repeated cycles of self-inflicted injuries in the presence of future pain, subsequent calm, the slow building of further tension, and, ultimately, further self-harm (Briere & Elliot, 1994).

In conclusion, it is possible that certain neurobiological and psychosocial factors might mediate the association between prior sexual abuse and subsequent psychiatric symptoms or disorders. Emerging evidence suggests that child sexual abuse may influence psychological adjustment by negatively affecting neurobiological and/or personality development. In other words, child sexual abuse might promote other biological (such as alterations in brain structure or function) or psychological (such as information processing biases and painful internal states) conditions which, in turn, might predispose to the onset of psychopathology. In these cases, child sexual abuse would not have a direct pathway to psychopathology but instead would have a direct relationship with another condition, which in turn would have a direct pathway to psychological problems. Thus, in some cases, child sexual abuse might be a "distal" and indirect cause, rather than a "proximal" and direct cause, of psychopathology. However, much more research is needed to discover potential mediating factors of the relationship between child sexual abuse and psychopathology.

CAUSATION

To date, research has provided clear evidence that the relationship between child sexual abuse and psychopathology does exist. The majorityof studies and literature reviews have suggested that child sexual abuse is a risk factor for the development of psychopathology. Indeed, several narrative reviews have concluded that survivors of early sexual victimization are at increased risk for psychiatric symptoms or disorders evidenced immediately after the event and often continuing for years. In addition, a number of meta-analytic reviews have found a statistically significant, although modest, association between child sexual abuse and a variety of psychiatric disorders, especially depression, anxiety disorders, substance-related disorders, and suicidal and non-suicidal self-injurious behaviors.

Nevertheless, despite these efforts, conclusions about the nature of such association have not yet been definitively drawn. More specifically, it is unclear whether child sexual abuse does have a causal role in the etiology of psychological disturbance.

Most reviews have implied a causal association between child sexual abuse and psychological problems, with some researchers explicitly stating that such association persists even when controlling for other variables that may be independently related to the development of psychopathology. For instance, some reviews have concluded that survivors of early sexual victimization are at increased risk for depression (Bagley, 1991; Holmes & Slap, 1998; Leeners et al., 2006) and substance abuse (Holmes & Slap, 1998; Margolin & Gordis, 2000), with some reviews strongly implying a causal relationship between child sexual abuse and later development of psychological problems, such as depression (Weiss et al., 1999) and substance-related disorders (Briere & Elliot, 1994; Miller & Downs, 1995; Prosser & Corso, 2007), or explicitly stating that such relationships persist even when controlling for other important variables that may be independently related to the development of such psychiatric symptoms or disorders (Downs & Harrison, 1998; Simpson & Miller, 2002; Weiss et al., 1999).

In contrast, other reviews have been more cautious, arguing that outcomes are variable, rather than being consistently and intensely negative (see Paolucci et al., 2001; Rind & Tromovitch, 1997; Rind et al., 1998; Sharpe & Faye, 2006; Smolak & Murnen, 2002). Some of these reviews have suggested that child sexual abuse is associated with psychological problems, such as depression (Alloy, Abramson, Smith, Gibb, & Neeren, 2006; Kendall-Tackett et al., 1993; Kuyken, 1995; Nurcombe, 2000), anxiety symptoms or disorders (Beitchman et al., 1992; Green, 1988; Kaysen et al., 2003; Kendall-Tackett et al., 1993; Kuyken, 1995; Nurcombe, 2000; Polusny & Follette, 1995; Terr, 1991), and alcohol or drug abuse (Arellano, 1996; Arnow, 2004; Cicchetti & Toth, 2005; Hecht & Hansen, 1999; Hurley, 1991; Johnson, 2004; Langeland & Hartgers, 1998; Murray, 1993; Nielsen, 1983; Nurcombe, 2000; Putnam, 2003; Sartor et al., 2008; Trickett & Putnam, 1993), without necessarily implying a causal relationship between child sexual abuse and later psychopathology. For example, it has been stated that the specific effects of sexual abuse, independent of family variables, such as parental psychopathology, are still to be clarified (e.g., Beitchman et al., 1992). Furthermore, it has been suggested that firm conclusions related to the relationship between child sexual abuse and posttraumatic stress disorder cannot be made because the researchers have not controlled for the influence of physical abuse or other traumatic experiences (Polusny & Follette, 1995). Finally, some reviews (e.g.,

Langeland & Hartgers, 1998; Moncrieff & Farmer,1998) have shown that studies on the association between childhood sexual abuse and later substance use or misuse have given conflicting results. Importantly, prospective studies (e.g., McCord, 1983; Pedersen & Skrondal, 1996; Widom, Ireland, & Glynn, 1995), which are well suited not only for inferring whether prior sexual victimization is significantly associated with subsequent substance problems but also for exploring the causality of this association, have reported mixed findings.

In sum, although efforts to summarize the empirical research on the topic have resulted in several literature reviews, even these have produced conflicting results. However, it should be noted that, to date, causal inferences cannot be made, because of the presence of both confounding variables and methodological weaknesses in the studies on the topic.

Although several theoretical explanations of how child sexual abuse affects children's development have been proposed (see Cicchetti & Toth, 2005; Freeman & Morris, 2001; Hulme, 2004), in the absence of consistent empirical evidence of/on a causal association between early abuse and later psychopathology, theories accounting for the impact of child abuse on human development lack support.

To date, it is unclear whether higher rates of psychological problems, especially depressive and anxiety disorders, substance problems, suicide, and non-suicidal self-injury, in subjects who have been sexually abused in childhood are truly due to child sexual abuse or whether they may be attributable to other risk factors that may precede, accompany, or follow the experience of child sexual victimization. An association between child sexual abuse and a variety of psychological problems, although statistically significant, does not imply a causal relationship between child sexual abuse and later psychopathology. It is possible that several antecedent or concurrent risk factors other than child sexual abuse may either act independently to cause psychological problems in people who were sexually abused as children or interact with early sexual victimization experiences to increase the likelihood of psychopathology in child abuse survivors.

Methodological Limitations

Most literature reviews addressing the relationship between child sexual abuse and psychopathology are characterized by imprecision and subjectivity (Rind & Tromovitch, 1997; Rind et al., 1998). For example, many reviewers have specified neither the data sources that were searched nor the criteria used for including studies, paying more attention to study findings indicating harmful effects. Although some meta-analytic reviews are available, even these are methodologically limited, because the vast majority of them have not assessed data quality and validity and have aggregated different study findings, particularly those with different levels of methodological quality.

In addition, it should be noted that the largest number of the individual studies addressing the relationship between child sexual abuse and psychopathology are characterized by a generally poor methodological quality. Indeed, most studies are methodologically limited, given that they are characterized by serious design, sampling, and measurement problems, such as poor sampling methods, absence of appropriate comparison groups, inadequate operationalization and measurement of abuse histories and outcomes, insufficient control for effect modifiers and confounders, or designs inappropriate to prove causality (see Briere, 1992b; Kilpatrick, 1987; Sharpe & Faye, 2006).

For example, with few exceptions, most of these studies have relied solely on self-report measures of child abuse and psychopathology of questionable reliability and validity (e.g., investigator-authored questions or only single item indicators of abuse experiences and depressive or anxiety symptoms) rather than employing well-established measures or formal classification systems to operationalize symptoms and disorders and/or child abuse.

Furthermore, many individual studies have sampled only subjects who were seeking or receiving psychiatric services, thus producing a high risk of sampling bias. Because clinical samples cannot be assumed to be representative of the general population, such convenience sampling raises questions concerning the generalizability and interpretation of research results. In addition, it has been showed that data coming from these samples are vulnerable to several biases that threaten their validity (Pope & Hudson, 1995; Rind & Tromovitch, 1997; Rind et al., 1998; Sharpe & Faye, 2006). For example, subjects drawn from clinical samples may be more likely than nonclinical participants to recall events of early traumatic experiences, including child sexual abuse, thus inflating the relationship between childhood abuse and adulthood psychopathology (Pope & Hudson, 1995). Moreover, the various forms of child maltreatment and family problems are highly confounded in clinical population; thus causality cannot be inferred from clinical samples (Beitchman et al., 1991; Pope & Hudson, 1995; Ney, Fung, & Wickett, 1994).

Importantly, the vast majority of studies investigating the potential relationship between child sexual abuse and psychopathology are retrospective in design, in that adults are asked about early experiences of sexual abuse. It has been suggested that research including reported data about an event or a series of events that occurred in the past may be threatened by the limitations of the individual's memory and the influence of disease or exposure status on the recalling process in humans (Grimes & Schulz, 2002; Hassan, 2006). Because retrospective designs may be subject to recall bias as they require participants to rely on their memory to identify what in the past might have caused their current disease which is most often of long latency, such designs might produce false positive results. For example, some studies that used prospective and retrospective victimization information (Raphael, Widom, & Lange, 2001; Widom, Weiler, & Cottler, 1999) have shown that retrospective self-reports of child abuse were linked to significant increases in risk for drug abuse and pain problems in adulthood. In contrast, prospectively, abused subjects were not at increased risk for drug abuse and pain symptoms. In a recent cross-sectional community survey with retrospectivereports of childhoodadversities (Green et al., 2010), the fact that associations of childhoodadversities with first onset of anxiety, mood, disruptive behavior, and substance use disorders increased in magnitude with length of recall raised the possibility of recall bias inflatingestimates. Because recall bias tends to inflate the estimated risk attributed to the exposure under investigation and this could potentially yield spurious association, such bias represents a major threat to the internal validity and credibility of studies using self-reported data (Grimes & Schulz, 2002; Hassan, 2006). Thus, results from studies employing retrospective designs should be interpreted with caution, given the demonstrated flaws of this methodology.

Most importantly, much of the traditional empirical research on the relationship between child sexual abuse and psychopathology have not controlled for the overlap with other biological, psychological, or social factors that increase the risk of psychopathology (see, e.g.,

Santa Mina & Gallop, 1998), such as family dysfunction, parental substance problems, and other forms of child abuse (e.g., psychological maltreatment), that often accompany early sexual victimization experiences.

Consequently, because of these methodological limitations, associations are confounded and causal inferences not feasible. Thus, findings must be interpreted with caution.

Confounders and Additional Risk Factors

Although most studies have not controlled for confounders and other risk factors of psychopathology in child abuse victims, it is possible that certain third variables, such as genetic and environmental factors, might better account for the higher levels of psychopathology reported by survivors of early sexual victimization rather than the experience of child abuse itself having a causal role in the etiology of psychological problems.

Speaking more broadly, multiple problems other than child sexual abuse, such as parental mental illness and/or substance abuse, high family conflict or dysfunction, and other forms of child maltreatment, might be present in an abused child's life or in the context in which the victim lives. Some of these problems might better account for the psychiatric symptoms or disorders found in subjects who have been sexually victimized as children rather than the experience of child sexual abuse itself having a causal role in the etiology of psychological disturbance.

It has been shown that childhood adversities, especially those associated with maladaptive family functioning (e.g., family violence and parentalmental illness, substance abuse, or criminality), are highly prevalent and intercorrelated in people with psychological problems. For example, Green, McLaughlin, and colleagues (Green et al., 2010; McLaughlin et al., 2010) examined the joint associations of 12 childhoodadversities with the first onset and persistence of anxiety, mood, disruptive behavior, and substance use disorders, using substantivelycomplex multivariate models. Results showed that childhoodadversities were highly prevalent and intercorrelated. Childhoodadversities associated with maladaptive family functioning(e.g., family violence and parentalmental illness, substance abuse, or criminality) were thestrongest correlates of disorder onset and persistence throughoutthe life course. Multiple childhoodadversities involving maladaptive family functioninghad significant subadditive associationswith the sameoutcomes.

There is evidence that the various forms of child maltreatment are highly prevalent and intercorrelated in dysfunctional families (Bagley, 1991;Briere, 1988b; Briere & Elliot, 1993; Sheldrick, 1991). Some reviews (Alloy, Abramson, Smith, Gibb, & Neeren, 2006; Kaplan, Pelcovitz, & Labruna, 1999) have shown that the evidence for an association between child emotional maltreatment and depression is more consistent than that for a relationship between child sexual abuse and depression. Indeed, it has been noted that a larger proportion of the studies of child emotional abuse that have controlled for the overlap of emotional maltreatment with child sexual abuse have found that child emotional abuse is more strongly related to depression than is child sexual abuse (Alloy, Abramson, Smith, Gibb, & Neeren, 2006). Thus, there might be greater confidence that the association of child sexual abuse with depression may be due to the emotional and psychological aspects that might also be present in the early experience of sexual abuse rather than any sexual or physical components of such experience. Further reviews have suggested that an increased likelihood of self-injurious and suicidal behavior in adolescence or adulthood is strongly associated with a history of child emotional abuse (e.g., Kaplan et al., 1999), child physical maltreatment (e.g., Gould et al., 2003; Malinosky-Rummell & Hansen, 1993), and concurrent physical abuse and sexual penetration by the perpetrator (Briere, 1988b). Therefore, it has been suggested that, to date, the influence of child sexual abuse alone on self-injurious and suicidal behavior is unclear and co-occurring forms of child maltreatment, such as physical and emotive abuse, might account, at least in part, for the increased risk of self-injurious and suicidal behavior in sexual abuse survivors, rather than early sexual victimization per se acting alone to increase the likelihood of self-harm and suicide (Polusny &Follette, 1995).

Because of the high prevalence of family problems and co-occurring forms of child maltreatment as well as histories of substance abuse, psychiatric disorders, and suicidal behavior among parents, it has been noted that, in these distressed families, it is difficult to determine the specific effects of child sexual abuse over and above the effects of dysfunctional environment and genetic contribution (Beitchman et al., 1991; Briere, 1988b; Briere & Elliot, 1993; Brent & Mann, 2005).

In many of these families, parents of sexually abused children may have histories of substance abuse, psychiatric disorders, and suicidal behavior that may be transmitted to their offspring.

It is well known that parental anxiety disorders confer significant risk for anxiety in offspring. A meta-analysis (Micco et al., 2009) has revealed that offspring of parents with anxiety disorders have greater risk for anxiety disorders than offspring of psychiatric and non-psychiatric controls. According to a series of meta-analyses of data from family and twin studies (Hettema et al., 2001), panic disorder, generalized anxiety disorder, phobias, and obsessive-compulsive disorder all have significant familial aggregation that is largely explained by genes. In fact, both family and twin studies indicate that genetic factors account for significant variance in the development of anxiety disorders (for reviews, see, e.g., Afifi et al., 2010; Gordon & Hen, 2004; Gregory & Eley, 2007; Hettema et al., 2001). Additional reviews also support a genetic contribution to the risk of completed and attempted suicide (Anguelova, Benkelfat, & Turecki, 2003; Arango, Huang, Underwood, & Mann, 2003; Baldessarini & Hennen, 2004; Bellivier, Chaste, & Malafosse, 2004; Bondy, Buettner, & Zill 2006; Lalovic & Turecki, 2002; Li & He, 2007; Lin & Tsai, 2004; Rujescu, Thalmaier, Miller, Bronisch, & Giegling, 2007; Voracek & Loibl, 2007), with the different serotonin (5-HT) receptors, including the serotonin transporter (5-HTT) gene, located at 17q11.1–q12, being considered promising candidate genes for suicide and suicidal behavior (Anguelova et al., 2003; Li & He, 2007). There is also evidence that depression (Leonardo & Hen, 2006; Levinson, 2008) and substance-related disorders (Crabbe, 2002; Dick & Bierut, 2006; Hopfer, Crowley, & Hewitt, 2003; Walters, 2002; McGue, 1999) result, at least in part, from genetic influences. It has been shown that major depressive disorder in parents may increase the risk of adult-onset depression in their offspring (Hammen, 2008; Goodman, 2007). Indeed, it has been estimated that the heritability of major depression is likely to be in the range of 31%-42% (Sullivan, Neale, & Kendler, 2000).

Thus, it is possible that psychiatric disorders in parents might independently increase the risk of their children themselves developing psychiatric symptoms or disorders in adolescence or adulthood. Consequently, in subjects who have been sexually victimized as children, psychiatric symptoms or disorders might be due, at least in part, to genetic components rather than child sexual abuse. Because parental psychiatric disorders, including substance-related disorders, may be risk factors for both child abuse and psychopathology in offspring, it is possible that, in some cases, parental mental illness might have direct effects on the occurrence of both sexual abuse events in childhood and psychiatric disorders in adolescence or adulthood. For example, it has been suggested that, since substance-related disorders in parents might independently increase the risk of both their children themselves developing substance problems in adolescence or adulthood (e.g., Campbell & Oei, 2010; Johnson & Leff, 1999; Wilens & Biederman, 1993) and their children experiencing maltreatment in childhood (e.g., Magura & Laudet, 1996), the association between early sexual victimization and later substance problems in offspring might be due to parental substance-related disorders, rather than child sexual abuse per se (Simpson & Miller, 2002; Sartor et al., 2008; Moncrieff & Farmer,1998; Downs & Miller, 1996).

Research also suggests that the impact of family on psychological adjustment goes beyond heritability. For example, several reviews have shown that dysfunctional family relationships and climate might promote the development of many psychological problems, such as depression (Restifo & Bögels, 2009; Sander & McCarty, 2005; Cummings, Keller, & Davies, 2005; Sexson, Glanville, & Kaslow, 2001; Goodman & Gotlib, 1999; Sheeber, Hops, & Davis, 2001), substance-related disorders (Denton & Kampfe, 1994; Repetti, Taylor, & Seeman, 2002; Sher, Grekin, & Williams, 2005; Vakalahi, 2001; Velleman, Templeton, & Copello, 2005), and suicidal behavior (Evans et al., 2004; Gould et al., 2003; Wagner, 1997; Wagner, Silverman, & Martin, 2003). More specifically, several reviews have found that a parenting style characterized by low levels of warmth and caring and high levels of overprotection, overcontrol, criticism, intrusiveness, guilt-induction, and rejection may increase the risk of childhood anxiety (Bögels & Brechman-Toussaint, 2006; Gerlsma, Emmelkamp, & Arrindell, 1990; McLeod, Wood, & Weisz, 2007; Rapee, 1997; Wood, McLeod, Sigman, Hwang, & Chu, 2003), childhood depression (McLeod et al., 2007), and adult-onset depression (Alloy, Abramson, Smith, Gibb, & Neeren, 2006; Gerlsma et al., 1990). Furthermore, impaired or unsatisfying parent-adolescent relationships, unsupportive parenting, high family conflict, low family cohesion, parental divorce, and ineffective family communication have been found to be significant risk factors for suicidal behavior and ideation (Evans et al., 2004; Gould et al., 2003; Wagner, 1997; Wagner et al., 2003). Moreover, substance-related disorders have been related to cold, distant, unsupportive, uninvolved, neglectful, and hostile parenting (Denton & Kampfe, 1994; Repetti, Taylor, & Seeman, 2002; Sher et al., 2005; Vakalahi, 2001; Velleman, Templeton, & Copello, 2005), a family environment lacking cohesion, cooperation, organization, and functioning (Denton & Kampfe, 1994; Repetti et al., 2002; Velleman et al., 2005), high family conflict, aggression, or violence (Repetti et al., 2002; Velleman et al., 2005), ineffective family communication (Denton & Kampfe, 1994; Velleman et al., 2005), severe family disruption (especially parental absence due to break-ups, death, or divorce; Denton & Kampfe, 1994; Zucker, 2006), inconsistent or excessively severe parental disciplinary practices (Donovan, 2004; Denton & Kampfe, 1994; Repetti et al., 2002; Velleman et al., 2005), inconsistent parental supervision (especially inadequate parental knowledge about and monitoring of children's activities, friends, and opportunities for substance use; Johnson & Leff, 1999; Repetti et al., 2002; Velleman et al., 2005), positive or tolerant parental attitudes towards substance use or inconsistent parental attitudes toward the harm of substance use (Johnson & Leff, 1999; Donovan, 2004; Sher et al., 2005; Denton & Kampfe, 1994; Velleman et al., 2005), and availability of substances in the home or substance use within the family (Campbell & Oei, 2010; Denton & Kampfe, 1994; Donovan, 2004; Finke & Bowman, 1997; Johnson & Leff, 1999; Vakalahi, 2001; Velleman et al., 2005; Wilens & Biederman, 1993; Zucker, 2006), including maternal substance use during pregnancy (Sher et al., 2005; Zucker et al., 2008).

Consequently, in sexually abused children, certain family factors might be better predictors of psychopathology than is child sexual abuse.

According to theoretical models of the impact of child abuse based on family dynamics (e.g., Finkelhor, 1984), a dysfunctional family environment, such as ineffective family functioning, inconsistent parental support and nurturance, confused family roles, parental separation or divorce, parental alcoholism, and other forms of child abuse, may contribute to adverse outcomes in victims of early abuse (see Hulme, 2004). Nevertheless, empirical research on the role of family variables in the etiology of psychopathology in child abuse victims is quite modest. However, some evidence suggests that the negative family circumstances in which many maltreated children are raised (e.g., other forms of child maltreatment or high family conflict or dysfunction), might independently account for the higher levels of psychopathology reported by subjects with a history of child sexual abuse (see, for example, Briere, 1988a; Briere & Elliot, 1993). A meta-analysis on the relationship between child sexual abuse and non-suicidal self-injury (Klonsky & Moyer, 2008) has found that those studies that controlled for family variables (such as childhood separation, attachment, neglect, physical or emotional abuse) revealed either minimal or negligible unique associations between child sexual abuse and self-injurious behavior. In a meta-analytic review on the association between child sexual abuse and a variety of outcomes (Rind et al., 1998), certain family variables (e.g., physical or emotional abuse and family structure, conflict, pathology, support, and bonding) were confounded with child sexual abuse and independently related to outcomes. Family environment explained considerably more variance than abuse, with the relationship between a history of abuse and later maladjustment generally becoming nonsignificant when studies controlled for family environment. More specifically, family variables were more strongly related to depression, anxiety disorders, and suicidal ideation and behavior than was child sexual abuse. In another review (Weiss et al., 1999) of eight studies addressing the association between family dysfunction, child sexual abuse, and adult-onset depression, six found a positive correlation between child sexual abuse and various markers of familial dysfunction (e.g., early parental separation, family violence, physical punishment, and lack of parental warmth) and/or a positive correlation between poor parenting and adult-onset depression, even in the absence of child sexual abuse; in one of these studies poor parental support was a better predictor of subsequent impaired psychological functioning than child sexual abuse. These results imply that family environment might be a better predictor of psychopathology than is child sexual abuse. Indeed, it may be possible that certain negative family circumstances environment might be directly responsible for the onset of psychiatric symptoms or disorders in people with a history of child sexual abuse. Nevertheless, it should be noted that, in the case of substance problems in people with histories of child sexual abuse, research findings are conflicting. In fact, when family variables (e.g., family conflict or violence, parental psychological and substance problems, cold, uncaring, and unsupportive parenting, or inconsistent parental discipline) have been statistically controlled, some studies (Bailey & McCloskey, 2005; Fergusson et al., 1996; Kendler et al., 2000; Spak, Spak, & Allebeck, 1997; Widom & White, 1997) have revealed that child sexual abuse contributed unique variance to later substance problems, whereas others (Dinwiddie et al., 2000; Fleming, Mullen, Sibthorpe, Attewell, & Bammer, 1998; Kilpatrick et al., 2000; Luster & Small, 1997; McCord, 1983) have found that both child sexual abuse and family factors made unique contributions to subsequent substance abuse.

In conclusion, it is possible that certain variables, other than child sexual abuse, might act independently to cause psychiatric symptoms or disorders in subjects who were sexually abused as children. It is clear that in abusive contexts or dysfunctional families, both environmental and biological factors may increase the risk of psychopathology in offspring. Multiple risk factors for psychiatric symptoms or disorders other than child sexual abuse, such as a parental mental illness, substance abuse, or suicidal behavior, dysfunctional family relationships and climate, and other forms of child abuse, might also be present in these dysfunctional contexts. Some of these factors may be directly responsible for psychiatric symptoms or disorders in survivors of child sexual abuse.

CONCLUSION

A large amount of studies and literature reviews provides clear evidence that the relationship between child sexual abuse and psychopathology does exist. To date, research has shown a statistically significant, although modest, association between child sexual abuse and a variety of psychological disorders, such as depression, anxiety disorders, substance-related disorders, and suicidal and non-suicidal self-injurious behaviors.

However, it is uncertain whether child sexual abuse does have a causal role in the etiology of psychological disturbance. To date, causal inferences cannot be made, because much of the traditional empirical research on the have not controlled for the overlap with other biological, psychological, or social factors that increase the risk of psychopathology in child abuse victims.

Several antecedent or concurrent risk factors other than child sexual abuse may either act independently to cause psychological problems in people who were sexually abused as children or interact with early sexual victimization experiences to increase the likelihood of psychopathology in child abuse survivors.

There is evidence that a number of third variables, especially genes and the adverse environmental factors that might accompany child sexual abuse, such as other forms of child maltreatment and dysfunctional family relationships and climate, may be directly responsible for the onset of psychopathology in people with a history of child sexual abuse. It is apparent that childhood adversities, especially those associated with maladaptive family functioning (e.g., family violence and parentalmental illness, substance abuse, or criminality), are highly prevalent and intercorrelated in an abused child's life and environment and play an important role in the etiology of many psychiatric disorders.

Therefore, it is possible that child sexual abuse may not have a primary role in the development of certain psychiatric disorders. Being a victim of child sexual abuse is a significant risk factor, but may not be the only important risk factor. It is clear that the etiology of many psychiatric disorders is multifactorial. Multiple factors interact with each other and contribute to the risk of developing psychological problems. Evidence to date suggests that child sexual abuse is a significant risk factor for a variety of psychiatric disorders, but not the only important one. Research clearly indicates that several other biological, environmental, and psychosocial factors enhance the likelihood of psychiatric disorders, although some factors might exert greater influence than others.

These findings should not be misinterpreted as suggesting that child sexual abuse is not related to psychopathology when, in fact, such findings emphasize, rather than exclude or minimize, the role of child sexual abuse in the etiology of a variety of psychiatric disorders, highlighting the childhood sexual abuse-related risk for developing psychological problems in adolescence or adulthood. However, speaking more broadly, since multiple risk factors enhance the likelihood of manifesting psychological disturbance in the general population, and given that some survivors of early sexual victimization are exposed to multiple risk factors for a variety of psychiatric disorders, it is possible that, in some cases, child sexual abuse may not have a primary role in the development and maintenance of psychopathology.

Individuals vary widely in their responses to traumatic experiences, such as child abuse. Some manifest serious or long-lasting psychiatric symptoms or disorders whereas others have not serious psychological sequelae or only suffer mild, short-lived psychiatric symptoms. It is apparent that an increased presence of biological, psychological, or social risk factors may interact with the effects of early traumatic experiences, such as child abuse, and increase the likelihood of deviating from the conditions that promote normal development and manifesting adverse developmental outcomes (Cicchetti & Toth, 1995).

Evidence to date suggests that the role of child sexual abuse in the etiology of psychiatric disorders is complex. Being a victim of child sexual abuse is a significant, although general, nonspecific, and modest in magnitude, risk factor for a variety of psychiatric disorders. However, child sexual abuse is not the only important risk factor and often has not a primary role in the genesis, maintenance, and recurrence of psychopathology. Additional biological, psychological, and social risk factors may, in some cases, be directly responsible for psychopathology, or, in other cases, contribute to the risk of psychological disturbance by mediating the relationship between child sexual abuse and psychopathology. However, it is apparent that being a victim of child sexual abuse may sometimes confer additional risk of psychopathology – a risk that is not fully accounted for by other risk factors – either as a "distal" and indirect cause or as a "proximal" and direct cause. Thus, child sexual abuse should be considered one of the several risk factors for a variety of psychiatric disorders and included in multifactorial etiological models in order to elucidate the mechanisms that contribute to the development of psychopathology in survivors of child abuse.

Because the methodological limitations of much of the traditional empirical research on the topic do not allow casual inferences to be made, it is clear that future empirical research on the role of child sexual abuse in the etiology of psychiatric disorders should be implemented. Further research should elucidate the causal mechanisms, processes, or pathways, both psychological and neurobiological, that contribute to the adverse consequences associated with child sexual abuse. Since the etiology of psychiatric disorders is complex and multifactorial, the development and empirical validation of more comprehensive, multifactorial etiological models are required in order to explain how risk factors work together to promote or maintain psychopathology in child abuse victims.

Furthermore, it is essential that future research determine not only the mechanisms by which child sexual abuse may result in psychological problems in adulthood, but also the compensatory processes whereby some abuse survivors achieve positive adaptation. Not all individuals who have been sexually abused in childhood manifest negative sequelae. Some survivors of child abuse develop and utilize compensatory mechanisms that enable them to function adaptively despite having experienced significant adversity (see Cicchetti & Toth, 2005). For example, there is some evidence that certain personality characteristics (e.g., high self-esteem) may be significant protective factors in child abuse victims (Cicchetti & Rogosch, 1997; Moran & Eckenrode, 1992).

In addition, research into those variables that might moderate or mediate the impact of child sexual abuse on health, such as neurobiological factors, personality traits, and cognitive styles, should be implemented. Importantly, further research is required to clarify the role of those variables concerning aspects of the abuse experience, especially those associated with traumatic forms of child abuse, such as contact, use of force, frequency, and duration of abuse.

To achieve all these goals, a number of methodological advances in research in this area must be implemented. Importantly, future investigations should (1) use prospective, longitudinal designs; (2) control for confounders; (3) employ study samples representative of the general population and matched comparison groups; (4) use formal classification systems, standard measures, and instruments designed to assess and operationalize child sexual abuse and outcomes.

REFERENCES

Abramson, L. Y., Metalsky, G. I., & Alloy, L. B. (1989). Hopelessness depression: A theory-based subtype of depression. *Psychological Review*, 96, 358-372.

Afifi, T. O., Asmundson, G. J., Taylor, S., & Jang, K. L. (2010). The role of genes and environment on trauma exposure and posttraumatic stress disorder symptoms: A review of twin studies. *Clinical Psychology Review*, 30, 101-112.

Alfano, C. A., Beidel, D. C., & Turner, S. M. (2002). Cognition in childhood anxiety: Conceptual methodological and developmental issues. *Clinical Psychology Review*, 22, 1209-1238.

Alloy, L. B., Abramson, L. Y., Smith, J. M., Gibb, B. E., & Neeren, A. M. (2006). Role of parenting and maltreatment histories in unipolar and bipolar mood disorders: Mediation by cognitive vulnerability to depression. *Clinical Child and Family Psychology Review*, 9, 23-64.

Alloy, L. B., Abramson, L. Y., Walshaw, P. D., & Neeren, A. M. (2006). Cognitive vulnerability to unipolar and bipolar mood disorders. *Journal of Social and Clinical Psychology*, 25, 726-754.

Anguelova, M., Benkelfat, C., &Turecki, G. (2003). A systematic review of association studies investigating genes coding for serotonin receptors and the serotonin transporter: II. Suicidal behavior. *Molecular Psychiatry*, 8, 646-653.

Arango, V., Huang, Y. Y., Underwood, M. D., &Mann, J. J. (2003). Genetics of the serotonergic system in suicidal behavior. *Journal of Psychiatric Research*, 37, 375-386.

Arellano, C. M. (1996). Child maltreatment and substance use: A review of the literature. *Substance Use and Misuse*, 31, 927-935.

Arnow, B. A. (2004). Relationships between childhood maltreatment, adult health and psychiatric outcomes, and medical utilization. *Journal of Clinical Psychiatry*, 65, 10-15.

Bachmann, G. A., Moeller, T. P., & Benett, J. (1988). Childhood sexual abuse and the consequences in adult women. *Obstetrics and Gynecology,* 71, 631-642.

Bagley, C. (1991). The long-term psychological effects of child sexual abuse: A review of some British and Canadian studies of victims and their families. *Annals of Sex Research,* 4, 23-48.

Bailey, D. B., Golden, R. N., Roberts, J., & Ford, A. (2007). Maternal depression and developmental disability: Research critique. *Mental Retardation and Developmental Disabilities Research Reviews,* 13, 321-329.

Baldessarini, R. J., &Hennen, J. (2004). Genetics of suicide: An overview. *Harvard Review of Psychiatry,* 12, 1-13.

Bardo, M. T., Williams, Y., Dwoskin, L. P., Moynahan, S. E., Perry, I. B., & Martin, C. A. (2007). The sensation seeking trait and substance use: Research findings and clinical implications. *Current Psychiatry Reviews,* 3, 3-13.

Bar-Haim, Y., Lamy, D., Pergamin, L., Bakermans-Kranenburg, M. J., & van Ijzendoorn, M. H. (2007). Threat-related attentional bias in anxious and nonanxious individuals: A meta-analytic study. *Psychological Bulletin,* 133, 1-24.

Baud, P. (2005). Personality traits as intermediary phenotypes in suicidal behavior. American Journal of Medical Genetics. Part C, *Seminars in Medical Genetics,* 133, 34-42.

Beck, A. T., Wright, F. D., Newman, C. F., & Liese, B. (1993). Cognitive therapy of substance abuse. New York: Guilford Press.

Beitchman, J. H., Zucker, K. J., Hood, J. E., daCosta, G. A., Akman, D., & Cassavia, E. (1992). A review of the long-term effects of child sexual abuse. *Child Abuse and Neglect,* 16, 101-118.

Beitchman, J. H., Zucker, K. J., Hood, J. E., daCosta, G. A., & Akman, D. (1991). A review of the short-term effects of child sexual abuse. *Child Abuse and Neglect,* 15, 537-556.

Bellivier, F., Chaste, P., &Malafosse, A. (2004). Association between the TPH gene A218C polymorphism and suicidal behavior: A meta-analysis. American Journal of Medical Genetics. Part B, *Neuropsychiatric Genetics,* 124, 87-91.

Black, C. A., & DeBlassie, R. R. (1993). Sexual abuse in male children and adolescents: Indicators, effects, and treatments. *Adolescence,* 28, 123-133.

Bögels, S. M., & Brechman-Toussaint, M. (2006). Family issues in child anxiety: Attachment, family functioning, parental rearing and beliefs. *Clinical Psychology Review,* 7, 834-856.

Bohn, D. K., & Holz, K. A. (1996). Sequelae of abuse. Health effects of childhood sexual abuse, domestic battering, and rape. *Journal of Nurse Midwifery,* 41, 442-456.

Bollerud, K. (1990). A model for the treatment of trauma-related syndromes among chemically dependent inpatient women. *Journal of Substance Abuse Treatment,* 7, 83-87.

Bondy, B., Buettner, A., &Zill, P. (2006). Genetics of suicide. Molecular *Psychiatry,* 11, 336-351.

Bornovalova, M. A., Lejuez, C. W., Daughters, S. B., Zachary Rosenthal, M., & Lynch, T. R. (2005). Impulsivity as a common process across borderline personality and substance use disorders. *Clinical Psychology Review,* 25, 790-812.

Brent, D. A., &Mann, J. J. (2005). Family genetics studies, suicide, and suicidal behavior. American Journal of Medical Genetics. Part C, *Seminars in Medical Genetics,* 133, 13-24.

Brezo, J., Paris, J., &Turecki, G. (2006). Personality traits as correlates of suicidal ideation, suicide attempts, and suicide completions: A systematic review. *Acta Psychiatrica Scandinavica*, 113, 180-206.

Briere, J., & Runtz, M. (1991). The long-term effects of sexual abuse: A review and synthesis. In J. Briere (Ed.), Treating victims of child sexual abuse. New Directions for Mental Health Services (Issue 51, pp. 3-13). San Francisco, CA: Jossey-Bass.

Briere, J. (1988a). Controlling for family variables in abuse effects research: A critique of the "partialling" approach. *Journal of Interpersonal Violence*, 3, 80-89.

Briere, J. (1988b). The long-term clinical correlates of childhood sexual victimization. *Annals of the New York Academy of Sciences*, 528, 327-334.

Briere, J. (1992a). Child abuse trauma: Theory and treatment of the lasting effects. Newbury Park, CA: Sage.

Briere, J. (1992b). Methodological issues in the study of sexual abuse effects. *Journal of Consulting and Clinical Psychology*, 60, 196-203.

Briere, J. N., & Elliot, D. M. (1994). Immediate and long term impacts of child sexual abuse. *The Future of Children*, 4, 54-69.

Briere, J. N., & Runtz, M. (1993). Childhood sexual abuse: Long-term sequelae and implications for psychological assessment. *Journal of Interpersonal Violence*, 8, 312-330.

Briere, J., & Elliot, D. M. (1993). Sexual abuse, family environment, and psychological symptoms: On the validity of statistical control. *Journal of Consulting and Clinical Psychology*, 61, 284-288.

Brodsky, B. S., & Stanley, B. (2008). Adverse childhood experiences and suicidal behavior. *The Psychiatric Clinics of North America*, 31, 223-235.

Browne, A., & Finkelhor, D. (1986). Impact of child sexual abuse: A review of the research. *Psychological Bulletin*, 99, 66-77.

Campbell, J. M., & Oei, T. P. (2010). A cognitive model for the intergenerational transference of alcohol use behavior. *Addictive Behaviors*, 35, 73-83.

Cicchetti, D., & Rogosch, F. A. (1997). The role of self-organization in the promotion of resilience in maltreated children. *Development and Psychopathology*, 9, 799-817.

Cicchetti, D., & Toth, S. L. (1995). A developmental psychopathology perspective on child abuse and neglect. *Journal of the American Academy of Child and Adolescent Psychiatry*, 34, 541-565.

Cicchetti, D., & Toth, S. L. (2005). Child maltreatment. *Annual Review of Clinical Psychology*, 1, 409-438.

Cisler, J. M., & Koster, E. H. W. (2010). Mechanisms of attentional biases towards threat in anxiety disorders: An integrative review. *Clinical Psychology Review*, 30, 203-216.

Clark, D. A., Beck, A. T., & Alford, B. A. (1999). Scientific foundations of cognitive theory and therapy of depression. New York: Wiley.

Conner, K. R., Duberstein, P. R., Conwell, Y., &Caine, E. D. (2003). Reactive aggression and suicide: theory and evidence. *Aggression and Violent Behavior*, 8, 413-432.

Connors, R. (1996). Self-injury in trauma survivors: Functions and meanings. *American Journal of Orthopsychiatry*, 66, 197-206.

Crabbe, J. C. (2002). Genetic contributions to addiction. *Annual Review of Psychology*, 53, 435-462.

Cummings, E. M., Keller, P. S., & Davies, P. T. (2005). Towards a family process model of maternal and paternal depressive symptoms: Exploring multiple relations with child and family functioning. *Journal of Child Psychology and Psychiatry*, 46, 479-489.

Daleiden, E. L., & Vasey, M. W. (1997). An information-processing perspective on childhood anxiety. *Clinical Psychology Review*, 17, 407-429.

Denton, R. E., & Kampfe, C. M. (1994). The relationship between family variables and adolescent substance abuse: A literature review. *Adolescence*, 29, 475-495.

Dick, D. M., & Bierut, L. J. (2006). The genetics of alcohol dependence. *Current Psychiatry Reports*, 8, 151-157.

Dinwiddie, S., Heath, A. C., Dunne, M. P., Bucholz, K. K., Madden, P. A. F., Slutske, W. S., et al. (2000). Early sexual abuse and lifetime psychopathology: A co-twin-control study. *Psychological Medicine*, 30, 41-52.

Donovan, J. E. (2004). Adolescent alcohol initiation: A review of psychosocial risk factors. *Journal of Adolescent Health*, 35, 529, e7-18.

Downs, W. R., & Harrison, L. (1998). Childhood maltreatment and the risk of substance problems in later life. *Health Soc Care Community*, 6, 35-46.

Downs, W. R., & Miller, B. A. (1996). Intergenerational links between childhood abuse and alcohol-related problems. In L. Harrison (Ed.), Alcohol problems in the community (pp. 14-51). Routledge: London.

Ehrenreich, J. T., & Gross, A. M. (2002). Biased attentional behavior in childhood anxiety: A review of theory and current empirical investigation. *Clinical Psychology Review*, 22, 991-1008.

Epstein, J. N., Saunders, B. E., Kilpatrick, D. G., & Resnick, H. S. (1998). PTSD as a mediator between childhood rape and alcohol use in adult women. *Child Abuse and Neglect*, 22, 223-234.

Evans, E., Hawton, K., &Rodham, K. (2004). Factors associated with suicidal phenomena in adolescents: A systematic review of population-based studies. *Clinical Psychology Review*, 24, 957-979.

Evans, E., Hawton, K., & Rodham, K. (2005). Suicidal phenomena and abuse in adolescents: A review of epidemiological studies. *Child Abuse and Neglect*, 29, 45-58.

Evans, K., & Sullivan, J. M. (1995). Treating addicted survivors of trauma. New York: Guilford Press.

Fergusson, D. M., Horwood, L. J., & Lynskey, M. T. (1996). Childhood sexual abuse and psychiatric disorder in young adulthood: II. Psychiatric outcomes of childhood sexual abuse. *Journal of the American Academy of Child and Adolescent Psychiatry*, 35, 1365-1374.

Field, M., Schoenmakers, T., & Wiers, R. W. (2008). Cognitive processes in alcohol binges: A review and research agenda. *Current Drug Abuse Reviews*, 1, 263-279.

Fine, C. G. (1990). The cognitive sequelae of incest. In R. Kluft (Ed.), Incest-related syndromes of adult psychopathology (pp. 161-182). Washington, DC: American Psychiatric Press.

Finke, L. M., & Bowman, C. A. (1997). Factors in childhood drug and alcohol use: A review of the literature. *Journal of Child and Adolescent Psychiatric Nursing*, 10, 29-34.

Finkelhor, D. (1984). Child sexual abuse: New theory and research. New York: Free Press.

Fleming, J., Mullen, P. E., Sibthorpe, B., Attewell, R., & Bammer, G. (1998). The relationship between childhood sexual abuse and alcohol abuse in women. A case-control study. *Addiction*, 93, 1787-1798.

Fossati, A., Madeddu, F., & Maffei, C. (1999). Borderline personality disorder and childhood sexual abuse: A meta-analytic study. *Journal of Personality Disorders*, 13, 268-280.

Freeman, K. A., & Morris, T. L. (2001). A review of conceptual models explaining the effects of child sexual abuse. *Aggression and Violent Behavior*, 6, 357-373.

Garnefski, N., & Diekstra, R. (1997). Child sexual abuse and emotional and behavioral problems in adolescence: Gender differences. *Journal of the American Academy of Child and Adolescent Psychiatry*, 36, 323-329.

Gerlsma, C., Emmelkamp, P. M. G., & Arrindell, W. A. (1990). Anxiety, depression, and perception of early parenting: A meta-analysis. *Clinical Psychology Review*, 10, 251-277.

Glanz, L. M., Haas, G. L., &Sweeney, J. A. (1995). Assessment of hopelessness in suicidal patients. *Clinical Psychology Review*, 15, 49-64.

Gold, S., Lucenko, B., Elhai, J., Swingle, J. M., Sellers, A. H. (1999). A comparison of psychological/psychiatric symptomatology of women and men sexually abused as children. *Child Abuse and Neglect*, 23, 683-692.

Goodman, S. H., & Gotlib, I. H. (1999). Risk for psychopathology in the children of depressed mothers: A developmental model for understanding mechanisms of transmission. *Psychological Review*, 106, 458-490.

Goodman, S. H. (2007). Depression in mothers. *Annual Review of Clinical Psychology*, 3, 107-135.

Gordon, J. A., & Hen, R. (2004). Genetic approaches to the study of anxiety. *Annual Review of Neuroscience*, 27, 193-222.

Gorman, D. M., & Derzon, J. H. (2002). Behavioral traits and marijuana use and abuse: A meta-analysis of longitudinal studies. *Addictive Behaviors*, 27, 193-206.

Gould, M. S., Greenberg, T., Velting, D., &Shaffer, D. (2003). Youth suicide risk and preventive interventions: A review of the past 10 years. *Journal of the American Academy of Child and Adolescent Psychiatry*, 42, 386-405.

Green, A. H. (1988). Child maltreatment and its victims. A comparison of physical and sexual abuse. *The Psychiatric Clinics of North America*, 11, 591-610.

Green, J. G., McLaughlin, K. A., Berglund, P. A., Gruber, M. J., Sampson, N. A., Zaslavsky, A. M., et al. (2010). Childhood adversities and adult psychiatric disorders in the national comorbidity survey replication I: Associations with first onset of DSM-IV disorders. *Archives of General Psychiatry*, 67, 113-123.

Gregory, A. M., & Eley, T. C. (2007). Genetic influences on anxiety in children: What we've learned and where we're heading. *Clinical Child and Family Psychology Review*, 10, 199-212.

Grimes, D., & Schulz, K. (2002). Bias and causal association in observational research. *Lancet*, 359, 248-252.

Hadwin, J. A., Garner, M., & Perez-Olivas, G. (2006). The development of information processing biases in childhood anxiety: A review and exploration of its origins in parenting. *Clinical Psychology Review*, 26, 876-894.

Hammen, C. L. (2008). Children of depressed parents. In I. H. Gotlib, & C.L. Hammen (Eds.), Handbook of depression (pp. 275-297). New York: Guilford Press.

Hans, S. L. (1999). Demographic and psychosocial characteristics of substance-abusing pregnant women. *Clinics Perinatology*, 26, 55-74.

Hasking, P. A., & Oei, T. P. S. (2008). Incorporating coping into an expectancy framework for explaining drinking behaviour. *Current Drug Abuse Reviews*, 1, 20-35.

Hassan, E. (2006). Recall bias can be a threat to retrospective and prospective research designs. *Internet Journal of Epidemiology*, 3, 2.

Hawkins, J. D., Catalano, R. F., & Miller, J. Y. (1992). Risk and protective factors for alcohol and other drug problems in adolescence and early adulthood: Implications for substance abuse prevention. *Psychological Bulletin*, 112, 64-105.

Hecht, D. B., & Hansen, D. J. (1999). Adolescent victims and intergenerational issues in sexual abuse. In V. B. van Hasselt, & M. Hersen (Eds.), Handbook of psychological approaches with violent offenders: Contemporary strategies and issues (pp. 303-328). New York: Kluwer Academic/Plenum Publishers.

Heim, C., & Nemeroff, C. B. (2001). The role of childhood trauma in the neurobiology of mood and anxiety disorders: Preclinical and clinical studies. *Biological Psychiatry*, 49, 1023-1039.

Herman, J. L. (1992). Trauma and recovery. New York: Basic Books.

Hettema, J. M., Neale, M. C., & Kendler, K. S. (2001). A review and meta-analysis of the genetic epidemiology of anxiety disorders. *American Journal of Psychiatry*, 158, 1568-1578.

Hittner, J. B., & Swickert, R. (2005). Sensation seeking and alcohol use: A meta-analytic review. *Addictive Behaviors*, 31, 1383-1401.

Holmes, W. C., & Slap, G. B. (1998). Sexual abuse of boys: Definition, prevalence, correlates, sequelae, and management. *Journal of the American Medical Association*, 280, 1855-1862.

Hopfer, C. J., Crowley, T. J., & Hewitt, J. K. (2003). Review of twin and adoption studies of adolescent substance use. *Journal of the American Academy of Child and Adolescent Psychiatry*, 42, 710-719.

Hulme, P. A. (2004). Theoretical perspectives on the health problems of adults who experienced childhood sexual abuse. *Issues in Mental Health Nursing*, 25, 339-361.

Hurley, D. L. (1991). Women, alcohol and incest: An analytical review. *Journal of Studies on Alcohol*, 52, 253-268.

Iacono, W. G., Malone, S. M., & McGue, M. (2008). Behavioral disinhibition and the development of early-onset addiction: Common and specific influences. Annual Review of Clinical Psychology, 4, 325-348.

Ingram, R. E., Miranda, J., & Segal, Z. V. (1998). Cognitive vulnerability to depression. New York: Guilford Press.

Ivanov, I., Schulz, K. P., London, E. D., & Newcorn, J. H. (2008). Inhibitory control deficits in childhood and risk for substance use disorders: A review. American Journal of Drug and Alcohol Abuse, 34, 239-258.

Johnson, C. F. (2004). Child sexual abuse. *Lancet*, 364, 462-470.

Johnson, J. L., & Leff, M. (1999). Children of substance abusers: Overview of research findings. *Pediatrics*, 103, 1085-1099.

Joiner, T. E., Brown, J. S., &Wingate, L. R. (2005). The psychology and neurobiology of suicidal behavior. *Annual Review of Psychology*, 56, 287-314.

Joiner, T. E., & Wagner, K. D. (1995). Attributional style and depression in children and adolescents: A meta-analytic review. *Clinical Psychology Review*, 15, 777-798.

Jones, B. T., Corbin, W., & Fromme, K. (2001). A review of expectancy theory and alcohol consumption. *Addiction*, 96, 57-72.

Jumper, S. A. (1995). A meta-analysis of the relationship of child sexual abuse to adult psychological adjustment. *Child Abuse and Neglect*, 19, 715-728.

Kaplan, S.J., Pelcovitz, D., & Labruna, V. (1999). Child and adolescent abuse and neglect research: a review of the past 10 years: Part I. Physical and emotional abuse and neglect. *Journal of the American Academy of Child and Adolescent Psychiatry*, 38, 1214-1222.

Kaysen, D., Resick, P. A., & Wise, D. (2003). Living in danger: The impact of chronic traumatization and the traumatic context on posttraumatic stress disorder. *Trauma, Violence & Abuse*, 4, 247-264.

Kendall-Tackett, K., Williams, L. M., & Finkelhor, D. (1993). Impact of sexual abuse on children: A review and synthesis of recent empirical studies. *Psychological Bulletin*, 113, 164-180.

Kendler, K. S., Bulik, C. M., Silberg, J., Hettema, J. M., Myers, J., & Prescott, C. A. (2000). Childhood sexual abuse and adult psychiatric and substance use disorders in women: An epidemiological and cotwin control analysis. *Archives of General Psychiatry*, 57, 953-959.

Khantzian, E. J. (1997). The self-medication hypothesis of substance use disorders: A reconstruction and recent applications. *Harvard Review of Psychiatry*, 4, 231-244.

Kilpatrick, D. G., Acierno, R., Saunders, B. E., Resnick, H. S., Best, C. L., & Schnurr, P. P. (2000). Risk factors for adolescent substance abuse and dependence: Data from a national sample. *Journal of Consulting and Clinical Psychology*, 68, 19-30.

Kilpatrick, A. C. (1987). Childhood sexual experiences: Problems and issues in studying long-range effects. Journal of Sex Research, 23, 173-196.

Klonsky, E. D. (2007). The functions of deliberate self-injury: a review of the evidence.*Clinical Psychology Review*, 27, 226-239.

Klonsky, E. D., & Moyer, A. (2008). Childhood sexual abuse and non-suicidal self-injury: Meta-analysis. *British Journal of Psychiatry*, 192, 166-170.

Kuntsche, E., Knibbe, R., Gmel, G., & Engels, R. (2006). Who drinks and why? A review of socio-demographic, personality, and contextual issues behind the drinking motives in young people. *Addictive Behaviors*, 31, 1844-1857.

Kuyken, W. (1995). The psychological sequelae of childhood sexual abuse: A review of the literature and implications for treatment. *Clinical Psychology & Psychotherapy*, 2, 108-121.

Lalovic, A., &Turecki, G. (2002). Meta-analysis of the association between tryptophan hydroxylase and suicidal behavior. *American Journal of Medical Genetics*, 114, 533-540.

Langeland, W., & Hartgers, C. (1998). Child sexual and physical abuse and alcoholism: A review. *Journal of Studies on Alcohol*, 59, 336-348.

Leserman, J. (2005). Sexual abuse history: Prevalence, health effects, mediators, and psychological treatment. *Psychosomatic Medicine*, 67, 906-915.

Leeners, B., Richter-Appelt, H., Imthurn, B., & Rath, W. (2006). Influence of childhood sexual abuse on pregnancy, delivery, and the early postpartum period in adult women. *Journal of Psychosomatic Research*, 61, 139-151.

Leonard, K. E., & Blane, H. T. (1999). Psychological theories of drinking and alcoholism. New York: Guilford Press.

Leonardo, E. D., & Hen, R. (2006). Genetics of affective and anxiety disorders. *Annual Review of Psychology*, 57, 117-137.

Levinson, D. F. (2008). Genetics of major depression. In I. H. Gotlib, & C. L. Hammen (Eds.), Handbook of depression (pp. 165-186). New York: Guilford Press.

Li, D., &He, L. (2007). Meta-analysis supports association between serotonin transporter (5-HTT) and suicidal behavior. *Molecular Psychiatry*, 12, 47-54.

Liebschutz, J., Savetsky, J. B., Saitz, R., Horton, N. J., Lloyd-Travaglini, C., & Samet, J. H. (2002). The relationship between sexual and physical abuse and substance abuse consequences. *Journal of Substance Abuse Treatment*, 22, 121-128.

Lin, P. Y., &Tsai, G. (2004). Association between serotonin transporter gene promoter polymorphism and suicide: Results of a meta-analysis. *Biological Psychiatry*, 55, 1023-1030.

Luster, T., & Small, S. A. (1997). Sexual abuse history and problems in adolescence: Exploring the effects of moderating variables. *Journal of Marriage and the Family*, 59, 131-142.

Magura, S., & Laudet, A. B. (1996). Parental substance abuse and child maltreatment: Review and implications for intervention. *Children and Youth Services Review*, 18, 193-220.

Malinosky-Rummell, R., &Hansen, D. J. (1993). Long-term consequences of childhood physical abuse. *Psychological Bulletin*, 114, 68-79.

Malouff, J. M., Thorsteinsson, E. B., Rooke, S. E., & Schutte, N. S. (2007). Alcohol involvement and the five-factor model of personality: A meta-analysis. *Journal of Drug Education*, 37, 277-294.

Maniglio, R. (2010). Child sexual abuse in the etiology of depression: A systematic review of reviews. *Depression and Anxiety*, 27, 631-642.

Maniglio, R. (in press). The role of child sexual abuse in the etiology of suicide and non-suicidal self-injury: A systematic review of reviews. Acta Psychiatrica Scandinavica.

Maniglio, R. (submitted, a). Child sexual abuse in the etiology of anxiety disorders: A systematic review of reviews.

Maniglio, R. (submitted, b). The role of child sexual abuse in the etiology of substance-related disorders: A systematic review of reviews.

Maniglio, R. (2009). The impact of child sexual abuse on health: A systematic review of reviews. *Clinical Psychology Review*, 29, 647-657.

Mann, J. J., Waternaux, C., Haas, G. L., &Malone, K. M. (1999). Toward a clinical model of suicidal behavior in psychiatric patients. *American Journal of Psychiatry*, 156, 181-189.

Mann, J. J. (2003). Neurobiology of suicidal behaviour. *Nature Reviews.* Neuroscience, 4, 819-828.

Margolin, G., & Gordis, E. B. (2000). The effects of family and community violence on children. *Annual Review of Psychology*, 51, 445-479.

McCord, J. (1983). A forty year perspective on effects of child abuse and neglect. *Child Abuse and Neglect*, 7, 265-270.

McCusker, C. G. (2001). Cognitive biases and addiction: An evolution in theory and method. *Addiction*, 96, 47-56.

McGrath, E., Keita, G. P., Strickland, B. R., Russo, N. F. (1990). Women and depression: Risk factors and treatment issues. Washington: American Psychological Association.

McGue, M. (1999). The behavioral genetics of alcoholism. *Current Direction in Psychological Science*, 8, 109-115.

McLaughlin, K. A, Green, J. G., Gruber, M. J., Sampson, N. A., Zaslavsky, A. M., & Kessler, R. C. (2010). Childhood adversities and adult psychiatric disorders in the national comorbidity survey replication II: Associations with persistence of DSM-IV disorders. *Archives of General Psychiatry*, 67, 124-132.

McLeod, B. D., Weisz, J. R., & Wood, J. J. (2007). Examining the association between parenting and childhood depression: a meta-analysis. *Clinical Psychology Review*, 27, 986-1003.

McLeod, B. D., Wood, J. J., & Weisz, J. R. (2007). Examining the association between parenting and childhood anxiety: A meta-analysis. *Clinical Psychology Review*, 27, 155-172.

Mezzich, A. C., Tarter, R. E., Giancola, P. R., Lu, S., Kirisci, L., & Parks, S. (1997). Substance use and risky sexual behavior in female adolescents. *Drug and Alcohol Dependence*, 44, 157-166.

Micco, J. A., Henin, A., Mick, E., Kim, S., Hopkins, C. A., Biederman, J., et al. (2009). Anxiety and depressive disorders in offspring at high risk for anxiety: A meta-analysis. *Journal of Anxiety Disorders*, 23, 1158-1164.

Miller, B. A., & Downs, W. R. (1995). Violent victimization among women with alcohol problems. Recent Developments in Alcoholism, 12, 81-101.

Miller, B. A., Downs, W. R., & Testa, M. (1993). Interrelationships between victimization experiences and women's alcohol use. *Journal of Studies on Alcoholism*. Supplement, 11, 109-117.

Moncrieff, J., & Farmer, R. (1998). Sexual abuse and the subsequent development of alcohol problems. Alcohol and Alcoholism, 33, 592-601.

Moran, P. B., & Eckenrode, J. (1992). Protective personality characteristics among adolescent victims of maltreatment. *Child Abuse and Neglect*, 16, 743-754.

Mullen, P. E., Martin, J. L., Anderson, J. C., Romans, S. E., & Herbison, G. P. (1993). Childhood sexual abuse and mental health in adult life. *British Journal of Psychiatry*, 163, 721-732.

Mulvihill, D. (2005). The health impact of childhood trauma: An interdisciplinary review, 1997-2003. *Issues in Comprehensive Pediatric Nursing*, 28, 115-136.

Murray, J. B. (1993). Relationship of childhood sexual abuse to borderline personality disorder, posttraumatic stress disorder, and multiple personality disorder. *Journal of Psychology*, 127, 657-676.

Musa, C. Z., & Lépine, J. P. (2000). Cognitive aspects of social phobia: A review of theories and experimental research. *European Psychiatry*, 15, 59-66.

Ney, P. G., Fung, T., & Wickett, A. R. (1994). The worst combinations of child abuse and neglect. *Child Abuse & Neglect*, 18, 705-714.

Neumann, D. A., Houskamp, B. M., Pollock, V. E., & Briere, J. (1996). The long-term sequelae of childhood sexual abuse in women: A meta-analytic review. *Child Maltreatment*, 1, 6-16.

Nielsen, T. (1983). Sexual abuse of boys: Current perspectives. *Personnel and Guidance Journal*, 62, 139-142.

Nurcombe, B. (2000). Child sexual abuse I: Psychopathology. *Australian and New Zealand Journal of Psychiatry*, 34, 85-91.

Oei, T. P. S., & Baldwin, A. R. (1994). Expectancy theory: A two-process model of alcohol use and abuse. *Journal of Studies on Alcohol*, 55, 525-534.

Okami, P. (1991). Self-reports of "positive" childhood and adolescent sexual contacts with older persons: An exploratory study. *Archives of Sexual Behavior*, 20, 437-457.

Ouimet, A. J., Gawronski, B., & Dozois, D. J. A. (2009). Cognitive vulnerability to anxiety: A review and an integrative model. *Clinical Psychology Review*, 29, 459-470.

Paolucci, E. O., Genuis, M. L., & Violato, C. (2001). A meta-analysis of the published research on the effects of child sexual abuse. *Journal of Psychology*, 135, 17-36.

Pedersen, W., & Skrondal, A. (1996). Alcohol and sexual victimization: A longitudinal study of Norwegian girls. *Addiction*, 91, 565-581.

Pilkington, B., & Kremer, J. (1995). A review of the epidemiological research on child sexual abuse. Clinical samples. *Child Abuse Review*, 4, 191-205.

Polusny, M. A., & Follette, V. M. (1995). Long-term correlates of child sexual abuse: Theory and review of the empirical literature. *Applied & Preventive Psychology*, 4, 143-166.

Pope, H. G., & Hudson, J. I. (1995). Does childhood sexual abuse cause adult psychiatric disorders? Essentials of methodology. *Journal of Psychiatry and Law*, 23, 363-381.

Prosser, L. A., & Corso, P. S. (2007). Measuring health-related quality of life for child maltreatment: A systematic literature review. *Health Qual Life Outcomes*, 5, 42.

Putnam, F. (2003). Ten year research update review: Child sexual abuse. *Journal of the American Academy of Child and Adolescent Psychiatry*, 42, 269-278.

Rapee, R. M. (1997). Potential role of childrearing practices in the development of anxiety and depression. *Clinical Psychology Review*, 17, 47-67.

Raphael, K. G., Widom, C. S., & Lange, G. (2001). Childhood victimization and pain in adulthood: A prospective investigation. *Pain*, 92, 283-293.

Repetti, R. L., Taylor, S. E., & Seeman T. E. (2002). Risky families: Family social environments and the mental and physical health of offspring. *Psychological Bulletin*, 128, 330-366.

Restifo, K, & Bögels, S. (2009). Family processes in the development of youth depression: Translating the evidence to treatment. *Clinical Psychology Review*, 29, 294-316.

Rind, B., & Tromovitch, P. (1997). A meta-analytic review of findings from national samples on psychological correlates of child sexual abuse. *Journal of Sex Research*, 34, 237-255.

Rind, B., Tromovitch, P., & Bauserman, R. (1998). A meta-analytic examination of assumed properties of child sexual abuse using college samples. *Psychological Bulletin*, 124, 22-53.

Rodriguez, N., Vande Kemp, H., & Foy, D. W. (1998). Postraumatic stress disorder in survivors of childhood sexual and physical abuse: A critical review of the empirical research. *Journal of Child Sexual Abuse*, 7, 17-45.

Roodman, A. C., & Clum, G. A. (2001). Revictimization rates and method variance: A meta-analysis. *Clinical Psychology Review*, 21, 183-204.

Rooke, S. E., Hine, D. W., & Thorsteinsson, E. B. (2008). Implicit cognition and substance use: A meta-analysis. *Addictive Behaviors*, 33, 1314-1328.

Rowan, A. B., & Foy, D. W. (1993). Post-traumatic stress disorder in child sexual abuse survivors: A literature review. *Journal of Traumatic Stress,* 6, 3-20.

Rujescu, D, Thalmaier, A, Miller, H-J, Bronisch, T, &Giegling, I. (2007). Molecular genetic findings in suicidal behavior: What is beyond the serotonergic system? *Archives of Suicide Research*, 11, 17-40.

Sander, J. B., & McCarty, C. A. (2005). Youth depression in the family context: Familial risk factors and models of treatment. *Clinical Child and Family Psychology Review*, 8, 203-219.

Santa Mina, E. E., &Gallop, R. M. (1998). Childhood sexual and physical abuse and adult self-harm and suicidal behaviour: A literature review. *Canadian Journal of Psychiatry*, 43, 793-800.

Sartor, C. E., Agrawal, A., McCutcheon, V. V., Duncan, A. E., & Lynskey, M. T. (2008). Disentangling the complex association between childhood sexual abuse and alcohol-related problems: A review of methodological issues and approaches. *Journal of Studies on Alcohol and Drugs*, 69, 718-727.

Sexson, S. B., Glanville, D. N., & Kaslow, N. J. (2001). Attachment and depression. Implications for family therapy. *Child and Adolescent Psychiatric Clinics of North America*, 10, 465-486.

Sharpe, D., & Faye, C. (2006). Non-epileptic seizures and child sexual abuse: A critical review of the literature. *Clinical Psychology Review*, 26, 1020-1040.

Sheeber, L., Hops, H., & Davis, B. (2001). Family processes in adolescent depression. *Clinical Child and Family Psychology Review*, 4, 19-35.

Sheldrick, C. (1991). Adult sequelae of child sexual abuse. *British Journal of Psychiatry*, 158, 55-62.

Sher, K. J., Grekin, E. R., & Williams, N. A. (2005). The development of alcohol use disorders. *Annual Review of Clinical Psychology*, 1, 493-523.

Sher, K. J., & Trull, T. J. (1994). Personality and disinhibitory psychopathology: Alcoholism and antisocial personality disorder. *Journal of Abnormal Psychology*, 103, 92-102.

Simpson, T. L., & Miller, W. R. (2002). Concomitance between childhood sexual and physical abuse and substance use problems. A review. Clinical Psychology Review, 22, 27-77.

Smolak, L., & Murnen, S. K. (2002). A meta-analytic examination of the relationship between child sexual abuse and eating disorders. *International Journal of Eating Disorders*, 31, 136-150.

Spaccarelli, S. (1994). Stress, appraisal, and coping in child sexual abuse: A theoretical and empirical review. *Psychological Bulletin*, 116, 340-362.

Spak, L., Spak, F., & Allebeck, P. (1997). Factors in childhood and youth predicting alcohol dependence and abuse in Swedish women: Findings from a general population study. *Alcohol and Alcoholism*, 32, 267-274.

Spirito, A, &Esposito-Smythers, C. (2006). Attempted and completed suicide in adolescence. *Annual Review of Clinical Psychology*, 2, 237-266.

Springer, K., Sheridan, J., Kuo, D., & Carnes, M. (2003). The long-term health outcomes of childhood abuse. *Journal of General Internal Medicine*, 18, 864-870.

Stanley, B, Winchel, R, Molcho, A, Simeon, D, &Stanley, M. (1992). Suicide and the self-harm continuum: Phenomenological and biochemical evidence. *International Review of Psychiatry*, 4, 149-155.

Stewart, S. H. (1996). Alcohol abuse in individuals exposed to trauma: A critical review. *Psychological Bulletin*, 120, 83-112.

Sullivan, P. F., Neale, M. C., & Kendler, K. S. (2000). Genetic epidemiology of major depression: Review and meta-analysis. *American Journal of Psychiatry*, 157, 1552-1562.

Suyemoto, K. L. (1998). The functions of self-mutilation.*Clinical Psychology Review*, 18, 531-554.

Teicher, M. H., Andersen, S. L., Polcari, A., Anderson, C. M., & Navalta, C. P. (2002). Developmental neurobiology of childhood stress and trauma. *Psychiatric Clinics of North America*, 25, 397-426.

Teicher, M. H., Andersen, S. L., Polcari, A., Anderson, C. M., Navalta, C. P., & Kim, D. M. (2003). The neurobiological consequences of early stress and childhood maltreatment. Neuroscience and Biobehavioral Reviews, 27, 33-44.

Terr, L. C. (1991). Childhood traumas: An outline and overview. *American Journal of Psychiatry*, 148, 10-20.

Thase, M. E. (2006). Major depressive disorder. In F. Andrasik (Ed.), Comprehensive handbook of personality and psychopathology (Vol. 2, pp. 207-230). Hoboken, NJ: John Wiley & Sons.

Tolin, D. F., & Foa, E. B. (2006). Sex differences in trauma and posttraumatic stress disorder: A quantitative review of 25 years of research. *Psychological Bulletin*, 132, 959-992.

Trickett, P. K., & Putnam, F. W. (1993). Impact of child sexual abuse on females: Toward a developmental, psychobiological integration. *Psychological Science*, 4, 81-87.

Vakalahi, H. F. (2001). Adolescent substance use and family-based risk and protective factors: A literature review. Journal of Drug Education, 31, 29-46.

Valente, S. M. (2005). Sexual abuse of boys. *Journal of Child and Adolescent Psychiatric Nursing*, 18, 10-16.

Velleman, R. D., Templeton, L. J., & Copello, A. G. (2005). The role of the family in preventing and intervening with substance use and misuse: A comprehensive review of family interventions, with a focus on young people. *Drug and Alcohol Review*, 24, 93-109.

Verdejo-García, A., Lawrence, A. J., & Clark, L. (2008). Impulsivity as a vulnerability marker for substance-use disorders: Review of findings from high-risk research, problem gamblers and genetic association studies. *Neuroscience and Biobehavioral Reviews*, 32, 777-810.

Voracek, M., &Loibl, L. M. (2007). Genetics of suicide: A systematic review of twin studies.*Wiener Klinische Wochenschrift*, 119, 463-475.

Wagner, B., Silverman, M., &Martin, C. (2003). Family factors in youth suicidal behaviors. *The American Behavioral Scientist*, 46, 1171-1191.

Wagner, B. M. (1997). Family risk factors for child and adolescent suicidal behavior.*Psychological Bulletin*, 121, 246-298.

Walters, G. D. (2002). The heritability of alcohol abuse and dependence: A meta-analysis of behavior genetic research. *American Journal of Drug and Alcohol Abuse*, 28, 557-584.

Weiss, E. L., Longhurst, J. G., &Mazure, C. M. (1999). *Childhood sexual abuse as a risk factor for depression in women: Psychosocial and neurobiological correlates. American Journal of Psychiatry*, 156, 816-828.

Widom, C. S., Ireland, T., & Glynn, P. J. (1995). Alcohol abuse in abused and neglected children followed-up: Are they at increased risk? *Journal of Studies on Alcohol*, 56, 207-217.

Widom, C. S., & White, H. R. (1997). Problem behaviours in abused and neglected children grown up: Prevalence and co-occurrence of substance abuse, crime, and violence. *Criminal Behaviour and Mental Health*, 7, 287-310.

Widom, C. S., Weiler, B. L., & Cottler, L. B. (1999). Childhood victimization and drug abuse: A comparison of prospective and retrospective findings. *Journal of Consulting and Clinical Psychology*, 67, 867-880.

Wilens, T. E., & Biederman, J. (1993). Psychopathology in preadolescent children at high risk for substance abuse: A review of the literature. *Harvard Review of Psychiatry*, 1, 207-218.

Wolfe, V. V., Gentile, C., Wolfe, D. A. (1989). The impact of sexual abuse on children: A PTSD formulation. *Behavior Therapy*, 20, 215-228.

Wood, J. J., McLeod, B. D., Sigman, M., Hwang, W. C., & Chu, B. C. (2003). Parenting and childhood anxiety: Theory, empirical findings, and future directions. *Journal of Child Psychology and Psychiatry*, 44, 134-151.

Yang, B., &Clum, G. A. (1996). Effects of early negative life experiences on cognitive functioning and risk for suicide: a review.*Clinical Psychology Review*, 16, 177-195.

Yates, T. M. (2004). The developmental psychopathology of self-injurious behavior: Compensatory regulation in posttraumatic adaptation. *Clinical Psychology Review*, 24, 35-74.

Zucker, R. A. (2006). Alcohol use and alcohol use disorders: A developmental-biopsychosocial system formulation covering the life course. In D. Cicchetti, & D. J. Cohen (Eds.), Developmental psychopathology: Risk, disorder and adaptation (pp. 620-656). New York: Wiley.

Zucker, R. A., Donovan, J. E., Masten, A. S., Mattson, M. E., & Moss, H. B. (2008). Early developmental processes and the continuity of risk for underage drinking and problem drinking. *Pediatrics*, 121, Suppl. 4, 252-272.

In: Child Abuse   ISBN: 978-1-62257-113-0
Editors: Raymond A. Turner and Henry O. Rogers   © 2012 Nova Science Publishers, Inc.

Chapter 7

CHILDHOOD SEXUAL ABUSE AND BORDERLINE PERSONALITY DISORDER

Randy A. Sansone[1] and Lori A. Sansone

Departments of Psychiatry and Internal Medicine at
Wright State University School of Medicine in Dayton, Ohio, US

ABSTRACT

In this chapter, we discuss the relationship between childhood sexual abuse and borderline personality disorder (BPD). We begin by presenting an overview of BPD, including the epidemiology, working definition of the disorder, diagnostic approaches, treatment strategies, and outcome. We next discuss the difficulties in assessing trauma in clinical populations, regardless of the individual's Axis II diagnosis. We then review the literature regarding the role of sexual abuse in BPD, which is generally conceptualized as one of several contributory variables to the development of the disorder. We conclude this chapter by integrating childhood sexual abuse into the other known causal factors for BPD.

INTRODUCTION

Many clinicians and investigators view borderline personality disorder (BPD) as a trauma-based syndrome, and identify sexual abuse as a contributory factor to its development. In this chapter, we will overview the clinical and diagnostic features of this intriguing Axis II disorder, describe the potential limitations of childhood trauma assessment, examine the empirical role of sexual abuse in relationship to BPD, and integrate the role of sexual abuse into the general etiological fabric of BPD.

---

[1] Corresponding author: Randy A. Sansone, M.D., 2115 Leiter Road, Miamisburg, Ohio, 45342. Telephone: 937-384-6850. FAX: 937-384-6938. E-mail: Randy.sansone@khnetwork.org.

AN OVERVIEW OF BPD

The "Borderline" Designation

The term *BPD* was first broached during the 1930s. During this era, mental health clinicians recognized a unique group of psychiatric patients who defied diagnostic classification, which at the time heavily relied on an initial symptom division between neurosis and psychosis. Oddly, these patients manifested multiple neurotic features but also periodically experienced transient psychosis. Because this patient cohort appeared to be sandwiched between the two general diagnostic categories of the era, they were perceived as "on the border" of neurosis and psychosis, or "borderline" (Stern, 1938).

Epidemiology of BPD

General US Population

Compared with other types of personality disorders, BPD is relatively common. To provide some context for this impression, in the US general population, the prevalence of all types of personality disorders is between 5% and 10% (Ellison and Shader, 2003). According to the *Diagnostic and Statistical Manual of Mental Disorders, 4th Edition, Text Revision* (*DSM-IV-TR*; American Psychiatric Association, 2000), the community prevalence of BPD is around 2%, although individuals with characteristics, traits, or subthreshold syndromes may account for up to 10% of the population (Stone, 1986).

Psychiatric Settings

Compared to individuals with other types of psychiatric disorders, those with BPD are seemingly over-represented in psychiatric settings (Quigley, 2005), most likely because of their engagement in chronic self-harm behavior. Indeed, approximately 25% of psychiatric inpatients as well as nearly 30% of outpatients are diagnosed with BPD (American Psychiatric Association, 2000; Widiger and Rogers, 1989). With regard to BPD *symptomatology*, which includes traits and subclinical or subthreshold syndromes, we have found prevalence rates of 50% and 22% among psychiatric inpatients and outpatients, respectively (Sansone, Rytwinski, and Gaither, 2003; Sansone, Songer, and Gaither, 2001).

Very little empirical work has been done in the area of prevalence rates in US subcultures. However, in a psychiatric sample, Chavira et al. (2003) found a higher prevalence rate of BPD among Hispanics, compared with Whites or Blacks.

Gender Patterns and Styles

According to the *DSM-IV-TR*, BPD is more commonly encountered in women than men. However, this seeming disparity may be an illusion and accounted for by sampling bias (Skodol and Bender, 2003). To explain this phenomenon, the two genders appear to manifest different types of BPD symptoms, which result in different types of social dispositions. Explicitly, women with BPD tend to have histrionic personality features, engage in self-directed self-harm behavior (e.g., self-cutting), and carry diagnoses of eating disorders and post-traumatic stress disorder (D. M. Johnson et al., 2003). Therefore, they tend to be treated in psychiatric settings where epidemiological studies frequently take place. Men, on the other hand, tend to manifest antisocial personality features, engage in externally directed self-harm behavior (e.g., bar fights), and have comorbid diagnoses of substance abuse (D. M. Johnson et al.; Zanarini et al., 1998). Therefore, a number of males with this disorder eventually end up in police custody and ultimately in prison settings, thereby eluding detection in epidemiological studies.

A Working Definition of BPD

Understandably, the borderline concept initially appears diffuse and ill-defined because of (a) the broad functional levels of affected patients (i.e., low versus high functioning), (b) the broad array of accompanying psychiatric symptoms, which are represented by high frequencies of comorbid Axis I and II diagnoses, and (c) the polythetic nature of the diagnostic criteria in the *DSM-IV-TR* (i.e., only five of nine criteria are required for diagnosis, resulting in various diagnostic permutations and clinical presentations; Jackson and Jovev, 2006).

However, regardless of the countless clinical variations in the presentation of this disorder, all affected individuals share three common clinical characteristics: (a) a transiently intact social façade or veneer, which tends to abruptly erode under stress; (b) chronic difficulties with self-regulation (e.g., eating disorders, substance abuse); and (c) chronic self-harm behavior. These features are consistently present in afflicted individuals and function as a practical working definition of BPD.

The Diagnosis of BPD

The DSM

While there are a number of diagnostic approaches to BPD, the criteria that are listed in the *DSM-IV-TR* remain the authoritative standard. These criteria are: (a) frantic efforts to avoid abandonment; (b) a history of unstable and intense relationships with others; (c) identity disturbance; (d) impulsivity in at least two functional areas such as spending, sex, substance use, eating, or driving; (e) recurrent suicidal threats or behaviors as well as self-mutilation; (f) affective instability with marked reactivity of mood; (g) chronic feelings of emptiness; (h) inappropriate and intense anger or difficulty controlling anger; and (i) transient stress-induced paranoid ideation or severe dissociative symptoms. As noted previously, five of the preceding nine criteria are required for the diagnosis of BPD.

Non-DSM Diagnostic Approaches

In addition to the *DSM* criteria, there are a number of available structured and semi-structured interviews for the diagnosis of BPD. Examples of these include the Diagnostic Interview for Borderlines-Revised (Zanarini, Gunderson, Frankenburg, and Chauncey, 1989), the Personality Disorder Examination (Loranger, 1988), the Structured Clinical Interview for DSM-III-R Personality Disorders (Spitzer, Williams, Gibbon, and First, 1990), and the

Diagnostic Interview for DSM-IV Personality Disorders (Zanarini, Frankenburg, Sickel, and Yong, 1996).

There are also various self-report measures for the diagnosis of BPD such as the Self-Harm Inventory (Sansone, Wiederman, and Sansone, 1998), the borderline personality scale of the Personality Diagnostic Questionaire-4 (Hyler, 1994), and the McLean Screening Inventory for Borderline Personality Disorder (Zanarini et al., 2003).

The selection of a particular approach or measure is typically based upon the level of diagnostic rigor required (i.e., research versus clinical purposes), ease of administration (i.e., interviews versus self-report measures), cost, and the suspected prevalence of BPD within a given clinical subpopulation (i.e., for populations with suspected high prevalence rates, such as in those with substance abuse and eating disorders, the clinician may want a rapid screening method for large numbers of patients).

The Treatment of BPD

According to the Practice Guideline for the Treatment of Patients with Borderline Personality Disorder (American Psychiatric Association, 2001), "The primary treatment for borderline personality disorder is psychotherapy..." (p. 4). Various psychotherapy approaches have been utilized and most consist of eclectic combinations of psychodynamic, interpersonal, and cognitive-behavioral therapies as well as contracting strategies, psychoeducation, and skills training (Sansone and Sansone, 2006). Several of these treatment components are available as packaged, intensive, time-limited, and highly structured programs that have predominant cognitive-behavioral components. Examples of these programs are Dialectical Behavior Therapy (DBT) (Linehan, 1993) and Systems Training for Emotional Predictability and Problem Solving (STEPPS) (Blum, Pfohl, St. John, Monahan, and Black, 2002). We are not aware of any totally manualized or computer-based approaches to the treatment of BPD.

Clinical Outcomes in BPD

There appear to be three general clinical outcomes for individuals suffering from BPD: (a) significant and gradual improvement over time in the overall personality pathology, which the majority experience (Zanarini, Frankenburg, Hennen, Reich, and Silk, 2006; Zanarini, Frankenburg, Hennen, and Silk, 2003); (b) ongoing and intense personality disorder symptoms, at least up to age 60, which seem to affect a minority (Sansone, Gaither, and Songer, 2002); and (c) suicide, which affects up to 10% of individuals (Paris, 2002).

Studies indicate that poor prognostic outcomes in patients with BPD are associated with histories of multiple suicide attempts (Mehlum, Friis, Vaglum, and Karterud, 1994), comorbid personality pathology (Links, Heslegrave, and van Reekum, 1998), high levels of impulsivity (Links, Heslegrave, and van Reekum, 1999), parental cruelty (Stone, 1993), and substance abuse (Zanarini, Frankenburg, Hennen, Reich, and Silk, 2004).

Childhood Sexual Abuse and Difficulties with Assessment

Regardless of the patient's Axis II diagnosis in adulthood (i.e., whether BPD or not), the accurate assessment of sexual abuse in childhood is an extremely challenging clinical undertaking. First, the abuse may have occurred during a time when the child was at a preverbal level of development. During this developmental period, infants and toddlers literally lack the cognitive, verbal, and psychological skills to interpret and intellectually encode an abuse experience. However, under such circumstances, there is likely to be emotional encoding of the trauma.

Second, young children have fairly limited and unsophisticated psychological defenses. As a result, in response to stress, they may employ somewhat primitive defenses, which tend to mirror their simplistic thought processes and absolutist (i.e., black/white) cognitive style. These defenses typically include: (a) repression (i.e., the *unconscious* relegation of unacceptable thoughts and feelings to the unconscious); (b) suppression (i.e., the *conscious* relegation of unacceptable thoughts and feelings to the unconscious); and (c) denial (i.e., the intentful disavowal of past experiences).

Third, patients may misinterpret the abuse experience (i.e., normalize the events or assume personal responsibility). For example, in the case of sexual abuse, the victim may have experienced some level of physical pleasure and/or benefited from a favored status in the family household. Some victims perceive this positive aspect of the experience as evidence that they were not actually "abused." Other patients may be too embarrassed by the experience to acknowledge or report the abuse, fearing its potential implications and/or subsequent meaning (e.g., a young male who is subjected to sexual abuse from an older male and is subsequently worried about sexual orientation).

To summarize, while the actual assessment of childhood sexual abuse is beyond the scope of this chapter, it is important to recognize the inherent difficulties in accessing traumatic histories from childhood victims, regardless of the measure used or the presence or not of an Axis II diagnosis. Repression, suppression, denial, misinterpretation, and embarrassment are all factors that may obscure the actual childhood events.

Childhood Sexual Abuse and BPD

As we noted earlier in this chapter, BPD is perceived by many clinicians and investigators as a trauma-based syndrome—one that ultimately has a profound effect upon the developing personalities of its victims. The effects of trauma may impair the development of affective and behavioral regulation, the ability to successfully achieve intimacy with other human beings, appropriate boundaries with others, and a healthy self-concept as well as precipitate a host of other developmental breaches.

In examining various trauma variables, childhood sexual abuse has historically and empirically been consistently identified as a non-specific risk factor for the development of BPD. In summarizing the research literature up through the mid 1990s, Pfeifer-Tarlowski (1997) concluded that *there appears to be a relationship between childhood sexual abuse and borderline-like symptoms* in adulthood.

Even in the most recent empirical literature, childhood sexual abuse continues to demonstrate significant correlations with BPD symptomatology in adulthood (e.g., Bandelow et al., 2005; Bradley, Jenei, and Westen, 2005; Chaudhry, 2005; Goodman and Yehuda, 2002; Hexel, Wiesnagrotzki, and Sonneck, 2004; Katerndahl, Burge, and Kellogg, 2005; Mclean, 2001). As an example, in a large study of a nonclinical population of over 5,000 18-year-olds, Trull (2001a) confirmed a relationship between childhood physical and sexual abuses, and BPD psychopathology.

However, like the historical literature in this area, not *all* recent studies support a relationship between childhood sexual abuse and the development of BPD (e.g., Bierer et al., 2003; Trull, 2001b). This seeming contradiction may be explained by the high rates of sexual abuse in the general population. Specifically, given that childhood sexual abuse is unfortunately common in the general population, comparing nonclinical subjects with BPD subjects may not evidence statistical differences, unless the BPD population under study manifests very extreme or severe personality psychopathology (i.e., individuals from inpatient populations, extremely self-harming individuals, those with frequent suicide attempts).

Even if there were *no* statistical differences between those with and without BPD, this mathematical finding would not necessarily exclude childhood sexual abuse as a contributory factor to BPD. This is because we know that, from a psychological perspective, some individuals fare reasonably well in the aftermath of trauma while others become psychologically dysfunctional. These varying outcomes are likely to be explained by the *context* of the childhood sexual abuse.

What contextual factors might affect outcome? Hyde and Kaufman (1984) describe several influential factors that may affect psychological outcomes following sexual abuse, such as the age at which the molestation first began, the frequency and duration of the abuse, the relationship of the perpetrator to the victim, the methods used to contain the "secret," the degree of isolation of the "secret," and the manner in which the exposure of the secret is handled. Additional factors may include a greater number of perpetrators, the lack of parental/family support, a threat to one's life or the life of a family member, and/or higher levels of aggression in conjunction with the sexual abuse (Sansone and Sansone, in press). We also suspect that the general psychological constitutions of the victims confer varying levels of resilience in the face of adversity.

OTHER TYPES OF CHILDHOOD ABUSES AND BPD

We have emphasized the meaningful contributory role of sexual abuse to the development of BPD. However, in addition to sexual abuse, other childhood trauma variables appear to contribute to BPD as well, including physical abuse and emotional abuses.

Childhood Emotional Abuse

While few in number, several recent studies have examined the relationship between emotional abuse in childhood and BPD in adulthood. In nonclinical populations, J. G. Johnson et al. (2001) found that verbal abuse was associated with a 3-fold risk of having

BPD. In the Collaborative Longitudinal Personality Disorders Study, Battle et al. (2004) found that both emotional and verbal abuses in childhood were associated with BPD.

Childhood Physical Abuse

Compared with other Axis II disorders, Golier et al. (2003) and Paris, Zweig-Frank, and Guzder (1994) found that those with BPD have a greater frequency of childhood physical abuse.

Combinations of Childhood Abuses

Contemporary investigators have recently examined the role of multiple types of abuses in childhood and their correlation with BPD symptoms in adulthood. In this regard, Renneberg, Wcibb, Under, Fiedler, and Brunner (2003) found that 87% of female psychiatric inpatients with BPD reported various traumatic childhood experiences (i.e., sexual and physical abuses). In an inpatient psychiatric sample, Zanarini, Williams, et al. (1997) found that, compared to those without the disorder, those with BPD reported significantly more emotional and physical abuses by a caretaker during childhood. In another inpatient sample, Zanarini, Dubo, Lewis, and Williams (1997) found that over 90% of the patients with BPD reported childhood abuse and neglect, 80% emotional or verbal abuse, and 60% physical and sexual abuses. In a sample of hospitalized adolescent females, Atlas (1995) found that those with early histories of physical and/or sexual abuse were significantly more likely to be diagnosed with BPD.

In addition to the preceding findings from psychiatric inpatient samples, several investigators have examined the relationship between childhood adversity and BPD symptoms in patients with various types of substance abuse. Ellason, Ross, Sainton, and Mayran (1996) examined inpatient substance abusers and found that, compared to those without histories of physical and/or sexual abuse, those with such histories had higher rates of BPD. In another sample of patients with substance abuse diagnoses, Ruggiero (1996) found that both physical and emotional abuses had diffuse relationships with most of the Axis II disorders under study, including BPD.

Finally, Bierer et al. (2003) examined a sample of 182 outpatients with various personality disorders. They found that global trauma severity was predictive of Cluster B diagnoses (i.e., in the *DSM-IV-TR*, those Axis II disorders characterized by dramatic, emotional, and/or erratic clinical features), particularly borderline and antisocial personality disorders.

In summary, these data indicate that childhood sexual abuse is but one of various types of abuses that may contribute to BPD. Other types include emotional and physical abuses. In addition, it appears that combinations of childhood abuse are apparent in many cases. The presence of various forms of childhood abuses in patients with BPD may suggest that: (a) the combination of abuse types are particularly predisposing to BPD and/or (b) a statistical "clustering" phenomenon is occurring. With regard to the latter, from a statistical perspective, clustering occurs when multiple variables are highly inter-related to each other. For example, in the case of BPD, it is unlikely that a single form of childhood abuse occurs in isolation from the others—i.e., various types naturally occur together (e.g., can one be physically abused without experiencing emotional abuse, as well?). Therefore, these types of variables are likely to cluster.

Non-Traumatic Pathways to BPD

Throughout this chapter, we have emphasized the role of childhood sexual abuse and other types of childhood trauma in the development of BPD. However, there may be other pathways to BPD that do not entail malignant adversity in childhood. According to Graybar and Boutilier (2002), such cases may develop from high-risk genetics and/or inherited temperaments, affective dysfunction, neurological deficits, and emotionality—all in the absence of childhood trauma. Many of these adjunctive predisposing factors will be discussed in the next section.

The only caveat we offer to the proposal by Graybar and Boutilier is the role of impaired childhood recollections. What if it only *appears* that some victims do not have trauma histories because of their well-honed psychological defenses, which may effectively and totally obscure the recollection of these types of events?

OTHER CONTRIBUTORY FACTORS TO BPD

While trauma appears to play a significant role in the majority of cases (Zanarini, Dubo, et al., 1997), other factors may also contribute to the development of BPD (i.e., BPD is a multi-determined disorder). These factors include: (a) genetic predisposition (Skodol et al., 2002); (b) parental psychopathology; and (c) family dysfunction.

Genetic Predisposition

Genetics appear to play a role in the development of BPD. The possibility of genetic predisposition does not mean that the personality disorder, itself, is directly inherited. Rather, investigators (Skodol et al., 2002) suggest that *temperamental characteristics* may be inherited, such as a genetic impairment in the ability to self-regulate or a tendency towards affective lability. Under conducive circumstances, these temperamental characteristics might then heighten the overall risk for developing BPD.

Parental Psychopathology

With regard to parental psychopathology, researchers describe a number of unhealthy patterns. These include parental neglect and a lack of empathy (Yatsko, 1996), "biparental failure" (Zanarini et al., 2000), and perceived low parental empathy and support (Fruzzetti, Shenk, and Hoffman, 2005). The overall theme of these studies is ineffectual parenting

(Norden, Klein, Donaldson, Pepper, and Klein, 1995), although Paris and Zweig-Frank (1997) also describe separation from or loss of parents in early life.

Family Dysfunction

In terms of family psychopathology, Fruzzeti et al. (2005) describe invalidating, conflictual, negative, and/or critical family interactions. In keeping with the preceding findings, Hogue (1999) emphasizes the overall *level* of family dysfunction.

Triggering Events

One final phenomenon may be of relevance in the ultimate manifestation of BPD symptoms—the role of triggering events. Zanarini and Frankenburg (1997) describe these events as acute psychosocial stressors that result in the abrupt precipitation and/or acute onset of BPD symptoms. We are not aware of extensive data regarding how frequently these triggering events occur among patients or the nature of the events, themselves. However, they are likely to be acute catalysts for chemical reactions that have been developing since childhood.

CONCLUSION

BPD is an insidious psychiatric disorder that, in the majority of cases, appears to have its primal roots in childhood. The childhoods of these individuals seem to be riddled with maltreatment, adversity, and neglect. Sexual abuse is common as well as other forms of abuse including emotional and physical abuses. While there may be non-traumatic pathways to BPD, this seems infrequent, particularly given what we know about the defensive operations of children under stress and their ability to "erase" the violations they incur. In addition to childhood trauma, other priming substrates appear to be parental psychopathology and dysfunctional family environments. While at first glance, these phenomena may appear independent of each other, in practical terms, these contributory variables are likely to be highly inter-related. In other words, bad genes are likely to be associated with psychologically impaired parents who, in turn, propagate abusive experiences upon their young charges, who have no options but to exist in these chaotic households. Are there individuals with BPD who do not come from such backgrounds? If so, they are very infrequent in psychiatric treatment settings.

REFERENCES

American Psychiatric Association. (2000). *Diagnostic and statistical manual of mental disorders, 4th edition, text revision.* Washington, DC: American Psychiatric Press.

American Psychiatric Association. (2001). Practice guideline for the treatment of patients with borderline personality disorder. *American Journal of Psychiatry*, *158*, S1-52.

Atlas, J. A. (1995). Association between history of abuse and borderline personality disorder for hospitalized adolescent girls. *Psychological Reports*, *77*, 1346.

Bandelow, B., Krause, J., Wedekind, D., Broocks, A., Hajak, G., and Ruther, E. (2005). Early traumatic life events, parental attitudes, family history, and birth risk factors in patients with borderline personality disorder and healthy controls. *Psychiatry Research*, *134*, 169-179.

Battle, C. L., Shea, M. T., Johnson, D. M., Yen, S., Zlotnick, C., Zanarini, M. C., et al. (2004). Childhood maltreatment associated with personality disorders: Findings from the Collaborative Longitudinal Personality Disorders Study. *Journal of Personality Disorders*, *18*, 193-211.

Bierer, L. M., Yehuda, R., Schmeidler, J., Mitropoulou, V., New, A. S., Silverman, J. M., et al. (2003). Abuse and neglect in childhood: Relationship to personality disorder diagnoses. *CNS Spectrums*, *8*, 737-740, 749-754.

Blum, N., Pfohl, B., St. John, D., Monahan, P., and Black, D. W. (2002). STEPPS: A cognitive-behavioral systems-based group treatment for outpatients with borderline personality—A preliminary report. *Comprehensive Psychiatry*, *43*, 301-310.

Bradley, R., Jenei, J., and Westen, D. (2005). Etiology of borderline personality disorder: Disentangling the contributions of intercorrelated antecedents. *Journal of Nervous and Mental Disease*, *193*, 24-31.

Chaudhry, B. R. (2005). Psychosocial risk factors associated with the development of borderline personality features. *Dissertation Abstracts International*, *65*, 6700B.

Chavira, D. A., Grilo, C. M., Shea, M. T., Yen, S., Gunderson, J. G., Morey, L. C., et al. (2003). Ethnicity and four personality disorders. *Comprehensive Psychiatry*, *44*, 483-491.

Ellason, J. W., Ross, C. A., Sainton, K., and Mayran, L. W. (1996). *Bulletin of the Menninger Clinic*, *60*, 39-51.

Ellison, J. M., and Shader, R. I. (2003). Pharmacologic treatment of personality disorders: A dimensional approach. In R. I. Shader (Ed.), *Manual of psychiatric therapeutics* (pp. 169-183). Philadelphia: Lippincott, Williams, and Wilkins.

Fruzzetti, A. E., Shenk, C., and Hoffman, P. D. (2005). Family interaction and the development of borderline personality disorder: A transactional model. *Development and Psychopathology*, *17*, 1007-1030.

Golier, J., Yehuda, R., Bierer, L. M., Mitropoulou, V., New, A. S., Schmeidler, J., et al. (2003). The relationship of borderline personality disorder to posttraumatic stress disorder and traumatic events. *American Journal of Psychiatry*, *160*, 2018-2024.

Goodman, M., and Yehuda, R. (2002). The relationship between psychological trauma and borderline personality disorder. *Psychiatric Annals*, *32*, 337-345.

Graybar, S. R., and Boutilier, L. R. (2002). Nontraumatic pathways to borderline personality disorder. *Psychotherapy: Theory, Research, Practice, Training*, *39*, 152-162.

Hexel, M., Wiesnagrotzki, S., and Sonneck, G. (2004). Psychiatric disorders and traumatic life events. *German Journal of Psychiatry*, *7*, 28-34.

Hogue, S. L. (1999). Relationship between family of origin history and personality pathology. *Dissertation Abstracts International*, *59*, 6067B.

Hyde, M. L., and Kaufman, P. A. (1984). Women molested as children: Therapeutic and legal issues in civil actions. *American Journal of Forensic Psychiatry*, *5*, 147-157.

Hyler, S. E. (1994). *Personality Diagnostic Questionniare-4*. New York: Author.

Jackson, H. J., and Jovev, M. (2006). Personality disorder constructs and conceptualizations. In R. A. Sansone and J. L. Levitt (Eds.), *Personality disorders and eating disorders: Exploring the frontier* (3-20). New York: Routledge.

Johnson, D. M., Shea, M. T., Yen, S., Battle, C. L., Zlotnick, C., Sanislow, C. A., et al. (2003). Gender differences in borderline personality disorder: Findings from the Collaborative Longitudinal Personality Disorders Study. *Comprehensive Psychiatry*, *44*, 284-292.

Johnson, J. G., Cohen, P., Smailes, E. M., Skodol, A. E., Brown, J., and Oldham, J. M. (2001). Childhood verbal abuse and risk for personality disorders during adolescence and early adulthood. *Comprehensive Psychiatry*, *42*, 16-23.

Katerndahl, D., Burge, S., and Kellogg, N. (2005). Predictors of development of adult psychopathology in female victims of childhood sexual abuse. *Journal of Nervous and Mental Disease*, *193*, 258-264.

Linehan, M. M. (1993). *Cognitive-behavioral treatment of borderline personality disorder*. New York: Guilford.

Links, P. S., Heslegrave, R., and van Reekum, R. (1998). Prospective follow-up study of borderline personality disorder: Prognosis, prediction of outcome, and Axis II comorbidity. *Canadian Journal of Psychiatry*, *43*, 265-270.

Links, P. S., Heslegrave, R., and van Reekum, R. (1999). Impulsivity: Core aspect of borderline personality disorder. *Journal of Personality Disorders*, *13*, 1-9.

Loranger, A. W. (1988). *Personality Disorder Examination Manual*. Yonkers, New York: DV Communications.

Mclean, L. M. (2001). The relationship between early childhood sexual abuse and the adult diagnoses of borderline personality disorder and complex posttraumatic stress disorder: Diagnostic implications. *Dissertation Abstracts International*, *62*, 2069B.

Mehlum, L., Friis, S., Vaglum, P., and Karterud, S. (1994). The longitudinal pattern of suicidal behaviour in borderline personality disorder: A prospective follow-up study. *Acta Psychiatrica Scandanavica*, *90*, 124-130.

Norden, K. A., Klein, D. N., Donaldson, S. K., Pepper, C. M., and Klein, L. M. (1995). Reports of the early home environment in DSM-III-R personality disorders. *Journal of Personality Disorders*, *9*, 213-223.

Paris, J. (2002). Implications of long-term outcome research for the management of patients with borderline personality disorder. *Harvard Review of Psychiatry*, *10*, 315-323.

Paris, J., and Zweig-Frank, H. (1997). Parameters of childhood sexual abuse in female patients. In M. C. Zanarini (Ed.), *Role of sexual abuse in the etiology of borderline personality disorder* (pp. 15-28). Washington, DC: American Psychiatric Association.

Paris, J., Zweig-Frank, H., and Guzder, J. (1994). Psychological risk factors for borderline personality disorder in female patients. *Comprehensive Psychiatry*, *35*, 301-305.

Pfeifer-Tarkowski, V. J. (1997). The role of childhood sexual abuse and the development of borderline personality disorder: A critical review. *Dissertation Abstracts International*, *57*, 4720B.

Quigley, B. D. (2005). Diagnostic relapse in borderline personality: Risk and protective factors. *Dissertation Abstracts International*, *65*, 3721B.

Renneberg, B., Weibb, M., Unger, J., Fiedler, P., and Brunner, R. (2003). Etiological factors in borderline personality disorder. *Verhaltenstherapie and Verhaltensmedizin, 24*, 347-364.

Ruggiero, J. S. (1996). The personality sequelae of child maltreatment in drug and alcohol dependent male veterans. *Dissertation Abstracts International, 56*, 4592B.

Sansone, R. A., Gaither, G. A., and Songer, D. A. (2002). Self-harm behaviors across the life cycle: A pilot study of inpatients with borderline personality disorder. *Comprehensive Psychiatry, 43*, 215-218.

Sansone, R. A., Rytwinski, D., and Gaither, G. A. (2003). Borderline personality and psychotropic medication prescription in an outpatient psychiatry clinic. *Comprehensive Psychiatry, 44*, 454-458.

Sansone, R. A., and Sansone, L. A. (2006). Borderline personality and eating disorders : An eclectic approach to treatment. In R. A. Sansone and J. L. Levitt (Eds.), *Personality disorders and eating disorders: Exploring the frontier* (197-212). New York: Routledge.

Sansone, R. A., and Sansone, L. A. (in press). *Borderline personality in the medical setting: Unmasking and managing the difficult patient.* Hauppauge, NY: Nova Science Publishers.

Sansone, R. A., Songer, D. A., and Gaither, G. A. (2001). Diagnostic approaches to borderline personality and their relationship to self-harm behavior. *International Journal of Psychiatry in Clinical Practice, 5*, 273-277.

Sansone, R. A., Wiederman, M. W., and Sansone, L. A. (1998). The Self-Harm Inventory (SHI): Development of a scale for identifying self-destructive behaviors and borderline personality disorder. *Journal of Clinical Psychology, 54*, 973-983.

Skodol, A. E., and Bender, D. S. (2003). Why are women diagnosed borderline more than men? *Psychiatric Quarterly, 74*, 349-360.

Skodol, A. E., Siever, L. J., Livesley, W. J., Gunderson, J. G., Pfohl, B., and Widiger, T. A. (2002). The borderline diagnosis II: Biology, genetics, and clinical course. *Biological Psychiatry, 51*, 951-963.

Spitzer, R. L., Williams, J. B. W., Gibbon, M., and First, M. B. (1990). *Structured Clinical Interview for DSM-III-R Personality Disorders (SCID-II).* Washington, DC: American Psychiatric Press.

Stern, A. (1938). Psychoanalytic investigation of therapy in the borderline group of neuroses. *Psychoanalytic Quarterly, 7*, 467-489.

Stone, M. H. (1986). Borderline personality disorder. In R. Michels and J. O. Cavenar (Eds.), *Psychiatry, 2nd edition* (pp. 1-15). Philadelphia: Lippincott.

Stone, M. H. (1993). Long-term outcome in personality disorders. *British Journal of Psychiatry, 162*, 299-313.

Trull, T. J. (2001a). Structural relations between borderline personality disorder features and putative etiological correlates. *Journal of Abnormal Psychology, 110*, 471-481.

Trull, T. J. (2001b). Relationships of borderline features to parental mental illness, childhood abuse, Axis I disorder, and current functioning. *Journal of Personality Disorders, 15*, 19-32.

Widiger, T. A., and Rogers, J. H. (1989). Prevalence and comorbidity of personality disorders. *Psychiatric Annals, 19*, 132-136.

Yatsko, C. K. (1996). Etiological theories of borderline personality disorder: A comparative multivariate study. *Dissertation Abstracts International, 56*, 4628B.

Zanarini, M. C., Dubo, E. D., Lewis, R. E., and Williams, A. A. (1997). Childhood factors associated with the development of borderline personality disorder. In M. C. Zanarini (Ed.), *Role of sexual abuse in the etiology of borderline personality disorder* (pp. 29-44). Washington, DC: American Psychiatric Press.

Zanarini, M. C., and Frankenburg, F. R. (1997). Pathways to the development of borderline personality disorder. *Journal of Personality Disorders, 11*, 93-104.

Zanarini, M. C., Frankenburg, F. R., Dubo, E. D., Sickel, A. E., Trikha, A., Levin, A., et al. (1998). Axis II comorbidity of borderline personality disorder. *Comprehensive Psychiatry, 39*, 296-302.

Zanarini, M. C., Frankenburg, F. R., Hennen, J., Reich, D. B., and Silk, K. R. (2004). Axis I comorbidity in patients with borderline personality disorder: 6-year follow-up and prediction of time to remission. *American Journal of Psychiatry, 161*, 2108-2114.

Zanarini, M. C., Frankenburg, F. R., Hennen, J., Reich, D. B., and Silk, K. R. (2006). Prediction of the 10-year course of borderline personality disorder. *American Journal of Psychiatry, 163*, 827-832.

Zanarini, M. C., Frankenburg, F. R., Hennen, J., and Silk, K. R. (2003). The longitudinal course of borderline psychopathology: 6-year prospective follow-up of the phenomenology of borderline personality disorder. *American Journal of Psychiatry, 160*, 274-283.

Zanarini, M. C., Frankenburg, F. R., Reich, D. B., Marino, M. F., Lewis, R. E., Williams, A. A., et al. (2000). Biparental failure in the childhood experiences of borderline patients. *Journal of Personality Disorders, 14*, 264-273.

Zanarini, M. C., Frankenburg, F. R., Sickel, A. E., and Yong, L. (1996). *The Diagnostic Interview for DSM-IV Personality Disorders (DIPD-IV)*. Belmont, MA: Authors.

Zanarini, M. C., Gunderson, J. G., Frankenburg, F. R., and Chauncey, D. L. (1989). The revised Diagnostic Interview for Borderlines: Discriminating BPD from other Axis II disorders. *Journal of Personality Disorders, 3*, 10-18.

Zanarini, M. C., Vujanovic, A. A., Parachini, E. A., Boulanger, J. L., Frankenburg, F. R., and Hennen, J. (2003). A screening measure for BPD: The McLean Screening Instrument for Borderline Personality Disorder (MSI-BPD). *Journal of Personality Disorders, 17*, 568-573.

Zanarini, M. C., Williams, A. A., Lewis, R. E., Reich, R. B., Vera, S. C., Marino, M. F., et al. (1997). Reported pathological childhood experiences associated with the development of borderline personality disorder. *American Journal of Psychiatry, 154*, 1101-1106.

INDEX

A

abusive, 141
academic problems, 11
access, 58, 72, 100
accessibility, 79
accounting, 14, 112
acid, 36, 37
acquaintance, 62
acute, 141
adaptation, 25, 109, 119, 132
adaptive functioning, 5
adjustment, 13, 16, 20, 23, 97, 98, 106, 107, 110, 116, 126
Administration for Children and Families, 2, 23
adolescence, 20, 67, 139, 143
adolescents, viii, 4, 7, 10, 21, 50, 64, 71, 72, 75, 76, 77, 78, 79, 80, 81, 83, 97, 121, 123, 126, 128
adulthood, 4, 7, 11, 12, 17, 20, 21, 24, 25, 107, 113, 115, 119, 123, 125, 129, 137, 138, 139, 143
adults, 10, 11, 16, 28, 34, 35, 37, 54, 59, 60, 72, 113, 125
adverse effects, 5, 100, 107
advocacy, 64
African-American, 24
age, 2, 3, 5, 8, 9, 10, 11, 14, 17, 29, 39, 40, 42, 58, 60, 63, 65, 72, 76, 77, 78, 105, 106, 136, 138
agencies, 2, 64
aggregation, 115
aggression, 15, 21, 24, 25, 108, 116, 122, 138
aggressiveness, 7
AIDS, 69
alcohol, 124, 131, 144
alcohol dependence, 123, 126, 130
alcohol problems, 104, 105, 128
alcohol use, 4, 7, 122, 123, 125, 128, 129, 130, 132
alcoholism, 117, 126, 127, 128
alternative causes, 45

ambiguous events, 108
American Psychiatric Association, 134, 136, 141, 142, 143
American Psychological Association, 128
amygdala, 107
anemia, 48
anger, 4, 7, 8, 23, 95, 103, 135
antecedents, 142
antisocial personality, 107, 109, 130, 135, 139
antisocial personality disorder, 130, 139
anxiety, 7, 11, 15, 86, 101, 102, 103, 105, 107, 108, 109, 110, 111, 112, 113, 114, 115, 116, 117, 118, 120, 121, 122, 123, 124, 125, 127, 128, 129, 132
anxiety disorder, 102, 107, 108, 109, 111, 112, 115, 117, 118, 122, 125, 127
apathy, 7
appointments, 76
arousal, 8, 87
ascorbic acid, 37, 48
assault, 7, 10, 12, 66, 93, 106
assessment, 19, 24, 34, 41, 49, 50, 54, 67, 74, 89, 95, 122, 133, 137
asymptomatic, 33, 34, 38, 41, 42, 44, 45
Atlas, 139, 142
attachment, 4, 15, 16, 17, 18, 22, 23, 88, 90, 95, 96, 97, 117
attachment theory, 15, 18, 88
attentional bias, 109, 121, 122
attitudes, viii, 53, 54, 66, 67, 74, 108, 116, 142
attributable fraction, 17
authorities, viii, 11, 53, 54, 55, 56, 61, 63, 64, 65
avoidance, 8, 88
awareness, ix, 85, 89, 95

B

barriers, ix, 72, 80
base, 88, 123, 133, 136, 137, 142

basic needs, 14

behavior, 7, 86, 124, 128, 134, 135, 144

behaviors, 3, 4, 11, 14, 20, 21, 68, 80, 100, 103, 104, 107, 109, 110, 111, 118, 131, 135, 144

Belgium, 71, 76

beneficial effect, 87

benign, 52

bias, 103, 109, 113, 121, 125, 134

biliary atresia, 45, 49

biochemistry, 32, 35

birth, 50, 142

black, 134, 137

blame, 73

bleeding, 28, 36, 38, 39

blood, 28, 34, 36, 37

BMI, 4, 72, 78, 79

body image, 72, 82

body mass index (BMI), 4, 72

body schema, 82

body weight, 37

bonding, 117

bone(s), vii, 6, 27, 28, 30, 31, 34, 40, 41, 42, 43, 44, 45, 46, 48, 49, 50, 51, 52, 86

bone form, 40, 48

borderline, x, 133, 134, 135, 136, 137, 139, 142, 143, 144, 145

borderline personality disorder, vii, x, 104, 128, 133, 136, 142, 143, 144, 145

boundary aware, viii, 54

BPD, x, 133, 134, 135, 136, 137, 138, 139, 140, 141, 145

brain, x, 7, 99, 107, 110

brain structure, x, 99, 107, 110

breaches, 137

breakdown, 72, 78

breast milk, 33

British, 144

brothers, 8

burn, 7

C

Ca^{2+}, 52

caesarean section, 42, 43, 46, 52

calcium, 34, 41, 52

carapace, 80

caregivers, 4, 5, 6, 11, 64

caretaker, 139

cartilage, 45

case study(s), 77, 78

catalysts, 141

causal inference, 94, 112, 114, 118

causal relationship, 100, 111, 112

causality, 112, 113

causation, 93

Central Europe, 83

central nervous system, 107

cerebral palsy, 40, 50

ceruloplasmin, 50

challenges, 55, 69, 88

chaotic, 141

chat rooms, 59

chemical, 141

chemical reactions, 141

Chicago, 52

child abuse, vii, ix, 1, 2, 4, 17, 18, 21, 22, 23, 24, 29, 39, 42, 43, 44, 45, 46, 47, 49, 50, 51, 52, 68, 69, 71, 73, 78, 86, 87, 88, 89, 90, 91, 92, 93, 94, 95, 97, 103, 106, 109, 110, 112, 113, 114, 116, 117, 118, 119, 120, 122, 127, 128

child maltreatment, vii, x, 1, 2, 5, 6, 7, 11, 13, 14, 15, 17, 18, 19, 20, 21, 22, 23, 24, 97, 100, 113, 114, 115, 117, 118, 127, 129, 144

child protection, 64, 68

child protective services, vii, 1, 89

childhood sexual abuse, x, 10, 18, 20, 22, 24, 67, 68, 69, 96, 97, 100, 112, 119, 121, 123, 124, 125, 126, 128, 129, 130, 133, 137, 138, 139, 140, 143

childrearing, 129

chromosome, 48

chronic, 134, 135

cities, viii, 53, 55

civil action, 142

classification, 82, 113, 120, 134

climate, x, 100, 116, 118

clinical, x, 133, 135, 136, 137, 139, 144

clinical problems, 75, 135

clinical symptoms, 12

clinician(s), 133, 134, 136, 137

close relationships, 88

clothing, 33

clubfoot, 52

clustering, 139

CNS, 142

coding, 28, 32, 120

cognition, 3, 129

cognitive, 122, 132, 136, 137, 142

cognitive function, 108, 132

cognitive style, 109, 120, 137

cognitive variables, 107

cognitive-behavioral therapies, 136

coherence, 76

cohort, 134

collagen, 28, 32, 33, 36, 38

college students, 96, 97

commercial, 48

communication, viii, 33, 53, 54, 57, 58, 60, 65, 67, 116
communication skills, viii, 53, 60
communication strategies, viii, 53, 57, 60, 65
community(s), 8, 12, 13, 16, 23, 25, 64, 66, 67, 68, 69, 106, 113, 123, 127, 134
comorbidity, 21, 79, 124, 128, 143, 144, 145
compilation, vii
complexity, 5
compliance, 76, 77, 78, 79, 81
complications, 3, 40, 49, 74, 76
components, 136
composition, 78
comprehension, 7
computer, 90, 94, 136
conception, 77
conceptual model, 124
conceptualization(s), 96, 143
conduct disorder, 7
confidentiality, 56
configuration, 74
confinement, 44
conflict, 88, 91, 92, 95, 114, 116, 117
confounders, x, 99, 101, 113, 114, 120
confounding variables, 112
confrontation, 62, 65
conscientiousness, 91, 94, 95
consent, 10, 64
conspiracy, 95
construction, ix, 72, 75, 78
consumption, 126
contradiction, 138
controversial, 28, 43
controversies, 68
convention, 89
conversations, viii, 53, 57, 58
cooperation, 116
coordination, 73
coping strategies, 109, 110
copper, vii, 27, 37, 38, 39, 41, 44, 45, 46, 48, 49, 50
corpus callosum, 107
correlation(s), 16, 33, 90, 91, 117, 138, 139
corticotropin, 107
cost, 2, 12, 136
covering, 132
criminal behavior, 15
criminal statutes, 10
criminality, 114, 118
cross sectional study, 82
CSA, 10, 11, 12, 13, 86, 87
cues, 109
cultural differences, 8
cultural heritage, 55

culture, ix, 85, 89, 94, 95
cycles, 110
cytomegalovirus, 40

D

danger, 31, 42, 104, 109, 126
data analysis, 100
data collection, 77
decoding, 97
defects, 28
defense mechanisms, 88
defenses, 137, 140
deficiency(s), vii, viii, ix, 27, 33, 35, 36, 37, 38, 39, 41, 44, 45, 46, 47, 48, 49, 71, 73, 78, 80, 81, 110
deficit, 49
definition, x, 133, 135
degradation, 81
degree, 138
demographic characteristics, 12
demographic factors, 15, 16
denial, 14, 137
Department of Health and Human Services, vii, 1, 23, 24
dependent variable, 93
depression, 3, 5, 7, 8, 11, 15, 16, 86, 88, 101, 102, 103, 104, 105, 107, 108, 110, 111, 114, 115, 116, 117, 118, 120, 121, 122, 124, 125, 126, 127, 128, 129, 130, 131
depressive symptoms, 101, 108, 109, 123
depth, viii, 53, 55, 57
detection, viii, 33, 53, 64, 109, 135
determinism, 80
developing countries, 37, 72
developmental process, 87, 132
developmental psychopathology, 122, 132
diagnostic, x, 133, 134, 135, 136
Diagnostic and Statistical Manual of Mental Disorders, 98, 134
diagnostic criteria, 135
differential diagnosis, 27, 45, 46, 50
disability, 7, 9, 121
disclosure, 13, 19
discomfort, 60, 65
diseases, 48, 73
disorder, ix, x, 9, 28, 37, 39, 40, 41, 42, 44, 71, 72, 74, 75, 77, 79, 81, 102, 104, 106, 111, 114, 115, 120, 123, 124, 126, 128, 129, 130, 131, 132, 133, 135, 136, 139, 140, 141, 142, 143, 144, 145
dissatisfaction, 79
dissociation, 8, 11, 22, 101, 103
distortions, 79
distress, 9, 14, 16, 18, 88, 93, 103, 110

distribution, 35, 43, 78
District of Columbia, vii, 1
diversity, 46
division, 134
doctors, 28, 44
DOI, 67
domestic violence, 16
donations, 5
draft, 46
drawing, ix, 71, 77, 79, 81
drug abuse, 16, 111, 113, 132
drugs, 4, 102, 109, 110
DSM, 134, 135, 139, 143, 144, 145
DSM-II, 135, 143, 144
DSM-III, 135, 143, 144
DSM-IV, 134, 135, 136, 139, 145
DSM-IV-TR, 134, 135, 139
duration, 138
dysfunctional, 138, 141
dysphoria, 67

E

Eastern Europe, 55
eating, 134, 135, 136, 143, 144
eating disorders, 76, 80, 101, 103, 130, 134, 135,
    136, 143, 144
economic development, 72
economic status, 16
education, viii, 8, 54, 55, 57, 63, 65, 66, 67, 68, 95
educators, 66, 69
elaboration, 80
emergency, 28, 42
emotion, 5, 9, 21, 109
emotion regulation, 5, 9, 21
emotional, 137, 138, 139, 141
emotional disorder, 7, 11, 86
emotional well-being, 90, 91, 95
emotionality, 108, 140
empathy, 88, 140
empirical studies, 21, 126
encoding, 137
endocrine, 76
endogenous depression, 108
energy, 73, 109
engagement, 134
enlargement, 34, 38
environment, 4, 6, 14, 15, 16, 19, 72, 78, 79, 82, 87,
    88, 91, 92, 93, 109, 115, 116, 117, 118, 120, 122,
    143
environmental conditions, 110
environmental factors, ix, x, 71, 72, 77, 81, 100, 114,
    118

environments, 5, 92, 129, 141
enzyme(s), 38, 39
epidemic, 17, 47, 83
epidemiological, 135
epidemiology, x, 125, 131, 133
erythrocytes, 39
ethnic background, 8
ethnic groups, ix, 85
ethnicity, 12, 20, 22
etiology, x, 52, 74, 99, 100, 101, 107, 108, 111, 114,
    117, 118, 119, 127, 143, 145
euphoria, 109
Europe, 64
everyday life, 94
evidence, x, 4, 27, 28, 33, 34, 36, 41, 42, 43, 44, 45,
    48, 61, 63, 66, 68, 79, 86, 96, 99, 101, 103, 104,
    105, 106, 107, 108, 110, 111, 112, 114, 115, 117,
    118, 120, 122, 126, 129, 130, 137, 138
evolution, ix, 71, 75, 77, 81, 127
examinations, 44
excess body weight, 78
exclusion, 76
excretion, 37
exploitation, vii, 1, 10, 14, 86
exposure, 10, 24, 35, 46, 86, 113, 120, 138
expressiveness, 91, 92, 95
external environment, 80
externalizing behavior, 3, 19
extraversion, 87, 91, 94, 95, 96, 108

F

fabric, 133
face validity, 94
factor analysis, ix, 71, 81
failure, 140, 145
failure to thrive, 15
faith, 89
false positive, 113
family(s), vii, viii, 5, 9, 12, 13, 17, 20, 23, 24, 27, 46,
    51, 53, 55, 56, 64, 69, 91, 95, 114, 115, 118, 121,
    129, 137, 138, 140, 141, 142
family conflict, 88, 114, 116, 117
family environment, viii, ix, 12, 22, 71, 73, 78, 81,
    87, 89, 90, 91, 92, 93, 95, 97, 116, 117, 122, 141
family factors, 17, 78, 117, 118
family functioning, 114, 117, 118, 121, 123
family history, 28, 29, 44, 45, 78, 141, 142
family members, 5, 56, 89
ffamily relationships, x, 100, 116, 118
family support, 21, 64, 130, 138
family violence, 68, 114, 117, 118
fat, 72

fear(s), 7, 12, 59, 102
federal law, vii, 1
feelings, 15, 66, 74, 90, 109, 110, 135, 137
femur, 30, 31, 34, 37, 38, 40, 42
fibroblasts, 32
fights, 135
financial, 2, 3, 5, 10, 100, 107
five-factor model, 96, 127
flashbacks, 109
flaws, 113
fluid, 38
food, 5, 72, 73, 74
force, 10, 11, 31, 44, 45, 104, 105, 106, 120
Ford, 121
formation, 36, 38
formula, 39
foundations, 122
fractures, vii, 6, 27, 28, 29, 31, 32, 33, 34, 35, 36, 37,
    38, 39, 40, 41, 42, 43, 44, 45, 46, 47, 48, 49, 50,
    51, 52
fragility, 52, 80, 81
fragments, 45
funding, 100

G

gene promoter, 127
generalizability, 113
generalized anxiety disorder, 115
genes, x, 28, 32, 99, 115, 118, 120, 141
genetic components, 115
genetic predisposition, 72, 140
genetics, 97, 121, 123, 128, 140, 144
Georgia, v, 53
Germany, 64
gestation, 38, 41, 42, 43
girls, 142
glasses, 98
globalization, 95
God, 88, 96, 97
grades, 15
group treatment, 142
growth, 23, 72
guidance, x, 99, 100
guidelines, 3, 61, 68
guilt, 86, 88, 116

H

hair, 6, 39, 49, 58, 86
happiness, 93, 94, 95, 96, 97, 98
harm, 103, 112, 134, 135, 144

Harvard, 143
head injuries, 6, 25
head trauma, 6, 19
healing, ix, 31, 40, 44, 51, 85
health, 2, 3, 4, 5, 7, 8, 20, 21, 22, 24, 67, 68, 74, 101,
    120, 125, 126, 127, 128, 129, 130, 134
health care, 2, 3
health effects, 126
health problems, 5, 24, 74, 125
height, 72, 77
helplessness, 109
heritability, 115, 116, 131
heterogeneous domain, ix, 85
high school diploma, 8
high-risk, 140
hippocampus, 107
Hispanics, 134
history, x, 5, 8, 9, 13, 31, 44, 87, 89, 91, 92, 94, 95,
    100, 105, 106, 110, 115, 117, 118, 126, 127, 135,
    142
HIV, 25, 69
homeostasis, 49, 52
homicide, 6
hopelessness, 108, 124
Hops, 116, 130
hormone, 35
hospitalization, 76, 82
hospitalized, 139, 142
host, 137
hostility, 15, 103
household(s), 137, 141
housing, 16
human, 2, 18, 58, 94, 97, 107, 112, 137
human development, 112
Hunter, 13, 19
husband, 63
hygiene, 3
hyperparathyroidism, 46, 52
hypertension, 79
hypothesis, 75, 79, 80, 87, 92, 94, 107, 126

I

identification, 13, 22
identity, 80, 81, 86, 135
illicit drug use, 19, 23
illusion, 110, 134
image(s), ix, 68, 71, 72, 73, 74, 75, 77, 78, 80, 81,
    82, 83, 96
immigration, 16
impairments, 3, 15, 20
impulsive, 5
impulsivity, 107, 108, 135, 136

in utero, 32
in vitro, 52
incidence, 2, 8, 11, 17, 33, 45, 86
income, 4, 9, 13, 55, 67
independent variable, 93
indirect effect, 90, 91, 94
individuals, ix, 6, 8, 28, 33, 35, 85, 86, 88, 90, 92, 93, 94, 100, 108, 109, 110, 119, 121, 130, 134, 135, 136, 138, 141
induction, 116
inequality, 10
infancy, 33, 48, 88, 89
infants, 5, 9, 19, 25, 28, 33, 34, 35, 38, 39, 40, 41, 42, 44, 45, 46, 47, 48, 50, 51, 52, 73, 137
infection, 40
inferences, 112, 114, 118, 119
information processing, x, 99, 108, 109, 110, 124
informed consent, 86
infrastructure, 66
inheritance, 47
inherited, 140
initiation, 123
injury(s), vii, 6, 7, 13, 27, 28, 33, 37, 38, 39, 40, 42, 43, 44, 45, 46, 47, 48, 49, 50, 52, 86, 101, 102, 103, 104, 108, 110, 112, 117, 122, 126, 127
innocence, 12, 55
instability, 135
instinct, 62, 65
integration, 131
integrity, 80, 100
intelligence, 16, 101, 103
intensive care unit, 46, 50, 51
interaction, 142
interaction effect(s), 90
intercourse, 104
internal validity, 113
internalizing, 3
intervention, vii, viii, 19, 24, 53, 54, 55, 56, 63, 65, 66, 69, 127
intervention strategies, vii, viii, 53, 54, 55, 63, 65
interviews, 136
intimacy, 137
Ireland, 112, 131
iron, 39, 49
irritability, 8
isolation, 14, 77, 138, 139
issues, 4, 5, 7, 20, 22, 55, 56, 57, 59, 66, 75, 96, 120, 121, 122, 125, 126, 128, 130, 142
Italy, 99

K

Kenya, 69

knees, 35

L

labeling, 10
latency, 113
later life, 107, 123
law enforcement, 64
laws, vii, ix, 1, 3, 10, 24, 56, 85, 89, 95
lead, 4, 5, 13, 15, 39, 40, 58, 64, 75, 79, 88, 107, 109, 110
learning, 7, 15, 101, 103
learning disabilities, 7
legal issues, 142
legislation, 22, 89, 95
lesions, 42, 43, 44, 45, 46, 48, 50, 51
level of education, 78
life course, 114, 132
life experiences, 132, 144
life satisfaction, 91, 93
lifetime, 2, 123
light, 33, 88, 95
limitations, 133
literature, x, 133, 137, 138
liver transplant, 40, 49
longitudinal study, 129
long-term, 143
Louisiana, 3
love, 14, 57, 58, 97
lying, 62

M

magnesium, 46, 52
magnitude, 113, 119
major depression, 21, 115, 127, 131
major depressive disorder, 115
majority, viii, 8, 12, 13, 28, 42, 45, 53, 54, 57, 61, 91, 92, 101, 111, 112, 113, 136, 140, 141
males, 135
malignant, 140
maltreatment, vii, ix, x, 1, 2, 3, 4, 5, 6, 10, 12, 13, 14, 15, 17, 21, 22, 24, 25, 71, 85, 89, 90, 91, 92, 94, 100, 113, 114, 115, 116, 117, 118, 120, 122, 123, 124, 127, 128, 129, 131, 141, 142, 144
management, 49, 50, 74, 75, 76, 77, 125, 143
marijuana, 7, 124
marital status, 8, 16
Marx, 88, 97
maternal support, 9
mathematical, 138
matrix, 5

matter, 82, 100
measurement, 112
measures, 136
media, 58
mediation, 93
medical, viii, 2, 3, 6, 12, 46, 51, 71, 76, 77, 79, 120, 144
medical care, 3, 51
medication, 109, 126, 144
medicine, 73
Mediterranean, 89
memory, 3, 94, 108, 113
men, 134, 144
mental disorder, ix, x, 71, 78, 81, 99, 100, 141
mental health, 5, 10, 12, 16, 23, 24, 74, 77, 78, 81, 128, 134
mental illness, 114, 116, 118, 144
messages, 55, 64, 66
meta-analysis, 11, 22, 23, 68, 96, 106, 115, 117, 121, 124, 125, 126, 127, 128, 129, 131
Metabolic, 50
metabolic disorder(s), 45
metabolism, 39, 49
metabolites, 50
methodology, 74, 77, 113, 129
Miami, 1
mice, 37
minority, 136
mirror, 137
misinterpretation, 137
mistreatment and obesity, vii
misuse, 86, 110, 112, 131
mobile phone, 58
models, viii, 54, 64, 73, 75, 93, 104, 114, 117, 119, 124, 130
moderators, x, 99, 101, 104, 105
mole, 22
mood disorder, 120, 135
moral reasoning, 15
morbidity, 72, 75
motivation, 16
motor skills, 73
MSI, 145
multiple personality disorder, 128
multivariate, 144
mutation(s), 28, 32, 33, 37, 52
mutilation, 74, 131, 135

neglect, vii, viii, ix, 1, 2, 3, 4, 5, 6, 9, 11, 17, 18, 19, 20, 21, 22, 23, 24, 25, 69, 71, 73, 79, 85, 86, 88, 95, 117, 122, 126, 127, 128, 139, 140, 141, 142
neocortex, 107
neonates, 47
nervous system, 107
neurobiology, 125, 131
neurological deficit, 140
neuroses, 144
neurotic, 134
neurotransmitter, 107
New York, 143, 144
New Zealand, 129
nightmares, 109
normal development, 87, 88, 119
North America, 122, 124, 130, 131
nurses, 22, 44
nurturance, 88, 117
nutritional status, 33

O

obedience, 10
obesity, vii, viii, ix, 4, 21, 25, 71, 72, 73, 74, 75, 76, 77, 78, 79, 80, 81, 82, 83
obesity prevention, 74
objectification, 75
obsessive-compulsive disorder, 115
ODS, 48
offenders, 65, 125
Ohio, 133
omission, 17, 86
openness, 107
openness to experience, 107
opportunities, 57, 58, 60, 69, 116
optimism, 9, 16
organize, 75
Osteogenesis, 28, 46, 47
osteogenesis imperfecta, vii, 27, 28, 29, 31, 32, 33, 34, 42, 45, 46, 47, 51
osteomalacia, 35, 48
osteopathy, 44, 45
osteoporosis, 28
outpatient(s), 134, 139, 142, 144
overlap, 113, 114, 118
overweight, 4, 82, 83

N

negative consequences, 6
negative effects, 9, 11, 93, 105
negative outcomes, 100, 109

P

pain, 6, 7, 25, 29, 104, 110, 113, 129
panic disorder, 115
parallel, 78

parathyroid, 34
parathyroidectomy, 52
parent-adolescent relationships, 116
parental attitudes, 116, 142
parental support, 117
parenting, 5, 16, 20, 21, 23, 25, 64, 68, 88, 116, 117, 120, 124, 128, 140
parenting styles, 88
parents, vii, viii, 4, 6, 8, 9, 11, 13, 16, 17, 20, 21, 27, 39, 44, 46, 47, 51, 53, 54, 55, 56, 57, 58, 59, 60, 61, 62, 63, 64, 65, 66, 69, 78, 86, 88, 115, 124, 141
Paris, 136, 139, 141, 143
participants, ix, 7, 8, 9, 10, 56, 75, 76, 85, 92, 94, 113
path model, 91
pathology, 72, 76, 78, 117, 136, 142
pathophysiological, 107
pathophysiology, 107
pathways, 5, 21, 119, 140, 141, 142
patients, 134, 135, 136, 137, 139, 141, 142, 143, 145
penis, 62
percentile, 76
permit, 94
perpetrators, 11, 54, 95, 104, 105, 106, 138
personal, 137
personal control, 5
personal responsibility, 137
personality, ix, x, 15, 23, 85, 86, 87, 89, 90, 91, 92, 93, 94, 95, 96, 101, 103, 107, 108, 109, 110, 120, 121, 124, 126, 127, 128, 130, 131, 133, 134, 136, 138, 139, 140, 142, 143, 144, 145
personality characteristics, 107, 109, 120, 128
personality dimensions, 87
personality disorder(s), x, 15, 86, 96, 101, 103, 124, 128, 130, 133, 134, 136, 139, 140, 142, 143, 144, 145
personality traits, 23, 93, 96, 107, 110, 120
phenomenology, 145
phenotypes, 47, 121
Philadelphia, 142, 144
phobia, 128
phosphate, 34, 41, 50
phosphorus, 41
physical abuse, vii, ix, 1, 2, 3, 4, 5, 6, 7, 8, 9, 11, 14, 17, 20, 23, 24, 25, 85, 86, 97, 98, 111, 115, 126, 127, 129, 130, 138, 139, 141
physical health, 4, 11, 23, 129
physical therapist, 6, 76
physicians, 100
pigs, 37, 48
pilot study, 67, 144
platform, 94

play, 140
pleasure, 81, 86, 137
police, 63, 64, 135
policy, 96, 101
policymakers, 100
pollution, 33
polymorphism, 121, 127
poor, 136
population, viii, ix, 8, 18, 24, 35, 44, 53, 71, 72, 74, 76, 77, 79, 82, 90, 95, 106, 113, 119, 120, 123, 130, 134, 138
positive correlation, 117
posttraumatic stress, 4, 102, 103, 104, 106, 109, 111, 120, 126, 128, 131, 134, 142, 143
poverty, 4
precipitation, 141
prediction, 143, 145
predictor variables, 91, 92
predisposing factors, 140
pregnancy, 11, 15, 38, 68, 117, 126
premature infant, 50, 51
prematurity, vii, 27, 44, 45, 50
preschool, 25, 82
preschool children, 25, 82
preterm infants, 41, 50, 51
prevalence rate, 134
prevention, vii, viii, 2, 12, 19, 20, 24, 53, 54, 55, 56, 57, 59, 60, 63, 64, 65, 66, 67, 68, 69, 76, 95, 125
primary caregivers, 54
primary hyperparathyroidism, 52
primate, 48
priming, 141
probability, 23, 87
problem drinking, 132
problem-solving, 108, 110
processing biases, x, 99, 108, 109, 110, 124
professionals, vii, x, 1, 99, 100
profit, 65
project, 55
promoter, 127
protection, viii, 53, 64, 67, 68
protective factors, 5, 13, 24, 120, 125, 131, 143
psychiatric diagnosis, ix, 71
psychiatric disorder(s), x, 17, 99, 100, 101, 107, 108, 110, 111, 115, 118, 119, 124, 128, 129, 134, 141
psychiatric illness, 4
psychiatric patients, 106, 127, 134
psychoanalysis, 22
psychological, 137, 138, 140, 142
psychological distress, 72, 88
psychological problems, x, 80, 82, 99, 100, 101, 103, 104, 105, 106, 107, 109, 110, 111, 112, 114, 116, 118, 119

psychological variables, 75
psychological well-being, 92, 97
psychology, 71, 94, 125
psychometric properties, 21
psycho-pathological perspective profile, ix, 71
psychopathology, vii, ix, 4, 5, 9, 15, 19, 21, 25, 73,
    80, 81, 99, 100, 101, 103, 104, 105, 106, 107,
    108, 109, 110, 111, 112, 113, 114, 116, 117, 118,
    119, 122, 123, 124, 130, 131, 132, 138, 140, 141,
    143, 145
psychosis, 134
psychosocial, 141
psychosocial factors, x, 8, 75, 99, 107, 110, 119
psychosocial stress, 141
psychotherapy, 87, 136
psychotic symptoms, 101, 104
PTSD, 18, 19, 21, 95, 123, 132
puberty, 28
public health, 11, 22, 67, 68
public policy, 89
punishment, 6, 66, 117

Q

qualitative research, 55
quality of life, 12, 76, 129
quantitative research, 66
questionnaire, ix, 71, 76, 77, 78, 81, 87

R

race, 22
radius, 35, 36, 38, 40
rape, 10, 121, 123
reactions, 55, 57, 141
reactivity, 4, 135
reading, 60
reality, 57, 80, 89, 90, 95
receptors, 115, 120
recognition, 46
recollection, 140
recommendations, 20
reconstruction, 126
recovery, 13, 16, 17, 97, 125
recurrence, 44, 119
regression, 90, 92
regulation, 137
rehabilitation, 81
rejection, 4, 14, 80, 86, 116
relapse, 143
relationship(s), x, 133, 135, 137, 138, 139, 142, 143,
    144

relatives, 55, 61, 66
relaxation, 109
relevance, 45, 86, 93, 96, 141
reliability, 91, 92, 113
relief, 110
religion, 97
religiosity, 16, 88, 91
religious beliefs, 97
remission, 145
renal osteodystrophy, 48
replication, 21, 67, 124, 128
repression, 137
research, 136, 137, 143
researchers, 17, 88, 100, 111, 140
Residential, 67
resilience, 5, 6, 16, 18, 19, 21, 87, 94, 122, 138
resistance, 108
resolution, 81
resources, 16, 17, 23, 56, 89, 96
response, 2, 11, 13, 33, 58, 61, 89, 101, 107, 137
responsiveness, 88
restoration, 52
rewards, 94
rickets, vii, 27, 28, 33, 34, 35, 37, 38, 41, 44, 46, 47,
    48, 50, 51
risk factors, x, 4, 5, 8, 12, 13, 15, 16, 19, 20, 21, 38,
    44, 88, 99, 101, 112, 114, 116, 118, 119, 123,
    130, 131, 142, 143
risks, viii, 54, 55, 63, 87, 107
roots, 141
routines, 14
rules, 58, 65, 88

S

sadness, 67
safe haven, 17, 88
safety, viii, 53, 57, 58, 59, 60, 65, 88
sample, 134, 139
sampling, 134
saturation, 37
scarcity, viii, 53
school, 9, 15, 16, 54, 59, 60, 63, 64, 66, 76, 106
school performance, 15
science, 94
scope, ix, 11, 18, 20, 85, 95, 137
secret, 138
self-concept, 86, 101, 103, 137
self-control, 9, 109
self-destructive behavior, 86, 144
self-efficacy, 108, 109
self-esteem, 4, 5, 6, 7, 15, 16, 83, 91, 101, 103, 109,
    120

self-image, 73, 79, 86, 108
self-mutilation, 131, 135
self-report(s), 113, 136
semi-structured interviews, 135
sensation(s), 107, 121
sensing, 52
sensitization, 107
separation, 141
sequelae, 144
serotonin, 115, 120, 127
serum, 34, 35, 39, 41, 50
services, 64, 113
SES, 13
severity, 139
sex, 59, 65, 72, 106, 135
sexual activities, 10, 66, 86
sexual behavior, 4, 8, 23, 25, 128
sexual contact, 10, 104, 129
sexuality, 22, 56, 57, 58, 59, 64, 65, 66, 68, 86
sexually transmitted diseases, 11
shame, 86, 95
showing, 32, 36, 43, 93
siblings, 9, 16, 46, 63, 78, 86
signs, 3, 28, 29, 34, 35, 51, 60, 65
skeleton, 34
skills, 136, 137
skin, 32, 33, 40, 80
skull fracture, 31
social,109, 134, 135
social construct, viii, 53, 55
social constructivism, 55
social environment, 23, 72, 82, 129
social network, viii, 53, 54
social phobia, 128
social relationships, 55
social situations, viii, 53, 60, 65, 94
social skills, 5, 109
social support, 9, 13, 16, 60, 65, 97
society, 45, 95
software, 77
somatization, 101, 103
special education, 2
spending, 135
spirituality, 88, 89, 91, 96, 97
SPSS software, 76, 77
standard deviation, 77
state, vii, 1, 10, 22, 48
states, vii, x, 1, 2, 3, 10, 24, 99, 109, 110
statistical processing, 77
statistics, 89, 94
stillbirth, 28
strategies, x, 133, 136

stress, 4, 5, 19, 20, 79, 102, 103, 104, 106, 107, 109,
    111, 120, 126, 128, 129, 131, 134, 135, 137, 141,
    142, 143
stress response, 107
stressful life events, 110
stressors, 4, 5, 141
stroke, 2
structure, x, 20, 95, 99, 107, 110, 117
style(s), 15, 72, 88, 96, 108, 109, 116, 126, 134, 137
subcutaneous tissue, 40
subjective well-being, 87, 88, 90, 91, 92, 93, 96
subjectivity, 74, 103, 112
substance abuse, 12, 13, 15, 21, 101, 103, 104, 105,
    111, 114, 115, 118, 121, 123, 125, 126, 127, 132,
    135, 136, 139
substance addiction, 12
substance use, 22, 23, 109, 112, 113, 114, 116, 120,
    121, 125, 126, 129, 130, 131, 135
substance use disorders, 113, 126
substrates, 141
suffering, 136
suicidal, 135, 143
suicidal behavior, 8, 12, 25, 68, 103, 108, 109, 115,
    116, 118, 120, 121, 122, 125, 126, 127, 130, 131
suicidal ideation, 17, 117, 122
suicide, 8, 15, 19, 101, 102, 103, 104, 112, 115, 121,
    122, 124, 127, 130, 131, 132, 136, 138
suicide attempts, 8, 122, 136, 138
supervision, vii, 1, 3, 116
support services, 64
suppression, 137
surgical intervention, 80
survival, 44, 88
survivors, x, 18, 96, 97, 99, 100, 101, 102, 103, 105,
    106, 109, 110, 111, 112, 114, 115, 118, 119, 122,
    123, 129
Sweden, 65
swelling, 29
sympathy, 63
symptom(s), 4, 8, 12, 13, 15, 22, 23, 28, 74, 93, 95,
    101, 102, 103, 105, 107, 108, 109, 110, 111, 113,
    114, 115, 117, 118, 119, 120, 122, 123, 134, 135,
    136, 137, 139, 141
syndrome, vii, 27, 39, 42, 46, 49, 51, 74, 102, 133,
    137
synthesis, 21, 33, 37, 74, 122, 126
syphilis, 40, 50
systems, 142

T

target, 67
target population(s), 67

Task Force, 72
teachers, 54
teams, 74
techniques, 60
teeth, 28
temporary brittle bone disease, vii, 27, 28, 42, 43, 45, 46, 51
tension, 8, 73, 110
test scores, 15
testing, 93
therapeutics, 142
therapy, 35, 48, 49, 52, 121, 122, 130, 144
thoughts, 15, 110, 137
threat(s), 3, 135, 138
tibia, 36, 38
time, 134, 136, 137, 145
time frame, 2
tissue, 37, 39
toddlers, 47, 137
total parenteral nutrition, 38
toxicity, 52
toys, 16
traditions, 67
training, 136
traits, 87, 97, 107, 110, 120, 121, 122, 124, 134
transference, 88, 122
transformation, 103
transmission, 21, 124
trauma, vii, x, 5, 8, 13, 18, 40, 41, 45, 51, 74, 86, 87, 88, 89, 90, 92, 94, 95, 107, 120, 121, 122, 123, 125, 128, 130, 131, 133, 137, 138, 139, 140, 141, 142
traumatic events, 18, 106, 142
traumatic experiences, 111, 113, 119
treatment, ix, x, 2, 13, 14, 16, 17, 18, 20, 21, 51, 52, 65, 71, 73, 74, 75, 76, 77, 78, 79, 81, 106, 121, 122, 126, 128, 129, 130, 133, 136, 141, 142, 143, 144
triggers, 58
tryptophan, 126
tumours, 40
twins, 31, 38, 43, 44
type 2 diabetes, 2

U

ulna, 35, 36, 38
ultrasound, 41
undernutrition, 82
uniform, ix, 85
United, vii, 1, 19, 21, 22, 33, 47, 61, 64, 68, 89, 94
United Kingdom, 22, 64
United Nations, 89

United States, vii, 1, 19, 21, 22, 33, 47, 61, 64, 68, 94
updating, 66
urban, 18, 19, 20
USA, 85, 86, 96, 133

V

vacuum, 87, 89
valgus, 34
validation, 119
variables, ix, x, 75, 77, 85, 87, 88, 89, 90, 91, 92, 93, 94, 95, 99, 101, 104, 105, 106, 107, 108, 111, 112, 114, 117, 118, 120, 122, 123, 127, 133, 137, 138, 139, 141
variations, 15, 135
varieties, 96
vector, 81
verbal abuse, 138, 139, 143
veterans, 144
victimization, vii, 2, 8, 10, 11, 12, 13, 18, 20, 23, 24, 69, 102, 104, 105, 109, 111, 112, 113, 114, 115, 116, 118, 119, 122, 128, 129, 132
victims, vii, ix, 1, 2, 3, 4, 5, 6, 7, 8, 9, 11, 12, 13, 14, 15, 17, 18, 33, 64, 65, 85, 87, 88, 89, 90, 92, 93, 94, 95, 102, 103, 105, 106, 110, 114, 117, 118, 119, 120, 121, 122, 124, 125, 128, 137, 138, 140, 143
violence, 6, 13, 14, 15, 73, 86, 104, 106, 114, 116, 117, 118, 127, 132
violent behavior, 4, 7
vitamin C, 36, 37, 48
vitamin C deficiency, 36, 37, 48
vitamin D, vii, 27, 33, 34, 35, 38, 40, 41, 45, 47, 48, 50
vitamin D deficiency, vii, 27, 33, 34, 35, 38, 40, 41, 45, 47
voiding, 103
vulnerability, 20, 72, 80, 108, 120, 125, 129, 131
vulnerability to depression, 108, 120, 125

W

Wales, 50
Washington, 23, 24, 123, 128, 141, 143, 144, 145
weight control, 76
weight loss, 74, 75, 76, 77, 79, 81
welfare, 2, 24, 67, 89, 100
well-being, ix, 23, 25, 85, 87, 89, 90, 91, 92, 93, 94, 95, 96, 97
wellness, 106
Western Australia, 65

Western countries, 89
WHO, 72
withdrawal, 3, 7, 15
women, 134, 144
workers, 56
World Health Organization, 72
worldwide, 11, 82
wrists, 35

X

x-linked recessive, 39
x-rays, 38

Y

yield, 113
young adults, 18
young people, 20, 74, 80, 82, 95, 126, 131

Z

zinc, 49